The Aesthetics of Discipleship

The Aesthetics of Discipleship

EVERYDAY AESTHETIC EXISTENCE
AND THE CHRISTIAN LIFE

Adrian Coates

FOREWORD BY
John W. de Gruchy

☙PICKWICK *Publications* · Eugene, Oregon

THE AESTHETICS OF DISCIPLESHIP
Everyday Aesthetic Existence and Discipleship

Copyright © 2021 Adrian Coates. All rights reserved. Except for brief quotations in critical publications or reviews, no part of this book may be reproduced in any manner without prior written permission from the publisher. Write: Permissions, Wipf and Stock Publishers, 199 W. 8th Ave., Suite 3, Eugene, OR 97401.

Pickwick Publications
An Imprint of Wipf and Stock Publishers
199 W. 8th Ave., Suite 3
Eugene, OR 97401

www.wipfandstock.com

PAPERBACK ISBN: 978-1-7252-7239-2
HARDCOVER ISBN: 978-1-7252-7237-8
EBOOK ISBN: : 978-1-7252-7238-5

Cataloguing-in-Publication data:

Names: Coates, Adrian, author. | De Gruchy, John W., foreword.

Title: The aesthetics of discipleship : everyday aesthetic existence and discipleship / Adrian Coates ; foreword by John W. de Gruchy.

Description: Eugene, OR: Pickwick Publications, 2021. | Includes bibliographical references.

Identifiers: ISBN: 978-1-7252-7239-2(paperback). | ISBN: 978-1-7252-7237-8 (hardcover). | ISBN: 978-1-7252-7238-5 (ebook).

Subjects: LCSH: Kierkegaard, Søren, 1813–1855. | Bonhoeffer, Dietrich, 1906–1945. | Faith development. | Christianity and the arts. | Aesthetics—Religious aspects—Christianity. | Theology.

Classification: BR115.C8 C520 2021 (print). | BR115.C8 (epub).

Unless otherwise indicated, Scripture quotations are from the New Revised Standard Version Bible, copyright © 1989, by the Division of Christian Education of the National Council of the Churches of Christ in the U.S.A., and are used by permission. All rights reserved.

Scripture quotations marked (NIV) are taken from the Holy Bible, New International Version®, NIV®. Copyright © 1973, 1978, 1984, 2011 by Biblica, Inc.® Used by permission of Zondervan. All rights reserved worldwide. www.zondervan.com The "NIV" and "New International Version" are trademarks registered in the United States Patent and Trademark Office by Biblica, Inc.®

Scripture quotations marked (NKJV) are taken from the New King James Version®. Copyright © 1982 by Thomas Nelson. Used by permission. All rights reserved.

Portions of chapters 2 and 6 originally appeared in "Beauty Lived towards Shalom: The Christian Life as Aesthetic-Ethical Existence." *Acta Theologica* 40, suppl. 29 (2020): 93–113, and are used here by permission.

Portions of chapter 3 originally appeared in "Bonhoeffer on Amusing Ourselves to Death: Mature Aesthetic Existence as Antidote to Everyday Aestheticism." *Stellenbosch Theological Journal* 6.2 (2020) 67–90, and are used here by permission.

Contents

Foreword by John de Gruchy vii
Acknowledgments ix

1. Introduction 1
2. The Nature of Aesthetic Existence 16
3. The Celebration of Aesthetic Existence in Christian Life 63
4. Aesthetic Existence as Fundamental in Being Human 102
5. Aesthetic Existence as Fundamental in Faith Formation 146
6. The Liturgical Orientation of Mature Aesthetic Existence 189
7. Conclusion: Toward Aesthetic Stewardship as a Spiritual Practice 222

Bibliography 237

Foreword

THE SUPERVISION OF DOCTORAL dissertations has often been the highlight of my life as an academic. What begins as an initial conversation exploring options and possibilities for research takes on a momentum analogous to a shared journey of discovery across a narrowing landscape as questions become sharper and focus more specific. But there is more to such supervision than the excitement and enrichment of intellectual endeavour; there is also the engagement of embodied minds, the mutual stimulation of shared insights and convictions that take form and gain clarity and precision through discussion. In the process I have often learnt as much from the dialogue as has the doctoral researcher. Not surprisingly, given the fact that this process sometimes lasts for five years, a relationship is established that lasts well into the future. And nothing is more satisfying than when what began as intellectual enquiry with the narrow goal of graduation, becomes a life-changing passion.

These thoughts came to mind as I began to write this Foreword to Adrian Coates' fine study on the fundamental connection between aesthetic existence, being human and Christian discipleship. What a joy it is to see his work now becoming more widely available through its publication, not just because I am delighted for Adrian himself, but also because I know that others will now have an opportunity to read and benefit from his labour of love. And it was nothing less than such an endeavour, not only because of Adrian's growing commitment to his enquiry, but also because during the years of his research and writing he had to endure periods of debilitating illness. That he did so, that he persevered so doggedly in pursuit of his goal, and that he managed to produce a dissertation of distinction, is remarkable.

It is not necessary for me to comment here on the content and argument of *The Aesthetics of Discipleship*. Coates sets this out in a clear manner in his Introduction, and the table of contents provides a concise overview of how his thesis develops. *The Aesthetics of Discipleship* is not only accessible to a wide readership of those who are eager to explore their faith commitments in fresh and significant ways, but also those who are engaged in Christian witness in today's world in which discipleship is too often sacrificed on the altar of a resurgent imperial Christendom, and too seldom engaged in costly yet transformative action in the life of the world.

Understandably, publishers are generally hesitant to publish doctoral dissertations for well-known reasons. I therefore salute Pickwick Publications for their willingness to do so, and especially for their support for this project. Not only is it a well-written and readable work of erudition, but it is also a timely and important study. Dissertations can be, and often are, so narrow in their scope that they are seldom of interest except to a small, select number of scholars. There is nothing wrong about that. But in this instance the same is not true. This is a book that will obviously be of interest to all those who want to explore the relationship between Christian faith and aesthetics, but hopefully also to all who simply want to know what it means to be a Christian and a human being in today's world.

—John W. de Gruchy

Acknowledgments

THIS BOOK BEGAN AS a PhD dissertation, and therefore I need to start by thanking my supervisor, John de Gruchy, who guided me through it with not only sage insight but deeply humanizing warmth, care, and hospitality in his home. John's own life depicts the inextricable unity of thoughtful faith, everyday aesthetics, and ethical action in being Christian, and it has been an honor not only to glean from his wisdom but to share a little of life together. He has been a consistent encouragement, offering practical help throughout the development of this book, for which I am deeply grateful. Thanks also to my dissertation examiners, Jens Zimmermann, Robert Vosloo, and Philip Ziegler, for their helpful input and advice.

Inevitably, a book such as this is the fruit of seeds sown long before. Thank you to those who set me on this trajectory many years ago, through shared encounters with beauty in the everyday. To all who journeyed alongside me during my time at Regent College, thank you for nurturing the seedlings of this study during that rich season together. (I am reluctant to name names as so many played a role, but I need to mention Loren Wilkinson, who personally modeled mature aesthetic existence in a life of faith and also practiced the "humane philosophy," which I refer to in the pages that follow.) Thanks also to Gill D'achada and Jordan Pickering for reading the manuscript and for the input and corrections you offered. And my deepest thanks to all those who have supported me throughout this process, notably Larry and Margaret Reimer and Lindsey Johnstone, without whom this book would not have been possible.

Finally, I owe my family—my children, Jude, Hannah, and Luke, and particularly my wife, Michelle—a deep debt of gratitude for all their understanding, support, and sacrifice. Thank you for your long-suffering love, belief, and encouragement. It is both a cliché and an understatement to say that I could not have done it without you, but it remains profoundly true.

Soli Deo gloria.

1

Introduction

DISCIPLESHIP IS EMBODIED. This obvious truth is easily lost amid an emphasis on discipleship as a "spiritual" process, along with the otherworldly focus that so often accompanies it. Yet, as a consequence of the incarnation, a life of discipleship, a life of following after Christ, is a life that is necessarily bound up with being fully human, as an embodied being in the world. This has implications for both sensory engagement with the world (aesthetics) and action in it (ethics). Failing to take the embodied nature of discipleship seriously dilutes its impact on both the aesthetic and ethical realms, but more than that, it is a failure to understand the interconnected and symbiotic relationships between aesthetics, ethics, and faith as they feed off and into one another. To put it differently, beliefs are continuously shaped and formed, both consciously and unconsciously, through our sensory and affective everyday life in the world. A practice of discipleship that ignores this embodied dynamic is certainly woefully lacking, but the void will be filled: sensory and affective, often preconscious person-formation *will* happen, whether it is through practice of the Christian life or via other means and contexts. The stakes are high. Recovering an understanding of discipleship through the lens of aesthetics is not merely an interesting conceptual exercise, but it has significant implications for a life of faith in the world.

We will attend to definitions shortly, but it should be immediately apparent that we are seeking to recover a broader and more integrated classical understanding of "aesthetics," relating to sense perception as apprehension, rather than a contemporary understanding that conflates aesthetics with beauty and the arts. Today, asking what aesthetics has to do with faith may seem a little like asking what Athens has to do with Jerusalem, as Tertullian famously did. Aesthetics, surely, belongs to the realm of culture, a Christian response to the aesthetic then being contingent on whichever approach one endorses regarding the relationship between Christianity and culture. At best, from this perspective, the aesthetic is validated as an aspect of life that is to be cherished and nurtured, in fulfillment of the cultural mandate to steward earthly life, perhaps even at its pinnacle functioning as a gateway to transcendence. At worst, it is to be rejected as a worldly distraction from that which carries eternal weight, the salvation of our souls. More often than not, in the everyday life of many Christians, their stance on the aesthetic lies somewhere in between these two poles: the aesthetic is there to be enjoyed (with moderation, according to the ethical bounds of the faith) but plays only a peripheral role in the serious business of life in Christ.

The aim of this book, however, is to approach the relationship between faith and aesthetics from a completely different paradigm. Rather than considering the aesthetic within the framework of cultural production, as a category named the arts, apparently distinct from much of our day-to-day life, we will be looking at the aesthetic as embedded in the everyday, as *lived* sensory existence, being absorbed in moments of aesthetic experience amid the ordinary. In other words, rather than exploring a Christian perspective *on* the arts, or a Christian attitude *toward* aesthetic production and engagement, we are asking the question from the inside: what role does experience of the aesthetic in the everyday play in living a life of faith? Is the Christian life solely one of religious existence, or does the aesthetic as lived (aesthetic existence) also have a role to play in discipleship? And how do both of these modes of existence relate to ethical life and action in the world? These are some of the questions before us. Underlying these questions, in turn, is another that lies at the heart of this inquiry: Is aesthetic existence fundamental to being human and becoming Christian?

The central claim of this book is that aesthetic existence does indeed play a fundamental role in human flourishing and a life of discipleship. We ignore this truth at our peril, both because this mode of existence ubiquitously pervades all human life (whether we acknowledge it or not), and also because it preconsciously contributes to paradigms whereby we apprehend the world and our place in it. Whatever our stance might be on Christianity and the arts, or aesthetic production and engagement as cultural stewardship, our everyday aesthetic experiences are quietly forming and shaping us, whether we acknowledge this or not. Perhaps now more than ever, being Christian demands responding well to this aspect of our beings. Whether we consider the influence of alluring advertising as it shifts our desires, the titillation of social and entertainment media, our burgeoning obsession with the sensory delights of food, the masses captivated by gaming, or even the visceral popularization of politics, we are the inhabitants of a world saturated with aesthetic stimuli impacting us most moments of our days. Virtual reality is not merely a name for a technological invention, but an increasingly viable mode of escaping from Reality into an aesthetic mode of existence that is the cultivation of a pseudoreality centered on the self. What should the Christian response be to this aestheticization of everyday life? Is it to be shunned or embraced? And what guides the practical application of this decision? What does it mean to follow Christ as embodied, sensory beings located in *this* time and place in the world?

The aesthetics of discipleship starts with an affirmation that embodied, sensory existence is a good gift to be celebrated and enjoyed as an expression of being fully human in Christian life. In an important sense, however, it is not aesthetic existence per se that is to be embraced, but a specific mode of enjoying the aesthetic in a life of discipleship. Aesthetic existence itself is not a choice. In this sense, *everyone* "embraces" it, intentionally or not, since it is a fundamental aspect of being human in the world. At points of time in our days, all of us are "in the moment," present to the all-consuming sensory immediacy of gazing at the stars, savoring a delicious meal, watching a film, laughing with friends, playing a game, listening to music, enjoying a kiss, chuckling at a meme, literally or figuratively smelling the roses. Such moments are not insignificant or neutral. They contribute to our apprehension of the world, to our formation, either for good or ill. The aesthetics of discipleship offers an account of two distinctive ways of engaging aesthetic existence. In contrast to an immature, self-seeking indulgence of the aesthetic, maturity in the Christian life requires that sensory existence be embedded in, and harmonious with, a broader life-narrative of worship. It is a mode of worship that is not limited to liturgy as practiced on a Sunday morning, but a liturgical embrace of all of life in the everyday.

Delineating an aesthetics of discipleship is important because a self-seeking, immature mode of aesthetic existence is pervasive not only in society as a whole, but in the church itself. Modes of being Christian all too often endorse the human desire for comfort, whether simply in the guise of a prosperity gospel or in the development of sophisticated models of Christendom that ally the church with affluence and power. The conflation of Christianity with empire is not a new phenomenon, but it remains as problematic as ever, as recent political events in the United States have once again highlighted. Amid the aestheticization of everyday life, the concomitant rise of consumerism, and the political manifestation of these realities and economies of desire in the life of the church, discipleship is all too often void of costly grace. As Dietrich Bonhoeffer famously reminded us, in the interests of cheap grace Christian discipleship is too easily sacrificed on the altar of comfortable Christendom. The task that lies before us is both, on the one hand, to critique cheap discipleship that desires to make the aesthetic absolute, and also, on the other, to integrate costly discipleship with mature aesthetic existence in the Christian life. The key to the success of such an enterprise is careful understanding of the dynamics of the aesthetic, particularly in relationship to the rational, and their mutual role in the nature of being human and becoming Christian.

Integrating Theological Aesthetics with a Theological Anthropology

The recent rising interest in theological aesthetics as a field of study in its own right offers an important lens on epistemological and anthropological questions. It is only in the last three decades or so that the field of theological aesthetics has become a major focus in theology, largely prompted by the "aestheticization of everyday life in postmodern society."[1] The postmodern context has cultivated a renewed interest in aesthetics by questioning the modern ratiocentric stance (a view of life oriented around and defined by rationality—marked by "rational exclusivism," "rational hegemonism," and "rational instrumentalism").[2] The essential claim of ratiocentrism is "that the good life can be understood in terms of and attained by reason and strength of will."[3] The subject-oriented paradigm of postmodernity challenges this claim, nurturing new

---

1. Thiessen, ed., *Theological Aesthetics*, 1.
2. Cottingham, *Philosophy and the Good Life*, 36.
3. Lacewing, "What Reason Can't Do," 140.

lines of thought around what it means to be human, and consequently, the basis of meaning, belief, and ultimately, action.

This postmodern critique of ratiocentrism has opened a door for richer epistemological dialogue in the area of theological aesthetics. The field has long acknowledged that experiencing the transcendent nature of beauty and the sublime contributes to the quest for knowledge of the divine, of the mysterious Other, and therefore, the life of faith. In the latter half of the twentieth century, Hans Urs von Balthasar exemplified this through his seminal work that sought to ground theology in aesthetics. Along with the other voices of the *Nouvelle Théologie* movement, Balthasar sought a *ressourcement*, which fueled his Platonic response to the modern understanding of beauty, thus reaffirming, and integrating the transcendental ideals of Beauty, Goodness, and Truth (in that order). While there is no doubt that Balthasar made an extremely valuable contribution to the field, his emphasis on the transcendent value of aesthetics has typified a prevailing paradigm of otherworldly orientation in theological aesthetics. (As Graham Ward puts it, "Balthasar's work breathes in a certain rarefied atmosphere, a post-resurrection perspective, as if the work was composed on the frosted heights of Thomas Mann's magic mountain".[4]) The danger of such an approach is that aesthetics becomes again dis-integrated from rationality. Here, aesthetic experience is seen primarily as a way of knowing beyond that which rationality can access. Whilst this represents a commendable reappropriation of the epistemic value of aesthetic experience, it still pits aesthetics against rationality. It also positions the primary value of aesthetic experience as oriented toward the transcendent, as opposed to a life of faith lived in this world, with the consequent ethical implications.[5] From this perspective, aesthetic experience that has epistemic value is limited to the overtly transformative, those vivid and explicit sensory encounters with transcendence that shape consciousness. But do *everyday* aesthetic experiences, which are often implicit and partly preconscious, shape our understanding, our beliefs and the way we act in the world? Answering this question requires grounding both aesthetic experience and belief formation in a holistic understanding of being human.

---

4. Ward, *Christ and Culture*, 205.

5. For a helpful exposition from the field of theological aesthetics on the problematic postmodern tendency to disconnect this-wordly, incarnational reality from transcendence, see Begbie, *Redeeming Transcendence in the Arts*.

The postmodern critique of ratiocentrism is an anthropological critique, a rejection of the Cartesian *homo rationale*, highlighting the need to recover a holistic Christian anthropology.[6] But even a description of humans as essentially *believing* beings does not necessarily free us from ratiocentric hegemony if our understanding of belief is assent to a series of rational propositions. Approaching belief in this sense means that understanding humans as fundamentally *believing* beings still leaves us in the realm of *homo rationale*, preoccupied with propositions and ideas. Consequently the brain is still in the vat, offering a disembodied and individualistic picture of the human person.[7] The key question is how human beings come to hold particular beliefs. Rather than understanding belief merely as a weak form of knowledge, belief is first and foremost *relational*, not rational. It is a relational commitment of trust; a disposition formed by drawing on multiple human faculties, including rationality, sensory experience, and affect as they collectively feed the imagination. Thus, while rationality does indeed have a role to play in belief, belief is grounded in a broader, integrated and embodied orientation toward the world. In this sense, belief (acting "as if") and the imagination ("seeing as") are not only inextricably connected, but fundamental to being human.[8]

If this assertion holds true, then it becomes important to consider the way the imagination is formed, and what role aesthetic experiences play in this formation. This is why, for our purposes, aesthetic experience encompasses far more than encounters with the fine arts, or even the broader arts. The emerging philosophical subdiscipline of everyday aesthetics affirms this formative role of aesthetic experience in our day-to-day lives. Aesthetics does not belong to a subset of human life, but is for every person and affects every person. Our aesthetic experiences in everyday life have "moral, social, political and environmental" ramifications.[9] For the same reasons, there are also significant implications for the life of faith, and the embodiment of that faith in the world as ethical action.

To explore these implications we will be engaging theological aesthetics through an existential lens, with an accompanying focus on

---

6. Smith, *Desiring the Kingdom*, 40.
7. Smith, *Desiring the Kingdom*, 41–45.
8. McGilchrist, *The Master and His Emissary*, 155–56.
9. Saito, *Everyday Aesthetics*, 2.

the everyday, for the purpose of shedding further light on a theological anthropology, ultimately highlighting consequences for the nature of discipleship. In a sense, then, similar to Maureen O'Connell's articulation of "beauty from below," it is an engagement with theological aesthetics "from below," emphasizing the significance of embodied, everyday life amid concrete contexts and relationships.[10] It is important to stress at this point, however, that this does not imply the priority of human agency in discipleship. The role of human agency in discipleship is always only in response to divine agency, an opportunity to participate in God's transforming work. While our focus will be on the role of aesthetic existence in this human response, exploring this relational process "from below" does not in any way prioritize or elevate the human role in following Christ. Rather it is simply a fitting participation, a receptive aesthetic attunement to the gracious transformative work of God in one's life. This is a point that always needs to remain at the forefront of an aesthetics of discipleship.

Tools for the Task

Exploring the relationship between everyday aesthetic existence and discipleship not only requires a clarification of terms, but a common understanding of the conceptual frameworks that undergird it. Both key terms, *aesthetic existence* and *discipleship*, will be further developed during the course of Chapters 2 and 3, through our engagement with the work of Kierkegaard and Bonhoeffer respectively. *Aesthetic existence* originates in the work of Kierkegaard as sensory immediacy. It refers to the lived dimension of sensory experience, typified by complete absorption of the senses to "being in the moment." For our purposes, the term is further developed by Bonhoeffer's taxonomy of it, wherein he locates aesthetic existence in the realm of freedom, unpacking it as art, play, friendship, and *Bildung* (formation).[11]

As a result, the definition of *aesthetics* that we will work with is a broad one that stems back to the classical use of the term as "sense perception." Alexander Gottlieb Baumgarten, the founder of aesthetics as a subject of study, initially defined *aesthetics* as "a science of how things

10. O'Connell, *If These Walls Could Talk*, 13–17.
11. See John de Gruchy's exploration of Bonhoeffer's taxonomy in de Gruchy, *Christianity, Art and Transformation*, 147–58.

are to be known by means of the senses."[12] Mark Johnson, writing on the basis of meaning being fundamentally embodied, describes aesthetics simply as "the study of how humans make and experience meaning."[13] While these broader perspectives inform the backdrop for our understanding of aesthetics, we will be grounding our discussion of aesthetics in the definition put forward by Frank Burch Brown. Aesthetics is "theoretical reflection regarding all aesthetic phenomena, including their modes of significant interrelation with, and mediation of, what is not inherently aesthetic: abstract ideas, useful objects, moral convictions, class conflicts, religious doctrines, and so forth."[14] The pivotal question that follows is how we define "aesthetic phenomena." Brown rightly suggests that we neither revert back to pre-Enlightenment models of aesthetics (thus considering aesthetic phenomena as anything perceptible), nor embrace modern conceptions of aesthetics (which attempt to hermetically seal aesthetic phenomena off exclusively in purist domains such as art or beauty, however defined). Brown thus proposes a neo-aesthetics, which harnesses both of these paradigms (along with an anti-aesthetics that critiques the latter: aesthetic phenomena inevitably deny strict purist boundaries such as beauty and art in their complex interrelationships with other aspects of human existence), suggesting that we locate aesthetic phenomena in the "sheerly delightful within perception, or the noticeable-for-its-own-sake."[15] Therefore, the distinction between the aesthetic and the nonaesthetic is relative, not binary, existing on a continuum from that which would traditionally be understood as purely aesthetic to that which is propelled by utility (most experiences of the aesthetic occurring somewhere in between).[16] Aesthetic phenomena are neither "perceptibles (as in Greek) or beautiful objects alone, but all those things employing a medium in such a way that its perceptible form and 'felt' qualities become essential to what is appreciable and meaningful."[17] Aesthetic experience then, is not solely limited to perceptions of harmony, light, proportion, or any other purist denotations of the aesthetic, but being absorbed in the sensory appreciation of the particular phenomenon.

12. As quoted in Kivy, ed., *Blackwell Guide to Aesthetics*, 15.
13. Johnson, *The Meaning of the Body*, 209.
14. Brown, *Religious Aesthetics*, 22.
15. Brown, *Religious Aesthetics*, 11.
16. Brown, *Religious Aesthetics*, 12.
17. Brown, *Religious Aesthetics*, 22.

Based on this definition, the description of "everyday" aesthetic experience may seem to be something of a tautology, since such an understanding of engagement with the aesthetic already encompasses the everyday. But it is used in the pages that follow to flag our specific focus not on the arts or beauty themselves (which also fit into our broad definition of aesthetics) but on a phenomenology of aesthetics dealing with aesthetic experience in everyday life. It is important to point out that the everyday is not a category distinct from arts and beauty. In other words, everyday aesthetics is not simply a third container for all that cannot be categorized as art or the beautiful. In fact, encounters with art and beauty may well occur within everyday aesthetic experience.[18] Rather, the modifier "everyday" is an attempt to liberate "aesthetic discourse from the confines of a specific kind of object or experience" in order to illuminate "how deeply entrenched and prevalent aesthetic considerations are in our mundane everyday existence."[19] Therefore, to confine our understanding of the "everyday" to specific attitudes, objects, or activities (distinguishing between the ordinary and extraordinary, for example) is not the point here, as it is in the philosophical debate on defining the field of everyday aesthetics.[20] Such categorizations are fluid, as the extraordinary can become the ordinary, and vice versa. Encounters with the aesthetic occur both in the mundane and unexpected, amid the ordinary routines of our days. Our use of "everyday" serves as a reminder that it is not only sensory encounters with beauty and the arts that are under consideration, but aesthetic experience of phenomena amid supposedly trivial or frivolous activity, such as engaging sports, music, gardening, cooking, playing, cleaning, hiking, shopping, dressing, socializing, and so on. The main point here is that it is in and through these everyday moments that the aesthetic has a significant impact on our formation, precisely because such moments are dismissed as trivial or insignificant, at times even flying below the radar of our consciousness, inculcating patterns of behavior through the repetition of aesthetic practices.

Locating aesthetics in the everyday foregrounds not only its relationship to daily practices but also the relationship between the imagination and action in the world. Since everyday aesthetics is not located in the realm of disinterested contemplation, a necessary relationship exists

18. Such an understanding of aesthetics in everyday experience stems back to Dewey, *Art as Experience*.
19. Saito, *Everyday Aesthetics*, 12.
20. Saito, "Aesthetics of the Everyday."

between the imagination and ethics.[21] This nexus of embodied, sensory existence, the paradigmatic nature of the imagination, and their mutual and symbiotic relationship with individual and social practices lies at the heart of the aesthetics of discipleship. A number of fields and conceptual frameworks make significant contributions to understanding this nexus, even if detailed articulation of their contributions lies beyond the limited scope of this book. They provide the foundation for our task, and therefore our discussion of the aesthetics of discipleship is informed by these frameworks, and is thus best read through the lens of the understanding they offer.

Recovering the significance of embodied, sensory existence for human perception and understanding is at the heart of these contributions. A phenomenological approach to anthropology, and in particular, Merleau-Ponty's *Phenomenology of Perception*, reminds us of the basic truth that perception occurs through existing as a body in the world. Further, bodily perception does not simply provide the raw data, which is then intellectually engaged as a distinct disembodied process; rather, perception is a "way of intending the world, of *meaning* the world *with* the body."[22] There is notable resonance here with the burgeoning field of embodied cognition. Embodiment not only shapes the way we think, but shapes the mind itself. "It may even be possible to say that bodily movement, transformed into the level of action, is the very thing that constitutes the self."[23] Embodied cognition is an emerging field and some of the claims remain contentious, but there is clearly sufficient evidence to justify the central claim that embodiment profoundly shapes consciousness.[24] It is particularly the aesthetic nature of this embodied experience that shapes meaning. Mark Johnson and George Lakoff's classic *Metaphors We Live By* speaks to the formative nature of aesthetic existence, Johnson further developing this with an aesthetic approach to embodied cognition.[25] Johnson argues that "image schemata" (which we will refer to as the paradigmatic production of the imagination) are shaped through bodily experience, and that consequently, "human rationality is imaginative through and through, insofar as it involves image-schematic

---

21. Fesmire, *John Dewey and Moral Imagination*, 60.
22. Smith, *Imagining the Kingdom*, 72 (italics original).
23. Gallagher, *How the Body Shapes the Mind*, 9.
24. Shapiro, *Embodied Cognition*.
25. Johnson, *The Body in the Mind*.

structures that can be metaphorically projected from concrete to more abstract domains of understanding."[26] Embodied cognition thus has obvious implications for a life of faith, as environmental experience shapes belief through the imaginative formation of paradigmatic religious frameworks.[27]

A number of theoretical models deepen our understanding of this relationship between embodied practice and the generation of imaginative paradigms. When considered together, in dialogue with one another, they provide a richly textured foundation for our discussion of the aesthetics of discipleship. Our use of "practice" is informed by both Pierre Bourdieu's practice theory and the interrelationship with the paradigmatic and normative impact of social practices, as explored by Alasdair MacIntyre among others.[28] Bourdieu's concept of *habitus* challenges the idea that embodied action in the world is merely the consequence of carefully reasoned conscious decisions.[29] Rather, embodied existence, as embedded in societal habits, dispositions, and attitudes, impacts perception of the world and action in it. In this sense, we are impelled not by abstract reflection but through embodied immersion in reality, through attunement to our environment akin to the sporting experience of "being in the game," where an athlete's body and being "just knows" how to act and react without extensive cognitive deliberation.[30] Thus, rather than consider perception of the world as an abstract, theoretical construct located in a cerebral sphere, it is more accurate to situate human meaning and action within the context of social imaginaries, described by Charles Taylor as, "the way ordinary people 'imagine' their social surroundings," which is "not expressed in theoretical terms, but is carried in images, stories, and legends . . . making possible common practices."[31] Again, this alignment with a social imaginary is significantly aesthetic; it is a relational attunement to reality by means of the senses.[32]

---

26. Johnson, *The Body in the Mind*, 194.
27. Barsalou et al., "Embodiment in Religious Knowledge."
28. MacIntyre, *After Virtue*.
29. Bourdieu, *Outline of a Theory of Practice*.
30. Bourdieu, *The Logic of Practice*, 66.
31. Taylor, *Modern Social Imaginaries*, 23.
32. Dreyfus and Taylor, *Retrieving Realism*, 118.

Synopsis

Before offering an overview of the argument presented in the chapters to come, it will be helpful to clarify that we are not attempting a practical theology or a biblical study on the aesthetics of discipleship. The purpose of this book is rather to provide a philosophical and theological introduction to the aesthetics of discipleship, thus serving as a theoretical basis for further study and application, with the hope of ultimately serving the church in its daily life and practice.

We will be exploring the aesthetics of discipleship through perspectives offered by five diverse, seminal thinkers (Dietrich Bonhoeffer, Søren Kierkegaard, Iain McGilchrist, Graham Ward, and Nicholas Wolterstorff), the work of each making an important contribution to a nuanced and multifaceted understanding of the role aesthetic existence plays in the Christian life. The focus is not on their work per se, but on dialoguing with their work as a lens through which to gain a better understanding of the aesthetics of discipleship. The diversity of the interlocutors selected reflects a desire to tap into the richness of both ecumenical and interdisciplinary dialogue, in order to offer a vision of the aesthetics of discipleship grounded in a holistic understanding of being human. In this sense, it is a theological inquiry in close conversation with "humane philosophy" (embracing the breadth of the humanities) and philosophy as a "form of life," as manifest in the likes of Pierre Hadot and Alexander Nehamas.[33]

Even though the focus of this book is not the practical outworkings of an aesthetics of discipleship (thus not dealing primarily with unique and concrete manifestations of aesthetic existence), each chapter will offer a short excursus, a "spotlight on music." The hope in briefly highlighting snapshots from the world of music, as specimens of aesthetic existence, at regular intervals throughout the project, is both to crystallize aspects of the argument and to allude to trajectories a practical theology might take.

We begin in Chapters 2 and 3 by drawing on the work of Kierkegaard and Bonhoeffer respectively, to clarify the nature of aesthetic existence and its place in the Christian life. The selection of Kierkegaard and Bonhoeffer is significant since they shared a mutual rejection of "cheap grace." If there is to be an argument for the endorsement of aesthetic existence in the Christian life, it needs to be one that takes the cost of

---

33. Cottingham, "What Is Humane Philosophy?"

discipleship seriously. Kierkegaard and Bonhoeffer are best positioned to help us do just that.

Chapter 2 will contribute to better understanding the nature of aesthetic existence through Kierkegaard's work on human existence, and in particular, the relationship of aesthetic to ethical and religious existence. A superficial reading of Kierkegaard seems to suggest that he proposed his three spheres of life (the aesthetic, ethical, and religious) as distinct stages, one replacing the other; aesthetic existence thus jettisoned as a person matures in their existential journey. However, a closer reading reveals Kierkegaard's limited and qualified endorsement of aesthetic existence in Christian life as poetic living. A life of discipleship is incompatible with the aestheticized Romantic notion of poetic living as self-creation, located in sensory immediacy amidst the play of unending freedom. This point is certainly not limited to Kierkegaard's Romantic context, but has almost uncanny prescient significance for the postmodern creation of self in contemporary society. Kierkegaard's attack on the potent combination of aestheticism and comfortable Christendom holds yet more contemporary relevance, a reminder of the perennial danger such an alliance holds. Despite these concerns, however, Kierkegaard endorses the formative role of the imagination and the concept of a second immediacy, or an "immediacy after reflection" in the Christian life, pointing toward the co-poeticizing role that one plays, in relationship with Christ, as one becomes Christian. Right at the outset of the project, therefore, we are confronted by a theme that we will follow throughout: not all modes of aesthetic existence are equal in relation to discipleship. While the aestheticized self-creation of Romantic aesthetic existence creates a fantastical and illusory sense of reality, there does appear to be a formational role for *mature* aesthetic existence in discipleship, in coming to apprehend christological reality.

Bonhoeffer helps us to further discover this role in Chapter 3 by locating aesthetic existence firmly within the Christian life, even amidst the self-same challenge Kierkegaard faced of distorted Christendom and the consequent call for costly discipleship. While it is too simplistic to say that Bonhoeffer's theological biography inverts Kierkegaard's "stages" of life (beginning with the religious, moving to the ethical, and finally the aesthetic), there is a sense in which this is true, as Bonhoeffer reflects more deeply on the aesthetic towards the end of his life journey. His basis for integrating aesthetic existence with the Christian life is his embrace of this-worldly existence as an incarnational response to imitating Christ.

Again, it is important to distinguish between, on the one hand, mature aesthetic existence, which is a polyphonous celebration of christological reality in the penultimate, and on the other, an aesthetic existence as ultimate, which is simply aestheticism. Even though Bonhoeffer does not provide us with a systematic treatment, his personal embrace of aesthetic existence in his own life, particularly in the form of his engagement with music from a young age, offers an insightful pointer to its formational significance, as seen through the impact of musical metaphors on his theology.

In Chapter 4, drawing on Iain McGilchrist's neuropsychological research integrated with his "humane philosophy," we delve into this formational significance of aesthetic existence as a fundamental aspect of being human. Neuroscience points toward the need for a holistic understanding of human faculties. Sense and sensibility, imagination and reason are not poles of opposites as they are often portrayed.[34] Drawing from research into the lateralization of brain function, McGilchrist argues for the fundamental integration of embodiment, imagination, and rationality in a holistic understanding of the human person. Brain lateralization appears to show that there are two primary ways of attending to the world: abstract, detailed (primarily) left-hemisphere attention and relational, contextual (primarily) right-hemisphere attention. While both are vital to healthy apprehension of reality, the modern world prioritizes the former, thereby neglecting the latter. Aesthetic existence plays a significant, partially preconscious role in the formation of contextual paradigms, or "metaphors we live by," through embodied and affective interaction with the world, grounded in right-hemisphere attention. Significantly, however, sensory engagement with the world dominated by left-hemisphere attention simply creates self-contained virtualities, the "formation" of simulacra. Aesthetic existence is thus not only an *expression* of being human, but more significantly, aesthetic existence plays a key role in the making of meaning, with consequences for ethical and religious life.

In Chapter 5 we explore the implications of this holistic understanding of being human for a life of faith. We take a closer look at the universal human commitment to belief, not as a weak form of knowledge, but as a relational disposition, informed, partially on a preconscious level,

---

34. On their integration, see in particular the work of eminent neuroscientists Jaak Panksepp and Antonio Damasio. For example, Panksepp, *Affective Neuroscience*; Damasio, *The Feeling of What Happens*; Damasio, *Descartes' Error*.

by aesthetic existence. Belief, therefore, is fundamentally connected to embodied action in the world, challenging the boundaries between aesthetics, ethics, and faith. *Making* sense, as a function of embodied action in relationship to the imagination, brings together poiesis and praxis, aesthetics and ethics. Such formation, or *making* of belief is universal, not limited to religious belief—but again, it can serve either faith-formation or virtualization. Graham Ward argues that the vital connection between embodied aesthetic existence and divine reality is analogical participation. The ontological connection with the divine hinges on the sacramental nature of all of life in the world, including aesthetic existence. Whether we endorse the entirety of Ward's sacramental, participatory metaphysics or not, his work challenges us to better understand the analogical and metaphorical as an embodied way of life, taking the this-worldly nature of discipleship seriously by framing it within a liturgical orientation to *all* of life.

Drawing on Nicholas Wolterstorff's analysis of liturgy and art, in Chapter 6 we then consider mature aesthetic existence as everyday liturgy. On the one hand, aesthetic engagement does not predominantly belong to the domain of disinterested contemplation, as the modern narrative suggests, but it is essentially action, and is best understood as social practice. On the other hand, liturgy, too, is best understood as informed and guided by social practice. By combining both of these analyses, it becomes clear that aesthetic existence has both an expressive and formative role to play in a liturgical orientation to all of life. Mature aesthetic existence is an expression of worship, as an incarnational celebration of this-worldliness, rightly oriented to God. Such celebration is not merely ornamental but *enhances* the ordinary as action in the world, thereby furthering shalom. But as with all liturgy, there is a circularity that should be noted here. Such expression functions as a practice, which is in turn formative, operating as a partially preconscious script for the liturgy of the everyday. To repeat the theme once more, such scripting does not automatically play a positive role in faith formation. Aesthetic existence is both an expression of worship and formative for worship, but the object or orientation of worship differs dependent upon which mode of aesthetic existence is embraced.

2

The Nature of Aesthetic Existence

DISMISSING EVERYDAY AESTHETIC EXPERIENCES as insignificant, or at best tangential, to the process of discipleship stems from misunderstanding the fundamental role that aesthetic existence plays in being human and becoming Christian. To fully appreciate why this is so problematic, we need to better understand the nature of aesthetic existence. Søren Kierkegaard (1813–1855) is a helpful ally in this quest. At first glance, drawing from Kierkegaard may seem counterproductive, for is it not precisely aesthetic existence that Kierkegaard suggests should be rejected in order to embrace religious existence? This narrow reading of Kierkegaard seems to affirm the commonly held view that a life of faith demands rejection of aesthetically saturated this-worldliness. Such a dichotomy, influenced by a spiritual/physical dualism, is often imposed upon Kierkegaard, the perception persisting that Kierkegaard drove a wedge between aesthetics on the one hand, and the ethico-religious on the other. Hans Urs von Balthasar recounts the story of Kierkegaard appearing before the queen for commendation, the queen misnaming his work *Either/Or* as "Either and Or," a title which Balthasar suggests ironically highlights the problematic disjunction in Kierkegaard's work.[1] However, beyond this superficial and reductionist caricature, Kierkegaard not only offers a rich and nuanced understanding of everyday aesthetics, but also points to the role of aesthetic existence in becoming Christian.

This chapter then has two objectives: First, to clarify the notion of aesthetic existence, particularly in relationship to discipleship. In order to

---

1. Balthasar, "Revelation and the Beautiful," 95–96.

do so, we will need to contextualize Kierkegaard's use of the concept within his reaction to both Romanticism and Danish Lutheran Christendom. Kierkegaard's concern was not constructing a systematic theory of aesthetics, but the question of what it meant to become Christian within his cultural milieu. While this is a helpful general principle to take away from Kierkegaard (aesthetic existence is always informed by a cultural context), the particular influences of Romanticism and a nationalized Christendom are particularly worth engaging, as they continue to offer particular resonance in our time. Christendom is all too often co-opted in service of political ends today, just as it was in Kierkegaard's time and has been so often in the past. And if Romanticism represents an early sensate attempt to respond to the social and anthropological fragmentation ushered in by the Enlightenment, then postmodernity only further exacerbates this fragmentation even while attempting to recover an affective and embodied response to it. In other words, an accurate understanding, not only of Kierkegaard's approach to aesthetic existence, but also our contemporary grasp and application of the concept, requires understanding it within the larger exploration of genuine Christian living and formation amidst societal forces such as these.

The second objective of this chapter is to articulate Kierkegaard's perspective, as a preliminary response to the question of the relation between aesthetic existence and discipleship. Kierkegaard's view is complex and defies reductionist readings, which either point exclusively to his vilification of the aesthetic or lean toward the temptation to massage his embrace of "poetic living" into an insufficiently qualified endorsement of the aesthetic. However, on close examination it is clear that there is not only an either/or but also a both/and in his approach to aesthetics. While offering a scathing rejection of the Romantic notion of self-creation, as a process defined by aestheticism (the either/or), he also embraces (his own qualified view of) existence as art, living poetically, and consequently the significant role the imagination plays in formation, even religious formation (the both/and). His response to the faculty of imagination is also complex. While he rejects the Romantic, imaginative creation of the ideal (which is disconnected from actuality), he acknowledges the role of the imagination in generating possibility for self-development. This healthy use of the imagination is anchored in the reality of Christ for us today, here and now (this theme is further developed by Bonhoeffer, as *promeity*, which we will further explore in the next chapter). Even if Kierkegaard does not explicitly take us that far, the implication that this raises is that everyday aesthetic existence is inherently connected, through our very bodies, to incarnational living as imitation of Christ. While we will need to go beyond Kierkegaard to explore this more deeply, he offers an important entryway into our exploration of aesthetic existence and discipleship.

Kierkegaard's Context: Calling for true discipleship amid aestheticism

In order to understand Kierkegaard's perspective on aesthetic existence we need to briefly situate his work within the context to which he was responding. In particular, for our purposes, it is his reaction to Romanticism and Danish Christendom (and their interaction) that informs his polemic on genuine Christian living. As we delve into his context, it should be apparent that these influences continue to mark aesthetic existence today, even if in a different guise. The postmodern creation of the self owes much to the legacy of Romantic self-creation, for example, being equally susceptible to aestheticism, albeit conveyed by technological media, which further blur the distinction between ideality and reality.

A Reaction to Romantic Self-Creation

At the heart of Kierkegaard's critique of Romanticism is the inability of the Romantic ideal to be integrated with reality.[2] While there is ample evidence of his engagement with Romanticism in his early papers and journal entries, it is in his academic dissertation, *The Concept of Irony*, where he deals extensively with the Romantic ideal of living poetically. The fragmentary and varied nature of his early papers and journals has led to a diversity of interpretations as to Kierkegaard's initial stance toward Romanticism. While some see this early work as a manifestation of Romantic youth in Kierkegaard, others argue that it represents reflections on Romanticism rather than an embrace of it.[3] Regardless, for our purposes the relevant point is that Romanticism, with its conception of the aesthetic self, was at the forefront of Kierkegaard's thinking and writing from early on. Romantics with which Kierkegaard engaged, Friedrich

---

2. Walsh, *Living Poetically*, 49.
3. Pattison, *Kierkegaard: The Aesthetic and the Religious*, 44.

Schlegel (1772–1829) and Friedrich Schiller (1759–1805) for instance, espoused the emergence of selfhood through freedom in an "aesthetic state," while Danish Romantic poets, such as Adam Oehlenschläger and Henrik Steffens, "used poetic means to master the expression of human truth and freedom . . . [claiming] it is poetic expression that best reveals human freedom as the ideal to which humans should aim."[4] This is the essential demand that Kierkegaard understood Romanticism to be making—that one should "live poetically"—and that consequently became the principal point of his critique.[5]

While there are aspects to the notion of living poetically that Kierkegaard wishes to recover (which we will later explore), he rejects aestheticism, as the absolutization of the aesthetic, and consequent disconnect from actuality, which lies at the heart of the Romantic version of living poetically. As Sylvia Walsh notes, Kierkegaard's claim is that the Romantics

> attempt to create themselves by imaginatively playing or experimenting with various poetic possibilities in life . . . But because the Romantic ironists flit from possibility to possibility, living, in his opinion, in a "totally hypothetical and subjunctive way," their lives lose continuity and lapse under the sway of moods and feelings that are themselves subject to sudden and drastic change (*Concept of Irony*, 284).[6]

The pursuit of "endless possibility" leads to immersion in the fantastical imagination, severed from finitude and actuality.[7] While it claims pursuit of the ideal, "every ideal is instantly nothing but an allegory hiding a higher ideal within itself, and so on into infinity."[8] It is precisely because of this that Kierkegaard "concludes that the romantic cannot be 'captured in a definition' . . . that 'the romantic lies essentially in flowing over all boundaries' (*Journals and Papers*, 3:3796)."[9] Behind the illusion of the ideal, Kierkegaard alludes to the ultimate bankruptcy of Romanticism by describing it as

---

4. Jothen, *Kierkegaard, Aesthetics, and Selfhood*, 15.
5. Kierkegaard, *The Concept of Irony*, 295–99; cf. Walsh, *Living Poetically*, 43.
6. Walsh, *Living Poetically*, 51.
7. Gouwens, *Kierkegaard's Dialectic of the Imagination*, 54.
8. Kierkegaard, *The Concept of Irony*, 306.
9. Walsh, *Living Poetically*, 46.

> restless (JP, 3806),[10] lacking integration (JP, 16), incapable of being given a permanent stable form (JP, 3815) . . . a constantly self-surpassing striving (JP, 5131), "a continual grasping after something which eludes one." (JP, 3816) No single image or expression can satisfy the Romantic consciousness for the "whole idea cannot rest and be contained in the actual expression," (JP, 3807) since the expression gives only "the image of the shadow." (JP, 3816)[11]

For Kierkegaard, there is no substance, "consistent principle of form" or "lifeview" that ultimately holds together the Romantic ideal in a sense of wholeness.[12] It is, therefore, the vacuity of this illusory self-creation that Kierkegaard wishes to confront. But herein lies the complexity of Kierkegaard's aesthetics: on the one hand he wishes to reject Romantic aestheticism while on the other to show that imaginative possibility and actuality can, and should, cohere in development of the self. He wants to affirm "a sense of our historical situatedness and finite limitations as well as freedom, and the construction of human personality through a process of self-development, rather than self-creation, in relation to the infinite or divine."[13] In other words, "his aesthetics is always intertwined with becoming a Christian."[14] Or, to put it in the terms of our discussion, to rightly understand his construal of "aesthetic existence" we need to consider it in light of his perspective on discipleship.

A Reaction to Danish Christendom and "Cheap Grace"

Kierkegaard's aesthetic critique was not merely directed at Romantic philosophers; his concern was with *existence*, lived reality, and the flourishing of aestheticism in the everyday. It is the manner in which these ideas affected Danish culture and the church, mutually coalescing in Christendom, which particularly provoked his ire. Therefore his critique does not traffic in the realm of abstraction but in everyday Danish existence. His use of three specific examples of aesthetic existence are helpful

---

10. Pattison is referencing Hong and Hong, eds., *Søren Kierkegaard's Journals and Papers*, published by Indiana University Press between 1967 and 1978. Unless otherwise indicated, all references to Kierkegaard's work are to the Hong's translations.

11. Pattison, *Kierkegaard: The Aesthetic and the Religious*, 49.

12. Gouwens, *Kierkegaard's Dialectic of the Imagination*, 70–71.

13. Walsh, *Living Poetically*, 2.

14. Jothen, *Kierkegaard, Aesthetics, and Selfhood*, 8.

to consider, since they not only illustrate this point but also, as we will see, illustrate how his attack on Christendom intersects with his commentary on everyday aesthetics: Østergade (East Street), Tivoli Gardens, and Deer Park.

The streets of Copenhagen make a regular appearance in Kierkegaard's writing and are especially prominent in "The Seducer's Diary," where particularly symbolic is the fashionable Østergade.[15] Østergade was described in 1852 by a British visitor as "the street where everyone walks one time of the day or other, where all the 'shopping' is done, for it contains the best shops in town, where youths go to saunter and smoke, ladies to gossip . . . A 'Dagdriver' (day-loiterer) is in Denmark much what a lounger is in England; and Östergade is the place where *par excellence* they exercise their calling."[16]

If lounging on Østergade typifies aesthetic existence for Kierkegaard, experiencing the amusement park Tivoli Gardens represents a concentration of such aesthetic existence, Tivoli thus later functioning as a key image in his attack on Christendom. Tivoli Gardens "opened, with nice irony, in the year that saw the publication of *Either/Or* (1843). Tivoli was not simply an empirical fact: it was a cultural product, imbued with the means given to it by its founder, George Carstensen . . . collaborators *and* by its devotees and critics."[17] While the collective creation of Tivoli as a cultural artifact is indeed a critical point, as the founder and designer of Tivoli, Carstensen himself, is for Kierkegaard a personification of reflective aesthetic existence, as we will momentarily see. Carstensen took both the name and concept of Tivoli "from pleasure gardens of the same name in Paris, 'Tivolis.'" In its first year, it drew 372,237 visitors, more than triple the population of Copenhagen at the time. It contained a diversity of amusements, including a steam roundabout, a roller-coaster, music, theater, fireworks, and so forth, "which created another world in which, for an afternoon or an evening, visitors could slip off their everyday identity and become tourists in some vaguely defined land . . . promenading up and down the allées, seeing and being seen."[18] It is not merely incidental that Tivoli continues to operate today, making it one of the oldest amusement parks in existence. In fact, not only is it still in operation,

---

15. Pattison, *Poor Paris!*, 65.
16. As quoted in Pattison, *Quest for Unambiguous Life*, 13.
17. Pattison, *Poor Paris!*, 2.
18. Pattison, *Poor Paris!*, 2.

but it continues to draw large numbers of visitors, being among the most visited theme parks in Europe. Its continued success points to the ongoing relevance of Kierkegaard's commentary, amid the contemporary influence of Disneyfication on culture and religion.[19]

Along very similar lines to Tivoli Gardens, for Kierkegaard, Deer Park represented another prototypical experience of aesthetic existence. Deer Park was an annual rural fair, described in 1857 as "all that the senses could desire. A motley chaos for ear and eye: tents and booths . . . swings . . . carousels . . . equestrian artists and menageries, wheels of fortune and panoramas, wax figures and waffle-sellers, public marionette theaters . . . [and] fire-eaters—in short: shrieking, noise, trumpet-blasts and shouting, as everyone seems to want to outbid all others in the art of working miracles and providing spectacles."[20]

Kierkegaard's critique of aesthetic existence, as represented in these examples, goes very much hand in hand with his attack on Christendom. On the one hand, he is condemning everyday bourgeois Danish aestheticism as expressed on buzzing streets like Østergade, the spectacle of the Theatre Royal, and ultimately the amusements and thrills of Tivoli Gardens and Deer Park. On the other, he is deeply troubled by the everyday apathy of the Danish church. In his estimation, these two existential realities overlap in the "*haute bourgeois* aestheticism" of leading clerical figures such as Bishop Jacob Peter Mynster, who bore the brunt of his attack.[21] In fact, Kierkegaard goes as far as equating Danish church leaders with entertainers like Tivoli's founder, Carstensen, their empty baptisms and confirmations being compared to "picnics" and "family delights."[22] "This is the highly respected activity of the pastor, a livelihood that prevents people from entering into God's kingdom. In return, 'the pastor' does his best by way of performances (for which producer Carstensen has a decided talent in grand style), beautiful, glorious festivities with—just as a little wine tastes good in lemonade—a little religion added, something Carstensen cannot do . . . but perhaps he could be ordained."[23]

Similarly, Kierkegaard equates the role of the clergy with "coachmen, hired to take visitors out to the Deer Park, (implying, further, that

19. Lyon, *Jesus in Disneyland*.
20. As quoted in Pattison, *Quest for Unambiguous Life*, 51.
21. Kirmmse, "Out with It!," 27.
22. Kierkegaard, *The Moment*, 249.
23. Kierkegaard, *The Moment*, 249.

the sacraments and offices of the Church are themselves no more than Deer Park entertainments)."[24] Later, after Carstensen had left Tivoli in 1848, writing in his journal Kierkegaard "notes under the heading 'Protestantism in Denmark' that, 'It is a shame that Carstensen has left us and that now Bournonville [Director of the Royal Ballet] is leaving us: these two would be best suited to serve and manage religion in Denmark.'"[25] This ecclesial connection with the carnival of Tivoli is telling if one correlates it with *Either/Or*'s aesthete "A" and his aspiration of "Copenhagen becom[ing] another Athens" as "the greatest artists, actors and dancers . . . stream to Copenhagen," to create a fantasia wherein, as Pattison puts it, "the fantastic [becomes] the factual and the factual [becomes] the fantastic."[26] It is a "fantasia" that is both self-perpetuating and economically sustainable since it not only creates a "reality," but sustains it through the commodification of leisure (Tivoli becoming "one of the most successful leisure 'products' of the nineteenth century").[27] A key point here, which we will further explore in later chapters, is that the religious realm is not immune to the virtualization of reality that accompanies aestheticism. Again, the contemporary relevance of Kierkegaard's critique should be clear. Disneyfication—the cyclical creation, commodification, and consumption of aestheticized pseudo-realities—has the potential to influence every aspect of societal existence, including the life of the church.

It is the combination of the influence of Romantic aestheticism, alongside the apathy and comfort of Danish Christendom, which led Kierkegaard to call for true discipleship and a rejection of cheap grace. The church had become aligned with culture for all the wrong reasons, succumbing to it rather than critically engaging it. It had become a "culture-religion."[28] As Kierkegaard's pseudonym Johannes Climacus reflects, if a Dane were to question whether they should call themselves a Christian, his wife would say, "Hubby, darling, where did you ever pick up such a notion? How can you not be a Christian? You are Danish, aren't you? . . . Aren't you a good subject in a Christian nation, in

---

24. Pattison, *Quest for Unambiguous Life*, 52. In reference to Kierkegaard, *The Moment*, 348.

25. Pattison, *Poor Paris!*, 24.

26. Kierkegaard, *Either/Or* 1:287; Pattison, *Poor Paris!*, 64.

27. Pattison, *Poor Paris!*, 64.

28. Johnson, "Kierkegaard and the Church," xxii.

a Lutheran-Christian state? So of course you are a Christian."[29] Central to Kierkegaard's frustration was the "marriage of convenience wherein the government was more than willing to pay clerical stipends and provide for the maintenance of church fabrics out of the public treasury in return for the modest, reciprocal favor that, on political and social issues, the Church remain irrelevant and confine itself to 'Quiet Hours.'"[30] Contrary to Schleiermacher, whose theology paved the way for affirming the relation between faith and nationality (and thus the established church), Kierkegaard saw the "whole phenomenon of established Christendom [as] a monstrous error."[31] "Christendom has done away with Christianity," Kierkegaard proclaimed, and he therefore saw the task before him to "introduce Christianity to Christendom."[32]

Kierkegaard launched his "attack on Christendom" through pieces published in the periodicals *Fatherland* and *Moment*, although, as Walter Lowrie notes, his journals contain far more, "ten times as much material as he needed."[33] The initial catalyst for the attack was an address by Professor Martensen, at the above-mentioned Bishop Mynster's memorial service, where Martensen named Mynster a "witness to the truth." Kierkegaard responded that he was nothing of the sort, but in fact the complete opposite. "Bishop Mynster's proclamation of Christianity (to take just one thing) tones down, veils, suppresses, omits some of what is most decisively Christian, what is too inconvenient for us human beings, what would make our lives strenuous, prevent us from enjoying life—this about dying to the world, about voluntary renunciation, about hating one-self, about suffering for the doctrine, etc."[34] To the contrary, there is a cost to discipleship, and a genuine understanding of "a truth-witness is a person whose life from first to last is unfamiliar with everything called enjoyment."[35] Kierkegaard explored these themes at length, his parable of the geese an example, wherein the geese are content to stay within the comforts of home, only talking of flying on Sundays ("Christendom's worship services") but never actually flying. All the while becoming "plump,

---

29. Kierkegaard, *Concluding Unscientific Postscript*, 1:50.
30. Johnson, "Kierkegaard and the Church," xxii.
31. Pattison, *Kierkegaard and the Theology of the Nineteenth Century*, 6.
32. Kierkegaard, *Training in Christianity*, 39.
33. Johnson, "Kierkegaard and the Church," xiii.
34. Kierkegaard, *The Moment*, 3–4.
35. Kierkegaard, *The Moment*, 5–6.

fat and delicate" (a sign of God's grace), ridiculing the geese that actually fly, who look "poorly and thin" (clearly not enjoying God's grace).[36]

While the "cost of discipleship," with its rejection of cheap grace, has come to be associated with Dietrich Bonhoeffer (as we will further explore in the next chapter), Bonhoeffer was clearly influenced by his engagement with Kierkegaard's work, amidst their common concern with the problem of Christendom. In calling attention to this mutual concern, Geoffrey Kelly describes Bonhoeffer's experience of Christendom as "the seductive lure of a comfortable Christianity, gliding along with an all-powerful ideology that promised law and order, stability and security, state-bestowed benefits that appealed to clerical interests and the churches' passion for survival as an institution enjoying civil privileges."[37] It is a description that could be applied equally to a number of different contexts over last few centuries of Christendom, and a "seductive lure" that remains relevant today. It certainly applied to Kierkegaard's context. Here we should remember the revolutionary European milieu, culminating in 1848, which in Denmark saw a bloodless revolution that for Kierkegaard "was a cataclysmic event for the spiritual health of the nation." Kierkegaard knew this was not the revolution that Denmark needed, and the apathy the church showed in its failure to protect the "common man" from being used and abused by the revolutionaries angered him.[38]

In their mutual frustration, Kierkegaard and Bonhoeffer share the call to a Christian life that comes at a cost and the rejection of "cheap grace." While both Kierkegaard and Bonhoeffer may have been aware of Luther's description of the abuse of Christ's grace as "cheap," there is a strong argument that Bonhoeffer's use of the phrase came from Kierkegaard.[39] Kierkegaard's study of Luther, translated and published in German as *Der Einzelne und die Kirche: Über Luther und den Protestantismus*, "served as a direct source for several sections" of Bonhoeffer's *Discipleship* (previously published as *The Cost of Discipleship*).[40] In his text, Kierkegaard

---

36. Kierkegaard, *Journals and Papers*, 3:391.

37. Kelly, "Kierkegaard as 'Antidote,'" 147.

38. Kirkpatrick, *Attacks on Christendom*, 30–33. See Kirkpatrick's text for an account of the interaction between Kierkegaard and Bonhoeffer in their mutual response to Christendom, which is both comprehensive and insightful.

39. In Luther's *Rationis Latominae Confutatio* of 1521, as pointed out in Kelly, "Kierkegaard as 'Antidote,'" 149.

40. Kelly and Godsey, "Editors' Introduction," 11.

uses the terms "cheap grace" and "costly grace," these being among the sections underlined by Bonhoeffer in his own copy of the book.[41] It is not merely a *phrase* that they share, but the concern that lies behind it. For both Bonhoeffer and Kierkegaard, the story of the rich young man in the Gospels speaks directly to the problem of comfortable Christendom.[42] And again, for both, the solution is simple: Bonhoeffer later echoes Kierkegaard's injunction that "if the gospel demands that we renounce this world . . . , then the simple thing to do is: do it."[43] But for Kierkegaard, the church is so caught up in the concerns of comfortable Christendom that it has lost sight of true Christianity, as he laments in *For Self-Examination*.

> Ah, we who still call ourselves Christians are from the Christian point of view so pampered, so far from being what Christianity does indeed require of those who want to call themselves Christians, dead to the world, that we hardly even have any idea of that kind of earnestness; we are as yet unable to do without, to give up the artistic and its mitigation, cannot bear the true impact of actuality—well then, let us at least be honest and admit it.[44]

Kierkegaard's allusion here, resonating with his rejection of aestheticism, is that "the artistic presentation and its soothing effect," the fantastical virtualization of reality, is an imaginative mechanism to escape (christological) actuality.[45] Later, in his "attack," he again emphasizes the disconnect between, on the one hand, the "unreality" of existence within finite, aestheticized Christendom, and on the other, discipleship as the embrace of christological reality.

> "Christendom" is by no means Christ's Church . . . "Christendom" is a pack of blather that has fastened itself to Christianity like a cobweb on fruit and that now is so good as to want to confuse itself with Christianity, just as when the cobweb considers itself to be the fruit because it . . . is something that clings to the fruit. The kind of existences manifested by the millions in Christendom has absolutely no relation to the New Testament, is an unreality that has no claim to Christ's promise concerning

---

41. Kelly, "Kierkegaard as 'Antidote,'" 149–50.
42. Kelly, "Kierkegaard as 'Antidote,'" 152.
43. As quoted in Kelly, "Kierkegaard as 'Antidote,'" 152.
44. Kierkegaard, *For Self-Examination/Judge For Yourself!*, 11–12.
45. Lowrie's translation in Kierkegaard, *For Self-Examination*, 37.

the believers; yes an unreality, since true reality is present only when a person has ventured decisively in this way, as Christ requires . . . But "Christendom" is this nauseating dalliance, to want to remain completely and totally in finiteness and then—to make off with the promises of Christianity.[46]

As Matthew D. Kirkpatrick succinctly puts it, "In the face of the absolute paradox [of Christ] and its offensiveness, of the extreme rigorousness of imitation, the secular world has converted Christianity into the palatable affirmation of life in all its peace, comfort, and security. Using a phrase that appears through his journals, in the face of anxiety, the fear and trembling of Christianity, 'The world wants to be deceived.'"[47]

Kierkegaard's Stages of Existence

This backdrop helps us to understand the motivation behind Kierkegaard's apparent rejection of aesthetic existence in becoming Christian. If the Christian life is one that faces up to christological reality, embracing sacrifice and suffering, and "unfamiliarity with enjoyment," then the proliferation of Romantic aestheticism, intermingled with comfortable Christendom, needs to be rejected in order to embrace religious existence. But is the equation as simple as this? This would seem to imply that aesthetic existence plays no part in discipleship, and therefore simply needs to be rejected in the Christian life. In some ways, Kierkegaard is indeed saying this, as we will shortly consider. But there is a danger in reading his apparent rejection of aesthetic existence too superficially and thereby drawing erroneous, sweeping conclusions, such as equating aestheticism with aesthetic existence. The critical point to note here is that Kierkegaard was responding to a particular context, as was Luther, and Bonhoeffer.[48] The task therefore befalls us to read Kierkegaard's

---

46. Kierkegaard, *The Moment*, 215.

47. Kirkpatrick, *Attacks on Christendom*, 154; cf. Kierkegaard, *Self-Examination/Judge for Yourself!*, 139; Kierkegaard, *Journals and Papers*, 3:21 (entry 50).

48. In fact, Kierkegaard himself highlights the significance of such contextualization by suggesting that Luther's message would have been quite different had he delivered it in Kierkegaard's time (*For Self-Examination/Judge for Yourself!*, 24), a point later affirmed in Bonhoeffer, *Letters and Papers from Prison*, 173: "Already one hundred years ago Kierkegaard said that Luther today would say the opposite of what he said back then. I think this is true—*cum grano salis* [within certain limits]."

perspective on aesthetic existence carefully, taking into account the rhetoric he employs, as he reacts to what he sees as the dangers of his context.

In doing so, it will become apparent that while Kierkegaard rejects aestheticism, he wishes to recover a sense of "poetic living," which includes aesthetic experience and the subsequent role of the imagination in formation (*Bildung*). In other words, there is a qualified sense of aesthetic existence, or a *mature* aesthetic existence, which is not rejected, but contributes to the formation of religious existence. The complexity of such an understanding is vital to accurately depicting the aesthetics of discipleship. A binary, reductionist view concerning the role of everyday aesthetic existence in faith formation is neither accurate nor helpful.

It is for this reason that exploring the question of aesthetic existence's relation to discipleship, as framed by Bonhoeffer and Kierkegaard, is particularly fruitful. Rather than engaging the question through the entryway of an unreserved embrace of the aesthetic, both Bonhoeffer and Kierkegaard's starting point of a critique of aestheticism, as well as the call to costly discipleship, allows for a sober evaluation of both the positive and negative aspects that aesthetic existence contributes to faith formation. The challenges, which both Christendom and aestheticism bring, have not disappeared from society. Therefore, we need to take the time to understand both Kierkegaard's critique of aesthetic existence and his subtler embrace thereof, which mutually provide an entryway to a robust account of the aesthetics of discipleship.

A superficial reading of Kierkegaard would conclude that aesthetic existence is an immature stage of life to be passed through, in a linear and progressive manner, as one matures to ethical and ultimately religious existence. It is rather obvious how one can come to such a conclusion based on reading selected passages and works from his corpus. However, such a reductionist reading does not take seriously the complexity of Kierkegaard's authorship. There are a number of aspects to take into account in this regard. The most obvious is the pseudonymous nature of much of his work. A critical point here is that Kierkegaard's views cannot be strictly equated with that of any of his pseudonyms. His suggestion that "in the pseudonymous books there is not a single word by me" should be taken seriously.[49] But the pseudonyms point to a deeper complexity: his extensive use of irony and Socratic method as a means of communicating indirectly, "without authority." Rather than presenting

---

49. Kierkegaard, *Concluding Unscientific Postscript*, 1:626.

his argument systematically, he uses "poet-communication."⁵⁰ His method reflects his objective, which is not merely to engage the intellect but to affectively and imaginatively provoke the reader toward existential reflection and action.⁵¹ While this should immediately, in itself, point to the fact that he values the formative role of the aesthetic, it also makes the systematizing of his work a challenging task. Although they are the words of a pseudonym (Johannes Climacus) describing the work *Either/Or*, the following quote succinctly reflects the existential nature and goal of Kierkegaard's indirect communication: "That there is no conclusion and no final decision is an indirect expression for truth as inwardness and in this way perhaps a polemic against truth as knowledge."⁵² In light of his method, articulating Kierkegaard's stance on the aesthetics of discipleship demands discerning the continuity in his thought in light of his corpus as a whole, approaching his pseudonymous work alongside his non-pseudonymous, direct communication.

Aesthetic Existence as a Stage of Life: Kierkegaard's Rejection of Aestheticism

While we ultimately need to move toward a layered, complex understanding of Kierkegaard's approach to aesthetic existence, it is nevertheless helpful for us to begin with the obvious, by encountering his apparent antipathy for aesthetic existence as the initial stage of life, which is significant because it points toward his rejection of aestheticism. For Kierkegaard, the central aspect of aesthetic existence as a stage of life is immediacy, living in the moment. This is to be superseded in the journey toward ethical and then ultimately religious existence. The initial stages are exposited at length in the two-part work *Either/Or* (the first concentrates on the aesthetic and the second on the ethical), and also in *Stages on Life's Way* (which refers to "spheres" of existence rather than stages). The pseudonym Frater Taciturnus outlines the stages,

> There are three existence-spheres: the esthetic, the ethical, the religious . . .The esthetic sphere is the sphere of immediacy, the ethical the sphere of requirement (and this requirement is so infinite that the individual always goes bankrupt), the religious

---

50. Kierkegaard, *Journals and Papers*, 6:248.
51. Jothen, *Kierkegaard, Aesthetics, and Selfhood*, 46.
52. Kierkegaard, *Concluding Unscientific Postscript*, 1:252.

the sphere of fulfillment, but, please note, not a fulfillment such as when one fills an alms box or a sack with gold, for repentance has specifically created a boundless space, and as a consequence the religious contradiction: simultaneously to be out on 70,000 fathoms of water and yet be joyful.[53]

In *Either/Or* II, another pseudonym, Judge William, further clarifies the distinction between the aesthetic stage and the ethical stage by locating ethical existence in the realm of volitional formation; in the ethical one chooses what one becomes, "to choose is an intrinsic and stringent term for the ethical."[54] By contrast, aesthetic existence is captive to the immediacy of moods, passions and circumstances. "But what does it mean to live esthetically, and what does it mean to live ethically? To that I would respond: the esthetic in a person is that by which he spontaneously and immediately is what he is; the ethical is that by which he becomes what he becomes."[55] We need to once again situate these comments in the context, and larger Kierkegaardian project, of self-development and concomitant rejection of Romantic self-creation. While the aesthete defines the self through the momentary gratification of desire, the ethical person *chooses* to embrace social responsibility. Existence in the aesthetic stage is simply a collection of moments, holding no coherence, as portrayed in *Either/Or*, through the figure of Don Giovanni. He "can become epic only by continually finishing and continually being able to begin all over again, for his life is the sum of *repellerende* [discrete] moments that have no coherence, and his life as the moment is the sum of moments and as a sum of moments is the moment."[56]

Not only is the immediate paramount, but the aesthetic stage of existence is a mode of freedom that aims to create the self by playful experimentation,

> In connection with Tivoli entertainments and literary New Year's presents it holds true for the catch-penny artists and those who are caught by them, that *variety is the highest law of life*. But in connection with the truth as inwardness in existence, in connection with a more incorruptible joy of life, which has nothing in common with the craving of the life-weary for diversion, the opposite holds true; the law is the same and yet changed, and

53. Kierkegaard, *Stages on Life's Way*, 476–77.
54. Kierkegaard, *Either/Or*, 2:166.
55. Kierkegaard, *Either/Or*, 2:178.
56. Kierkegaard, *Either/Or*, 1:96.

still the same. That is why lovers of Tivoli are so little interested in eternity, for it is the nature of eternity always to be the same, and the sobriety of the spirit is recognizable in the knowledge that a change in externalities is mere diversion, while change in the same is inwardness.[57] (Italics added)

In the aesthete's effort to bring coherence to these discrete and diverse moments, a fantastical world is created: "It is a fantasy-existence in esthetic passion."[58] The attempt to reflectively create such a fantastical reality distinguishes two types of aesthetic existence for Kierkegaard. While the more primitive mode of aesthetic existence dwells solely in the momentary hedonistic experience, in a more sophisticated mode the intellect too can be seized by aesthetic existence, thereby creating an ideality of ceaseless aesthetic reflection. In *Either/Or* this is most clearly seen in the "The Seducer's Diary," where we find both "the seducer, the very embodiment of unalleviated reflectivity and absolute artfulness, and Cordelia, the unplucked flower of pure immediacy"; while they may reflect distinct iterations of immature aesthetic existence they are "shown to complement each other perfectly."[59] These two senses of existence in the aesthetic stage are further explained in the introduction to the diary,

> In the first instance he enjoyed the aesthetic personally, in the second instance he enjoyed his own aesthetic personality. In the first instance the point was that he enjoyed egoistically and personally what in part was reality's gift to him and in part was that with which he himself had impregnated reality; in the second instance his personality was effaced, and he enjoyed the situation. In the first instance he constantly needed reality as occasion, as factor: in the second instance, reality was submerged in the poetic.[60]

In other words, reality disappears amid the fantastical ideality created by the reflective aesthete. Or perhaps more accurately, a pseudo-reality replaces actuality as this "second level of enjoyment wins an autonomy for the resulting poetic world that allows it to forget itself as poetic so that its

---

57. Kierkegaard, *Concluding Unscientific Postscript* (trans. Swenson and Lowrie), 254–55. For the Hong and Hong translation see Kierkegaard, *Concluding Unscientific Postscript*, 1:286.

58. Kierkegaard, *Concluding Unscientific Postscript*, 253.

59. Connell, *To Be One Thing*, 83; cf. Kierkegaard, *Either/Or*, 1:380.

60. Kierkegaard, *Either/Or* (trans. Swenson and Swenson), 1:53. For the Hong and Hong translation, see Kierkegaard, *Either/Or*, 1:305.

writer becomes unselfconsciously his own character and, thus, myth."[61] At its most developed, therefore, the life stage of aesthetic existence is not merely a preoccupation with momentary, sensory pleasure, but the reflective creation (incorporating both intellect and affect) of "reality" which absolutizes the aesthetic.

It is *this* conception of aesthetic existence, as aestheticism, that Kierkegaard argues should be rejected and left behind on the path to becoming Christian. *Concluding Unscientific Postscript to Philosophical Fragments* and *Practice in Christianity* (both pseudonymous works, the former attributed to Johannes Climacus and the latter Anti-Climacus) clearly express this view by arguing that a self wholly devoted to God is not concerned with the aesthetic. Anti-Climacus argues that Christendom is full of "admirers" who "will make no sacrifices, renounce nothing, give up nothing earthly, will not transform [their lives]."[62] But being a disciple of Christ requires "imitators," who are willing to "die to the world, to surrender the earthly," to deny the self, for here lies the transformation of a life, and its reality.[63]

Consequently, art that is disconnected from the reality of lived discipleship provokes Kierkegaard's scorn. There is no place here for aesthetic simulacra amid this christological reality, even "admiring" artistic depictions of Christ himself. "I do not comprehend how the artist would maintain his calm, that he would not notice Christ's displeasure, would not throw it all out, brushes and paints, far, far away, just as Judas did with the thirty pieces of silver, because he suddenly understood that Christ has required only imitators."[64] In fact, Johannes Climacus, resonating with the problematic nature of being an "admirer," goes as far as to suggest that not only does art have no place in Christian formation, but its "disinterested" nature means that it is not fundamentally a necessary aspect of human existence. "Poetry and art have been called an anticipation of the eternal. If one wants to call them that, one must nevertheless be aware that *poetry and art are not essentially related to an existing person*, since the contemplation of poetry and art, 'joy over the beautiful,' is disinterested, and the observer is contemplatively outside himself *qua* existing

---

61. Connell, *To Be One Thing*, 99.
62. Kierkegaard, *Practice in Christianity*, 252.
63. Kierkegaard, *Practice in Christianity*, 252.
64. Kierkegaard, *Practice in Christianity*, 255.

person."[65] Little wonder then that Kierkegaard has been perceived to drive a wedge between the aesthetic and the ethico-religious.[66]

Two points are important to note from this cursory reading of Kierkegaard's aesthetics: First, Kierkegaard *appears* to reject any role for aesthetic existence in becoming Christian. While we want to acknowledge that our engagement with Kierkegaard in this section is via pseudonyms, and therefore needs to be understood through the lens of rhetorical irony, Kierkegaard clearly had strong views on the dangers of aestheticism for Christian formation (particularly when situated amid apathetic Christendom). Second, we will need to read Kierkegaard more carefully, particularly alongside his direct communication, to ascertain if he does indeed allow aesthetic existence a role in becoming Christian. But even in so doing, we will do well to bear in mind the clarity and strength of the first point: his rejection of aestheticism and the virtual reality it creates.

Aesthetic Existence and Poetic Living: A Clarification of Terms

In order to appreciate the complexity of Kierkegaard's perspective on the role of aesthetic existence in becoming Christian, we need to delve deeper and delineate his multifaceted approach to aesthetics. Clarifying the terminology he uses is important, not only for better understanding his work, but also because it will provide a helpful framework for discussing the aesthetics of discipleship as we move beyond Kierkegaard. As already noted, Kierkegaard's engagement with aesthetics is not systematic, resulting in multiple interpretations that accentuate particular aspects of his work. The most obvious of these selective readings is outlined above: equating Kierkegaard's treatment of aesthetics solely with aesthetic existence as a stage of life, which is superseded on the path to ethical and then religious existence. But, as Jothen shows, this is only one of four "fragments" of Kierkegaard's aesthetic that we need to piece together to provide an accurate picture of his perspective. In addition to a stage of existence, his aesthetic also includes an explicit critique of art; his authorship style as poet-communicator; and his endorsement of formative

---

65. Kierkegaard, *Concluding Unscientific Postscript*, 1:313 (italics added).

66. For a helpful overview of the schools of thought regarding Kierkegaard's various approaches to aesthetics, including his apparent rejection of art, see Jothen, *Kierkegaard, Aesthetics, and Selfhood*, 7–46.

"poetic living."[67] Interpreters focusing on any one of these four elements in isolation lose sight of the "ontological moorings that tie his fragmentary aesthetics together": the formation of the human self.[68] "These fragments are all part of a rich, tactical method that seeks to provoke, awaken and enliven each reader. But to do so, Kierkegaard develops a conception of the self built upon the importance of the imagination, will, and passion as means to enact human becoming."[69] In other words, as we have already mentioned, we cannot approach Kierkegaard's understanding of aesthetics other than through the lens of self-formation; his aesthetic is inseparable from his anthropology.

The "Aesthetic" as the Lived Dimension of Sensory Experience

For Kierkegaard, therefore, *aesthetics* is fundamentally existential. As Terry Eagleton argues, "For [Kierkegaard], as for the originators of the discourse, aesthetics refers not in the first place to art but to the whole lived dimension of sensory experience, denoting a phenomenology of daily life before it comes to signify cultural production."[70] This is a helpful starting point, not only as a lens through which to interpret Kierkegaard, but also for revisiting the definition of *aesthetics* that we will be working with as it relates to discipleship.

However, we need to exercise caution as to how we proceed. For Eagleton, "cultural production" is the nexus of thought and action. Aesthetic existence is therefore a mode of existence that precedes "cultural production" either due to the immediacy that marks the first type of aesthete, such as Don Juan (action alone), or the reflectivity of the second, such as the Seducer (thought alone). In aesthetic existence, devoid of "cultural production," the self is then lost either through "flattening it out into external reality or plunging it fruitlessly into its own vertiginous depths."[71] While these two modes of aesthetic existence may seem polar opposites, Eagleton points out that, "Reflectiveness negates immediacy, but thereby shatters it to an infinite indeterminacy not wholly untypical

---

67. Jothen, *Kierkegaard, Aesthetics, and Selfhood*, 2.
68. Jothen, *Kierkegaard, Aesthetics, and Selfhood*, 5.
69. Jothen, *Kierkegaard, Aesthetics, and Selfhood*, 46.
70. Eagleton, *The Ideology of the Aesthetic*, 173.
71. Eagleton, *The Ideology of the Aesthetic*, 175.

of immediacy itself."⁷² Either way, the end result is the "radically empty" self.⁷³ The danger however, is equating one of the "fragments" of Kierkegaard's aesthetics with his aesthetics as a whole. While Eagleton is offering an accurate analysis of Kierkegaard's critique of the *life stage* of aesthetic existence, specifically as aestheticism, which Kierkegaard certainly sees as hindering self-formation, it does not necessarily follow that the *entire* "lived dimension of sensory experience," (as "phenomenology of daily life," which precedes "cultural production") is vacuous, making no contribution to self-formation. In Chapters 4 and 5 we will see that it is not feasible to separate such "cultural production" from preconscious aesthetic existence, since the actions of immediacy (preconscious though they may be) influence formation of self and thereby play a role in discipleship. But before we move beyond Kierkegaard, it is helpful to further probe his own response to the interrelationship between aesthetic and ethico-religious existence. Clearly, aestheticism, aesthetic existence as absolute, is problematic for Kierkegaard. But are his stages of existence mutually exclusive? Or, does he see formative value in a qualified, or mature aesthetic existence, as a subset of Christian existence?

"Existence" as the Lived Reality of Self-Formation

In order to appreciate the relationship between the stages of existence we need to approach Kierkegaard's work as he intended it to be read, as provocative discourse to be lived rather than a systematic treatise. Eagleton's error, along with that of others who reduce Kierkegaard's aesthetics to the life stage of aesthetic existence, is a reductionist approach in the interests of systematic neatness.⁷⁴ This fails to take into account both the nature of his "poet-communication" and the way in which Kierkegaard's indirect communication was an effort to deflect focus from himself to the reader, provoking participation (ideally formation) as a living subject. "The stages are about living and breathing, about choosing and willing, rather than merely how a self thinks and organizes thought into a conclusive system. And by describing the aesthetic as a system, merely one of the

---

72. Eagleton, *The Ideology of the Aesthetic*, 174.

73. Eagleton, *The Ideology of the Aesthetic*, 174.

74. For another example of this approach, see Dunning, *Kierkegaard's Dialectic of Inwardness*.

stages, the aesthetic is thereby reduced in its complexity, relegated to the world of logic and thought."[75]

This is why *existence* is a key term for Kierkegaard, pointing to the fact that reality is first and foremost lived. While Kierkegaard is seen as the father of existentialism, we should be cautious of reading anachronistically into his work. For Kierkegaard,

> the term "existential" always connotes the concrete or historical actualization of those factors that are essential to the formation of human personality or the qualitative life of the individual (*Journals and Papers* 1:1054, 1059, 1060, 1062, 1063). These factors are to be realized in the individual's own being and personal relations, not merely in the form of a conceptual, or ideal, actuality envisioned by the imagination and represented in external products of art.[76]

For our purposes, therefore, we are not exploring existentialism as further developed in the twentieth century by the likes of Jean-Paul Sartre, but limiting discussion of existence to the concrete and historical lived reality of self-formation amid the everyday. This is the subjective lens through which Kierkegaard's aesthetic needs to be read. He is not engaging an objective, disinterested approach, as is the case with traditional aesthetics. Even his treatment of aesthetic phenomena, from the everyday experience of Deer Park or Tivoli to the products of "literary, plastic and musical art," is subject to "an existential aesthetics that has as its object the edification, or upbuilding and fulfillment, of the human subject."[77]

The "Poetic" as an Existential Aesthetic Category

A final key term for understanding Kierkegaard's existential aesthetic is the "poetic," which he uses in an attempt to recover and rehabilitate the Romantic notion of "poetic living." He uses *poetry* not simply as a literary genre, or even in relation to the classical notion of *making* an external artistic product. But for Kierkegaard, the "poetic" "and its synonym 'poetry' are generally used in a very broad sense to encompass all forms and expressions of the creative or artistic imagination."[78] In a sense, he *is* allud-

---

75. Jothen, *Kierkegaard, Aesthetics, and Selfhood*, 22.
76. Walsh, *Living Poetically*, 5.
77. Walsh, *Living Poetically*, 6.
78. Walsh, *Living Poetically*, 18.

ing back to classical usage, but the *poiesis* (producing, or making) that he is referring to is that of self-formation. In other words, his use of *digtning*, the process of poeticizing, "describes the act of becoming a self as a creative, and thus an aesthetic, act."[79] There is therefore an obvious overlap in Kierkegaard's use of the "aesthetic" and the "poetic," and often they are employed interchangeably.[80] Because of the nature of Kierkegaard's authorship, caution should therefore be shown in imposing an artificial, systematic distinction, but it may nevertheless be fair to suggest that for the most part, "the aesthetic refers to those elements that are constitutive of the immediate, sensate life, whereas the poetic connotes sensate representation of an idea or ideal in works of art and in human life."[81]

The key point to note is that both his usage of "aesthetic" and "poetic" are inextricably bound up within the existential formation of the self, particularly in relation to the human faculty of imagination. Kierkegaard's authorship, as a self-proclaimed poet-communicator, expresses precisely this sense of formative "poeticizing," as opposed to the understanding of a poet who is primarily concerned with creating an external artistic product—poetry. While his authorship is sometimes divided into an initial aesthetic phase and a subsequent religious phase, Kierkegaard himself refutes this.[82] Repeatedly, in his later journal entries, he describes himself as essentially a poet, and even more specifically "a 'poet of the religious' and even more narrowly as a 'Christian poet and thinker' (*Journals and Papers*, 6:6511, 6521, 6391)."[83] His concern to qualify the type of poet he is reflects his rejection of Romantic poeticizing, which cannot integrate the ideal with the real. But he nevertheless believes that God has ordained him to imaginatively stir "a 'poetic awakening' in his readers (*Journals and Papers*, 6:6337, 6528, 6727)" by introducing the productive possibility of true Christian existence.[84] His pseudonym, Vigilius Haufniensis, suggests that psychological development requires "poetic originality" in the imaginative ability "to create the totality and the invariable from what in the individual is always partially and variably present."[85] Vigilius Haufniensis

---

79. Jothen, *Kierkegaard, Aesthetics, and Selfhood*, 8.
80. Walsh, *Living Poetically*, 20.
81. Walsh, *Living Poetically*, 20.
82. Walsh, *Living Poetically*, 224–25.
83. Walsh, *Living Poetically*, 224.
84. Walsh, *Living Poetically*, 239.
85. Kierkegaard, *The Concept of Anxiety*, 55.

is here pointing to a fundamental component of both Kierkegaard's affirmation of the aesthetic, as well as his rejection of Romantic aestheticism: The imagination, along with its necessary relationship to the aesthetic, has the ability to either fragment a fantastical ideal from actuality, or, to provide a cohesive and consistent understanding of reality and the aesthetic phenomenon encountered therein. We will discuss this further as the paradigmatic nature of the imagination in chapters 4 and 5, but here this emanates from Kierkegaard's aesthetic concern for unity or wholeness, which we will shortly engage.

Kierkegaard's framing of the poetic has significance for our further discussion of the aesthetics of discipleship. If the aesthetic, as sensory immediacy, plays any role in becoming Christian, then this connection cannot be explored without explicating the creative and formative (poetic) role of the imagination therein. Poiesis here is the imaginative production of existential possibility in symbiotic relationship with aesthetic existence. The crucial question is whether such poiesis leads solely to fantastical ideality, or whether it can contribute to a perception, and living, of christological reality, or Christian existence. Before taking this question beyond Kierkegaard, we will briefly survey his concern around the danger of the former option, and outline his limited and qualified endorsement of the latter.

Christian Poetic Living: The role of mature aesthetic existence in discipleship

Kierkegaard's positive affirmation of the aesthetic is reserved for, and situated firmly within, the stability, continuity and unity of the absolute paradox of christological reality. He contrasts this Christian mode of poetic living with the vacuous and illusory Romantic alternative of perpetual aesthetic self-experimentation. Failure to take into account this complex relationship with the aesthetic is what lies behind the perception that Kierkegaard rejects the aesthetic in the life stages of ethical and ultimately religious existence.

The Continuity of the Aesthetic in Ethico-Religious Existence

As we have already seen, a cursory reading provides ample evidence for Kierkegaard's apparent stance that the aesthetic and poetic play no positive role in Christian existence. On the surface, and without the broader context of his work, we can point, for instance, to his claims that

> a union between the aesthetic and the ethical is a "misalliance" (*Stages on Life's Way*, 442); that a poetic relation to actuality is a "misunderstanding" and a "retrogression" (*Concluding Unscientific Postscript*, 1:388); . . . that the poet cannot help one to understand life (*Works of Love*, 63); and that one must move away from the poetical to a religious, more specifically a Christian, mode of life (*The Point of View*, 74 [Lowrie translation]).[86]

But, on the other hand, Kierkegaard also claims, seemingly paradoxically, that the aesthetic and poetic continue to play a productive role throughout the life stages or spheres. In *Either/Or II*, for example, depicting the ethical stage, Judge William sets out to show that one can "preserve the aesthetic even in everyday life."[87] Two long letters from that work vividly point toward this end: "The Esthetic Validity of Marriage" and "The Balance Between the Esthetic and the Ethical in the Development of the Personality." Continuity is a logical necessity between the stages since "it is the total esthetic self that is chosen ethically."[88] Further he expresses the point differently, "the ethical is posited by the absolute choice, but it by no means follows that the esthetic is excluded. In the ethical, the personality is brought into a focus in itself; consequently, the esthetic is absolutely excluded or it is excluded as the absolute, but relatively it is continually present."[89]

It becomes clear on closer inspection that Romantic aestheticism is the problem for Kierkegaard, not the aesthetic in its entirety. In fact, the poetic and aesthetic are "continually reinterpreted in an ethical-religious manner as essential elements in that sphere."[90] Kierkegaard's Judge William suggests that ethico-religious existence reorients the aesthetic; it "does not want to destroy the esthetic but transfigure it."[91] Even when Kierkegaard rhetorically portrays the pinnacle of Christian existence in *Works of Love*, a direct work published under his own name, the immediate inclinations and desires are not to be left behind or destroyed, but to

---

86. Walsh, *Living Poetically*, 167.
87. Kierkegaard, *Either/Or* 2:9.
88. Kierkegaard, *Either/Or*, 2:222.
89. Kierkegaard, *Either/Or*, 2:177.
90. Walsh, *Living Poetically*, 15.
91. Kierkegaard, *Either/Or*, 2:253.

be "dethroned" and "transformed" as they are subsumed into Christian living.⁹²

George Price suggests that one way of articulating this continuity between the life stages, or spheres, is to describe them as "existential attitudes," the respective ways one can respond to self-same sensory stimuli. Kierkegaard

> himself answers it clearly. He says *Nothing is ever lost. Nothing that we have experienced, loved and treasured is ever thrown away.* What is discarded in the Leap from one level to another is not the content of experience but the mood, the existential attitude, in which we hold it. What is changed is the quality, not the content of the self. For example, the aesthetic as an attitude towards life must inevitably disappear, but the ethical, which replaces it, does not annihilate its content, it simply transforms it, gathers it up and redirects it.⁹³

To put it differently, the immature "life attitude" of aesthetic existence, which can be equated with Romantic aestheticism, needs to be discarded in the discipled life, but aesthetic existence per se, as sensory immediacy, inevitably continues to play a role in discipleship.

The continuity of the aesthetic throughout the stages of existence is most clearly seen in Kierkegaard's affirmation that existence itself, as an art, is aesthetic formation. It is important to note that it is a qualified aesthetic formation, or *mature* aesthetic existence, as subsumed within ethico-religious existence, but it nevertheless remains a fundamental aspect of being human and becoming Christian. Contrary to the earlier quotes, which taken out of context in pseudonymous isolation seem to question whether the aesthetic is fundamental to being human, his corpus as a whole clearly points to existence being an aesthetic category, with faith itself considered a "work of art."⁹⁴ Interestingly and significantly, it is amid a phase of authorship particularly marked by a critique of the aesthetic and poetic that the pseudonym Johannes Climacus affirms existence as aesthetic formation, even while crystallizing Kierkegaard's rejection of Romantic poetic creation.⁹⁵

---

92. Kierkegaard, *Works of Love*, 45, 61–62, 139.

93. Price, *The Narrow Pass*, 159 (italics original).

94. Walsh, *Living Poetically*, 3. This point is a central thesis, comprehensively argued, in both Walsh's *Living Poetically*, as well as Jothen's, *Kierkegaard, Aesthetics, and Selfhood*.

95. Walsh, *Living Poetically*, 167, 195–221.

All existence-issues are passionate, because existence, if one becomes conscious of it, involves passion. To think about them so as to leave out passion is not to think about them at all, is to forget the point that one indeed is oneself an existing person. Yet the subjective thinker is not a poet even if he is also a poet . . . but is also a dialectician and is himself essentially existing, whereas the poet's existence is inessential in relation to the poem . . . The subjective thinker is not a scientist-scholar; he is an artist. *To exist is an art.* The subjective thinker is esthetic enough for his life to have esthetic content, ethical enough to regulate it, dialectical enough in thinking to master it.[96]

This expression—of being a poet, even while not being a poet—points to Kierkegaard's dual perspective on "poetic living," capturing his stance on existence as art.

Poetic Living as Discipleship

A key to understanding Kierkegaard's approach to "poetic living" is the Romantic notion of *Bildung*, a significant concept, not only in framing Kierkegaard's argument, but also for our continuing exploration beyond Kierkegaard (specifically the connection Bonhoeffer makes between *Bildung* and aesthetic existence). *Bildung* can be understood as "self-cultivation," in the sense used within German neoclassicism, which focused on *Bildung* "and the achievement of wholeness of the individual personality as the goal of life and art."[97] The concept is theoretically articulated in Friedrich Schiller's *On the Aesthetic Education of Man*, and artistically in *Bildungsromane*, "novels of individual development."[98] While on the one hand critiquing Romantic "poetic living," with its perception of *Bildung* as self-creation, Kierkegaard nevertheless does not reject the concept, but rather wishes to recover it by arguing that *Bildung*, as self-development, is an integral part of becoming Christian.[99]

While Romantic "poetic living" may be problematic, Kierkegaard still sees the poetic as an important aspect of becoming Christian to the

---

96. Kierkegaard, *Concluding Unscientific Postscript*, 1:351 (italics added).
97. Walsh, *Living Poetically*, 31.
98. Walsh, *Living Poetically*, 31.
99. In fact, understanding *Either/Or* as an intentional *Bildungsroman* offers an insightful cohesion to the work, which otherwise appears somewhat fragmentary (Walsh, *Living Poetically*, 63–64n1).

extent that it is grounded in actuality, as informed by the absolute reality of Christ. Here it is worth quoting him at length, as he articulates the essence of this Christian approach to living poetically, in contradistinction to the poetic living of the Romantic ironists. It is, therefore, a key passage for understanding his contribution to the aesthetics of discipleship.

> By "living poetically" irony understood . . . something more than what any sensible person . . . understands by this phrase. It did not take this to mean *the artistic earnestness that comes to the aid of the divine in man, that mutely and quietly listens to the voice of what is distinctive in individuality, detects its movements in order to let it really be available in the individual and to let the whole individuality develop harmoniously into a pliable form rounded off in itself*. It did not understand it to be what the pious Christian thinks of when he becomes aware that *life is an upbringing, an education, which . . . is specifically supposed to develop the seeds God himself has placed in man*, since the Christian knows himself as that which has reality for God. Here, in fact, the Christian comes to the aid of God, becomes, so to speak, his *co-worker in completing the good work God himself has begun*.[100]

This passage explicates the core of Kierkegaard's perspective on the role of poetic living, or mature aesthetic existence, in discipleship. Becoming Christian by "completing the good work" of God certainly does not reject the aesthetic. To the contrary, it is precisely here where the poetic finds its true and most meaningful expression as "artistic earnestness" working "harmoniously" with God in the process of formation, as an act of existential co-poeticization. The crucial point here is the *co-*poeticizing. Aesthetic existence becomes problematic when it plays out in individualistic isolation. However, "life as an upbringing, an education," *life as discipleship, is stewarding aesthetic existence*, "earnestly" taking this mode of living seriously, by both submissively and attentively "quietly listening" to that which God has already deposited in both the self and the environment, and subsequently nurturing these "seeds" through mature aesthetic existence, thereby co-poeticizing with Christ.

Kierkegaard is here highlighting a pivotal truth for our understanding of the aesthetics of discipleship, regarding the dance between human and divine agency in Christian formation. While the essential argument of this book is that everyday aesthetic experiences play a significant role

---

100. Kierkegaard, *The Concept of Irony*, 280 (italics added).

in Christian formation, this always needs to be understood within the context of divine agency. In other words, mature aesthetic existence is a mode of stewardship, a discipled human *response* to the gift of the "good work of God." In Bonhoeffer's terms, as we will explore in the next chapter, mature aesthetic existence is not the ultimate, but operates in the penultimate, preparing the way for the ultimate. This strikes at the heart of the distinction between mature and immature aesthetic existence, the former a surrendered, harmonious, co-poeticizing response to the existential agency of Christ, the latter a grasping to maintain independent agency in self-formation by making the aesthetic absolute.

It is precisely this latter approach to aesthetic existence that Kierkegaard sees in the Romantic attempt to create a sense of self through playful experimentation, as an expression of freedom, thinking, "everything is possible. Our God is in heaven and does whatever he pleases; the ironist is on earth and does whatever he desires."[101] For Kierkegaard, this approach is ultimately vacuous, and precisely the opposite of true poetic living, since the self is lost in virtuality, disconnected from reality. "As the ironist poetically composes himself and his environment with the greatest possible poetic license, as he lives in this totally hypothetical and subjunctive way, his life loses all continuity. He succumbs completely to mood. His life is nothing but moods."[102] In other words, the "reality" that the Romantic has created holds no relation to actuality. It is simply the product of aesthetic immediacy in isolation, "At times he is a god, at times a grain of sand . . . He poetizes everything, poetizes his moods, too. In order to be genuinely free, he must have control of his moods; therefore one mood must instantly be succeeded by another."[103] This is not to say that "moods" are the problem. To the contrary, they play a role in "a sound and healthy life" as "an intensification of . . . life that . . . stirs and moves within a person"; for the Christian they are grounded in the "continuity" of Christ.[104] But for the Romantic, moods are disconnected from any grounding reality. Amid this aesthetic immediacy, to sustain the illusion of self-creation requires being severed from the givenness of one's actual material environment.

---

101. Kierkegaard, *The Concept of Irony*, 282.
102. Kierkegaard, *The Concept of Irony*, 284.
103. Kierkegaard, *The Concept of Irony*, 284.
104. Kierkegaard, *The Concept of Irony*, 284.

> [Given] context... has no validity, and since it is not his concern to form himself in such a way that he fits into his environment, then the environment must be formed to fit him—in other words, he poetically composes not only himself but he poetically composes his environment also... In so doing, he continually collides with the actuality to which he belongs. Therefore it becomes important for him to suspend what is constitutive in actuality, that which orders and supports it: that is, morality and ethics.[105]

Hence Kierkegaard's depiction of the immature life stage of aesthetic existence; Romantic "poetic living" is here disconnected from ethico-religious existence.

However, Kierkegaard wishes to show that Christian existence is true poetic living, since self-development occurs not by disconnecting ideality and actuality, but by uniting the finite and infinite in the absolute paradox of Christ, as the true Poet.[106] "Romanticism... thinks it is living poetically, but... the poetic is the very thing it misses, because true inward infinity comes only through resignation, and only this inner infinity is truly infinite and truly poetic."[107] Rather than attempting to "compose oneself poetically... the Christian lets himself be poetically composed, and in this respect a simple Christian lives far more poetically than many a brilliant intellectual."[108] The key difference in the Christian sense of poetic living is the submission of aesthetic existence to both the sovereignty of God and the concomitant givenness of material actuality. "An individual who lets himself be poetically composed does have a definite given context into which he has to fit and thus does not become a word without meaning because it is wrenched out of its associations."[109] While the Romantic seeks, but fails, to unite the ideal and the actual, merely offering "an emigration from actuality [rather] than a continuance in it... only the religious is able to bring about the true reconciliation, because it infinitizes actuality."[110] Existential freedom then, is not found in fantastical aesthetic experimentation, but through embracing the paradox of

---

105. Kierkegaard, *The Concept of Irony*, 283.

106. For the theme of God as poet throughout Kierkegaard's work, see Rasmussen, *Between Irony and Witness*, 55–84.

107. Kierkegaard, *The Concept of Irony*, 289.

108. Kierkegaard, *The Concept of Irony*, 280.

109. Kierkegaard, *The Concept of Irony*, 283.

110. Kierkegaard, *The Concept of Irony*, 297.

the "infinite" reality of Christ, as grounded in the historical actuality of material givenness. Anchored in this "inner infinity," one "lives poetically only when [one] is oriented and thus integrated in the age in which [one] lives, [being] positively free in the actuality to which [one] belongs."[111]

Imitating Christ: The Unification of the Infinite with Finite Aesthetic Existence

The "art of living," therefore, is to subsume aesthetic existence within Christian existence, thereby integrating the material actuality of finite immediacy with infinite Reality in a cohesive whole. Here, existence is an art because, for Kierkegaard, as influenced by the Romantics, "every true work of art is an essential unity."[112] It is a theme that is central throughout Kierkegaard's work, as seen in his "'quest for unambiguous life', a life figured ... as involving a sense for 'the whole' and which is to be sought not only in isolated moments of ecstasy but in 'every moment' so as to bring about a lasting and productive inner unification of the self."[113] As Connell exposits at length, this is the Kierkegaardian quest "to be one thing," bringing cohesion to the fragmented immediacy of life that is an inevitable consequence of being historical, sensate beings. "As temporal, the self is forced to live moment by moment. If it would exist in such a way as to deserve the description 'one,' it must gather all the discrete moments of its life into a unity."[114] In the words of Kierkegaard's pseudonym, Johannes Climacus, "In the life of the Individual the task is to achieve an ennoblement of the successive within the simultaneous."[115]

Kierkegaard, therefore, wishes on the one hand to reject aestheticism, which may seem to be taking material existence seriously, but really

---

111. Kierkegaard, *The Concept of Irony*, 326.

112. Connell, *To Be One Thing*, 19. Connell notes that "For some time, this world [Denmark, as influenced by German philosophy and culture] had been dominated, perhaps even possessed, by the idea of unity ... The idea was already at work as an aesthetic principle in the writings of Goethe and Herder," then subsequently "asserting itself as absolute" in the "joint literary and philosophical movement of Romanticism" (Connell, *To Be One Thing*, 11).

113. Pattison, *Quest for Unambiguous Life*, 4.

114. Connell, *To Be One Thing*, xii.

115. Kierkegaard, *Concluding Unscientific Postscript* (trans. Swenson and Lowrie), 311. For the Hong and Hong translation, see Kierkegaard, *Concluding Unscientific Postscript*, 1:348.

devalues material actuality by escaping into a fantastical ideal, and ultimately, virtuality.[116] On the other hand, he affirms that religious existence is embedded in everyday aesthetic engagement with physical actuality. Genuine religious existence needs to be integrated with concrete and material daily reality, by being Christian "in the actuality of daily life ... here in Copenhagen, in the market on Amagertorv [Amager Square], in the middle of the daily bustle of weekday life!"[117] Religious "loftiness" needs to be integrated with everyday actuality. Recall Kierkegaard's parable of the geese, a scathing critique of Danish Christendom as an expression of Romantic aestheticism, wherein the "poet or orator illustrates this loftiness," affectively moving people for "only one hour" on a Sunday—a reflective ideal bearing no connection to everyday reality.[118] The consequence is a neutering of the Christian message, disconnected from sensory existence in everyday life. Such "loftiness" of the gospel is removed from daily life so that "people are not so familiar with loftiness that they really dare to believe in it."[119] By contrast, the "absolute paradox" of the incarnation points to the essential affirmation of material actuality in Christian existence. "It is indeed an enormous contradiction—that the loftiest of all has become the everyday!"[120]

As with his aesthetic, Kierkegaard offers no systematic account of his Christology, but as Joel Rasmussen puts it, the latter infuses the former through Kierkegaard's "Christomorphic poetics."[121] If we cannot understand the aesthetic in Kierkegaard without situating it in the context of existence then equally, we cannot approach his perspective of aesthetic existence and poetics without situating it, in turn, within Christian existence as the imitation of Christ. "God's initiative in Christ is paradigmatic for Kierkegaard's many explorations of the possibility or impossibility of

116. William Cavanaugh affirms the same point in the economic realm, by arguing that consumerism is not fundamentally about material attachment, but in fact quite the opposite: consumerism is a product of *detachment* from material reality driven by hunger for the novel. See Cavanaugh, *Being Consumed*, 33–58.

117. Kierkegaard, *Practice in Christianity*, 59.

118. Kierkegaard, *Practice in Christianity*, 59, 60.

119. Kierkegaard, *Practice in Christianity*, 60.

120. Kierkegaard, *Practice in Christianity*, 60.

121. "Kierkegaard's theological poetics has a specifically 'Christomorphic' character because he believes it is God's incarnation in Christ, a self-introduction of the poet into the poem, that warrants the claim that God 'fulfills' in actuality what every other poet only achieves in imagination, namely, a 'reconciliation' between the actual world and the divine ideal." Rasmussen, *Between Irony and Witness*, 3, 55.

human fulfillment through artistic creativity."[122] Only in Christ is it possible to unite the ideal and actual. It is logically necessary that the discrete moments of everyday aesthetic existence can only cohere in the eternal. But as Kierkegaard shows, Romantic attempts to unite the finite and infinite result unavoidably either in the proliferation of sensory immediacy (Don Juan) or fantastical idealism (the Seducer). For it is solely within Christ that the finite and infinite cohere, since "only the eternal can be and become and remain contemporaneous with every age; temporality, on the other hand divides within itself, and the present cannot become contemporaneous with the future, or the future with the past, or the past with the present."[123]

While Romantic aestheticism, wedded to Danish Christendom, fails to integrate the ideal with the actual, it is in imitating Christ, as the prototypical "witness to truth," that both poetic ideal and poetic action are united. Kierkegaard's attack on Christendom may appear to be a critique of the church's apathy and materialism, as it prioritized this-worldly comfort. In this sense, his call to costly discipleship seems to entail a rejection of the aesthetic in favor of the spiritual. To be sure, he is indeed critical of materialism and aestheticism, but even amid the rhetorical urgency needed to deal with the crisis of his day, it is important to note that imitating Christ does not equate to rejecting this-worldly reality, and consequently the aesthetic. To the contrary, it is precisely in Christ where the poetic and aesthetic find their rightful place. "In Kierkegaard's Christomorphic poetics the divine poet proclaims true love and also manifests it existentially, such that Word and flesh, imagination and will, ideality and actuality, all accord perfectly with one another in a reconciliation that, for Christian faith, unites truth and art in 'true art.'"[124] Discipleship, therefore, as the "imitation" of Christ (as opposed to Christendom's "admiration" of Christ) is true poetic living.[125]

---

122. Rasmussen, *Between Irony and Witness*, 4.

123. Kierkegaard, *Works of Love*, 31.

124. Rasmussen, *Between Irony and Witness*, 173.

125. A Kierkegaardian trajectory which we will not be pursuing here, but has much to offer an aesthetics of discipleship, particularly as unfolding in the coming chapters, is Kierkegaard's concept of "repetition," especially in relation to mimetic discipleship—a life of imitating Christ—which is elaborated upon by Catherine Pickstock's "non-identical repetition," wherein "human identity, and the identity of all things... is secured through the historical reduplicating, and so continuous representation of the atonement achieved by the God-Man." Pickstock, *Repetition and Identity*, 147.

"By believing in, by becoming contemporaneous with, by following and imitating Christ, the self repeats this incarnation within itself . . . [allowing] the self to relate to itself properly and truly, to exist as it was created to exist: simultaneously finite and infinite, temporal and eternal."[126] It is only here, in imitating Christ, that existence is truly poetic, truly formative, that self-development truly occurs, since Christ is the "criterion," the prototypical human being.[127]

In sum, it is only through the incarnation of Christ that the actual and ideal cohere, and thus only to the extent that the disciple is "in Christ" that the self is truly living poetically, both present in the discrete moments of everyday, this-worldly actuality, but also existing in a sense of ultimate coherence through the infinite and eternal grace of God. In this sense, aesthetic existence, or sensory immediacy, matters because this is a fundamental aspect of being historical, finite beings, an aspect of being human affirmed by the incarnation. Kierkegaard is clear that the everyday, "in the market on Amager Square," is a fundamental aspect of Christian existence. This affirmation is significant, but the question that remains unresolved at this point is whether aesthetic existence is formative. What role, if any, does sensory immediacy play in faith formation? Kierkegaard does not directly answer this question. His focus is on exposing Romantic sensory immediacy as problematic. However, there are two concepts that he deals with which offer pointers to the positive role that aesthetic existence may play in discipleship. The first is his limited treatment of the notion of a "second immediacy," as an attribute of faith. The second is his more robust engagement with the formative role of the imagination. We will delineate his perspective on both briefly here, before moving beyond Kierkegaard to explore them more deeply.

Second Immediacy

Kierkegaard refers to a "second immediacy" as an attribute of faith, pointing to the passionate and aesthetic nature of life in Christ. Yet, precisely what he means here, and the nature of its relation to sensory immediacy, is difficult to interpret, due both to his fragmentary treatment of the concept and the rhetorical context within which he employs the term. In a number of places in his journals he describes faith as a second

---

126. Connell, *To Be One Thing*, 185–86.
127. Kierkegaard, *Sickness Unto Death*, 113–14.

immediacy; faith being an "immediacy or spontaneity after reflection."[128] Some of the pseudonyms also discuss this second immediacy, although, unsurprisingly, they do not all concur on the role of immediacy and the aesthetic in faith formation. For Judge William, "the poetic is given a higher and more authentic expression in the second immediacy of the ethical-religious."[129] For Johannes de Silentio, in *Fear and Trembling*, "Faith is not an 'esthetic emotion' or a 'spontaneous inclination of the heart,' he says, but rather a 'new interiority' and a 'later immediacy,' that is, a form of immediacy or spontaneity that Kierkegaard describes elsewhere as being acquired after reflection by virtue of a relation to God (*Fear and Trembling* 47, 69, 82; *Journals and Papers*, 5:6135)."[130] In other works, Kierkegaard offers clues as to the nature of this second immediacy, as an expression of the "infinite task" of imitating Christ's love in material actuality, in the here and now, as Connell shows,

> Anti-Climacus writes that the more the self accepts the infinite task, "the more personally present and contemporaneous it becomes in the small part of the task that can be carried out at once." [*Sickness unto Death*, 32] Following Jesus' exhortation to take no thought for the morrow, the Christian self's temporal horizons contract to leave it wholly within the moment. But it is within the moment that time and eternity meet... the Christian self lives as an eternal being within time, as the Paradox writ small. Presence and its corresponding concept, the moment, are the common denominators of time and eternity... [see *Concept of Anxiety*, 86].[131]

While it is difficult to build a conceptual framework on his fragmentary exploration of this "second immediacy," two conclusions are fairly clear. First, Kierkegaard is quite obviously keen to rhetorically distinguish the immediacy of Christian existence from that of aestheticism, labeling the immediacy of aestheticism a "first immediacy" as opposed to the "second immediacy" of Christian existence.[132] Second, however,

---

128. Kierkegaard, *Journals and Papers*: 1:9, 49, 84, 85, 214, 235, 972, 1032; 2:1101, 1123, 1215, 1335, 1942, 1943; 3:3560, 3561; 5:6135; cf. Walsh, *Living Poetically*, 139.

129. Walsh, *Living Poetically*, 184.

130. Walsh, *Living Poetically*, 140.

131. Connell, *To Be One Thing*, 189–90.

132. Kierkegaard, by articulating this second immediacy as an "inner" immediacy is also here responding to Hegel, "who holds that the outer is higher than the inner" (Walsh, *Living Poetically*, 140).

in spite of this rhetorical agenda, his exploration of faith as second immediacy points to the "fundamentally aesthetic nature of faith insofar as it is a passion or a form of immediacy."[133]

Of course it would be speculation to hypothesize about whether Kierkegaard would have explored the notion of a "second immediacy" differently had he been writing in a different time, responding to different contextual challenges. But his cryptic treatment of a second immediacy raises important questions for us to further explore beyond Kierkegaard, specifically regarding the relationship between sensory immediacy and reflection in the formation of faith. Kierkegaard seems to be arguing that a "second immediacy" is, first, internal, rather than external, and second, temporally subsequent to conscious reflection. The question this raises is whether this is an anthropological possibility. Is conscious reflection completely distinct from sensory immediacy? Is there both a chronological and epistemological hierarchy, or is there, to an extent at least, a symbiotic coherence that needs to be taken into account? In Chapters 4 and 5 we will explore the integrated nature of embodiment, affect, and belief, which suggests that Kierkegaard's second immediacy is best simply thought of as a discipled first immediacy, or *mature* aesthetic existence. The key point at this stage is acknowledging the distinction between these two modes of immediacy, and by extension, two modes of aesthetic existence, even if the distinction demands more subtle and complex development than Kierkegaard offers.

The Imagination

The formative role of the poetic and aesthetic in becoming Christian is arguably most clearly seen in Kierkegaard's affirmation of the imagination.[134] At the outset though, it needs to be clear that Kierkegaard wants to make a distinction between the imagination (*Phantasien*) and the Romantic employment of the imagination as the fantastic (*det Phantastiske*).[135] On the one hand, he wishes to reject the fantastical imagination of poetic Romanticism, wherein the imagination creates a self through playful

---

133. Walsh, *Living Poetically*, 140.

134. See both Gouwens, *Kierkegaard's Dialectic of the Imagination*; and Ferreira, *Transforming Vision*.

135. Walsh, *Living Poetically*, 231.

experimentation, ultimately leading to virtuality.[136] Here the imagination is simply reveling in the freedom of ideal possibility, without any relationship to actuality. However, on the other hand, Kierkegaard shows that rightly employed, the imagination can do the complete opposite: it allows one to see the ideal of Christ as Reality, and consequently opens one's eyes to possibility, beyond the finitude of an independent self, to the actuality of life as imitation of Christ.[137] For Kierkegaard then, the power of the imagination in faith formation is its ability to move one from the ideal to action. As he writes in a journal entry from 1854 (not during his early, so-called aesthetic phase, but amid the "attack on Christendom," the year before he died), "Imagination is what providence uses to take men captive in actuality, in existence, in order to get them far enough out, or within, or down into actuality. And when imagination has helped them get as far out as they should be—then actuality genuinely begins."[138]

The power of the imagination, thus construed, leads the pseudonym Anti-Climacus to proclaim that the human faculty of imagination is "the capacity *instar omnium* [for all capacities]. When all is said and done, whatever of feeling, knowing and willing a person has depends upon what imagination he has."[139] Readings of Kierkegaard that prioritize the will in the formation of self are reductionist. Imagination, as the *instar omnium*, provides the paradigmatic perception of reality within which choices are made. The role of volition, then, in self-formation can only be understood alongside the imagination and another prominent Kierkegaardian theme, passion, both of which feed off everyday aesthetic existence. "Aesthetically, the imagination can create images of how to exist as well as store images received from culture, experience, and education. Passion, a form of desire, moves a self towards sensual beauty and images as well as ideas of selfhood."[140] In other words, the symbiotic interrelationship between everyday aesthetic experience, the imagination, and desire has a significant impact on the movement and definition of the self. This framing of existence coheres with contemporary constructions of being human and creating meaning within the context of a presiding narrative, as elucidated by the likes of Alasdair MacIntyre, Stanley Hauerwas,

136. Kierkegaard, *Practice in Christianity*, 185–88.
137. Walsh, *Living Poetically*, 229–39.
138. Kierkegaard, *Journals and Papers*, 2:313–14.
139. Kierkegaard, *Sickness unto Death*, 31.
140. Jothen, *Kierkegaard, Aesthetics, and Selfhood*, 4.

Charles Taylor, Sallie McFague, William Cavanaugh, and Paul Ricoeur. Kierkegaard's conception of the imagination, therefore, is "poetic" not in the sense of Romantic "poetic living," fantastical self-creation, but in the sense of "poetry as act, 'living poetically,' [that] not only provides narrative but also testifies to an imaginative ideal by putting it to work in real life."[141]

For our purposes, the critical question is the nature of the relation between everyday aesthetic experience and the shaping of the imagination. If the imagination holds a store of images received from culture and experience, then implicitly, by acknowledging the role of the imagination in faith formation, Kierkegaard is also thereby affirming the role of everyday sensory immediacy in faith formation (or deformation). This is a suggestive implication that we will have to further probe and test in moving beyond Kierkegaard, for he does not offer any explicit indication that this relation exists, at least in a positive sense. However, he certainly holds the inverse to be true: the Romantic imagination, as shaped by sensory immediacy creates a virtual reality. Such "free play of fantasy . . . makes life a dream," thereby "exhaust[ing] and anesthetiz[ing] the soul."[142] Sensory life in Tivoli, and the magic of the theater, blurs the boundaries, "the make-believe of masks, disguises, and possibilities spills over into real relationships."[143]

Summary: Christian existence amid the sensory immediacy of Deer Park

The question we have put to Kierkegaard is whether aesthetic existence, as sensory immediacy, plays a role in Christian living. His answer is difficult to discern, since his focus is on the destructive nature of Romantic sensory immediacy, but a careful reading shows that he offers a tentative and qualified yes. As a means of summary, it is helpful to consider a specific passage in *Concluding Unscientific Postscript* that crystallizes his perspective. It is significant that the author, Kierkegaard's pseudonym Johannes Climacus, is not a Christian, and is therefore reflecting on

---

141. Rasmussen, *Between Irony and Witness*, 173.
142. Kierkegaard, *The Concept of Irony*, 292.
143. Pattison, *Quest for Unambiguous Life*, 20. See also Pattison, *Kierkegaard: The Aesthetic and the Religious*, 95–124.

religious existence from the outside, an important point to which we will return.

Climacus considers how religious existence could be lived in the everyday, and not merely on a Sunday, in church, or amidst the more earnest moments of life.[144]

> Nowadays the religious address, although it preaches against the monastery, observes the most strict monastic propriety and distances itself from actuality just as much as the monastery and thereby indirectly betrays quite adequately that everyday existence is actually in other categories, or that the religious does not assimilate daily life.[145]

Therefore, he proposes a thought experiment: how would "Christians" from the different stages of life (aesthetic, ethical and religious) respond to the prospect of an outing to enjoy the amusements of Deer Park? Here, we need to remember Kierkegaard's context of Christendom, wherein Climacus is working from the assumption that the subjects of his thought experiment are churchgoing Christians by name (as such, not only someone in the religious stage of life would self-describe as Christian, but equally a person in the aesthetic or ethical stage would self-describe as Christian). The thought experiment therefore has continued relevance and implications for contemporary Christendom, which too for Kierkegaard would consist of subjects labeled the Aesthete, the Ethical, and Religious.

How does the Christian relate to the sensory immediacy of everyday entertainment, such as Deer Park, the "most trivial of trivialities"?[146] For the aesthete, this is a nonissue. By living entirely in the moment, it matters not whether this is in church, for an hour on Sunday, enjoying the idealistic oration of the pastor, or whether it is reveling in the sensory thrills of Deer Park. There is no contradiction since these discrete, existential moments are entirely distinct. The consequence, however, is a fragmentation of self, a complete absence of "poetic living," as Kierkegaard employs the term. Consumed by the individual's fragmentary enjoyment of the moment, it is an existence entirely void of the cohesion offered when "being poetically composed" by Christ, the ultimate poet.

---

144. Kierkegaard, *Concluding Unscientific Postscript*, 1:470–503.
145. Kierkegaard, *Concluding Unscientific Postscript*, 1:481.
146. Kierkegaard, *Concluding Unscientific Postscript*, 1:481.

The subject in the ethical stage also finds no contradiction, embracing an equally fragmented perspective, but for different reasons. Ethically, the key question is whether it is permissible. Does it contravene moral bounds? If not, it is harmless fun. "To go out to the amusement park—if one can afford it, if one's business affairs allow it, if one takes along wife and children, yes, and the servants, and comes home at a decent time—is an innocent joy and one ought to participate in the innocent joys."[147] The joy is "innocent" because, as spontaneous sensory immediacy, it defies ethical evaluation. A theme found both in *Either/Or II* and *Stages on Life's Way* is that, "Spontaneity lies within the realm of immediacy and, strictly speaking, cannot be ethically judged."[148] Due to this fundamental rift in these two modes of existence, the ethical person states that "it never occurs to me to bring such trifles as going out to the amusement park into connection with the thought of God—indeed to me it seems to be an insult to God, and I know that it does not occur to a single one of the many people I know, either."[149] For Kierkegaard this too represents the self-same problematic fragmentation of self.

Climacus spends the bulk of his time on the religious person, wrestling with the challenge of reconciling the absolute with the immediate, in the unity of true poetic living. While the *principle* of embracing everyday actuality may be laudable, "in the concretion of daily life . . . practicing it is so very difficult. Nowadays a pastor hardly dares to speak in church about going to the amusement park or even mention the word—so difficult is it even in a godly discourse to join an amusement park and the thought of God."[150] But Climacus suggests that this is precisely the test of Christian existence: "the absoluteness of the religious placed together with the specific."[151] The pastor, therefore, should be able "to transform even speaking about this into an upbuilding discourse. If he is unable to do that, if he thinks it cannot be done, he must warn against it."[152] While such integration may be a worthy goal in theory, Climacus finds navigating the paradox a weighty task. On the one hand, God consumes one "like the fire of the summer sun when it refuses to set," thereby obliterating

---

147. Kierkegaard, *Concluding Unscientific Postscript*, 1:476.
148. Connell, *To Be One Thing*, 178.
149. Kierkegaard, *Concluding Unscientific Postscript*, 1:477.
150. Kierkegaard, *Concluding Unscientific Postscript*, 1:481.
151. Kierkegaard, *Concluding Unscientific Postscript*, 1:483.
152. Kierkegaard, *Concluding Unscientific Postscript*, 1:481.

the "relativity of immediacy."[153] External sensory immediacy ceases to hold traction due to this inner, second immediacy. Yet paradoxically, it is in the trivial everyday, in the apparently unimportant that "the relationship with God will be known."[154] A rejection of everyday materiality is therefore a rejection of given humanness. "The monastic movement is an attempt at wanting to be more than a human being, an enthusiastic, perhaps pious attempt to be like God."[155] So where does this leave the religious person as he approaches the outing to Deer Park, attempting to navigate this paradoxical tension?

> So he goes out there. "But he does not enjoy himself," someone may say. Yes, he does indeed. And why does he enjoy himself? *Because the humblest expression for the relationship with God is to acknowledge one's humanness, and it is human to enjoy oneself.*[156]

So far, so good: Despite the paradox—embracing the infinite, being consumed by God, while living concretely in the finite—everyday Christian existence is possible because of life *in* Christ, the "paradox writ small."[157]

Yet, it is here where Climacus falters, as he analytically considers faith from the outside. He cannot conceive how it is rationally possible for the religious person to enjoy Deer Park. He concedes that it may be possible for someone else, but personally, he would not be able to enjoy it. His first problem is a question at the heart of the aesthetics of discipleship: how does one distinguish between aestheticism (making the aesthetic absolute) and mature aesthetic experience (a valid expression of sensory immediacy in this-worldly Christian living)? How can he "ascertain that it is not a momentary inclination, a fancy of immediacy, that determines him"?[158] The only way to know with certainty is to delay the outing, thereby proving that his motives are pure. The process perpetually repeats itself, and the outing to Deer Park never materializes. Even if he *were* in the amusement park, as a religious, Climacus cannot conceive the possibility of enjoying the outing within the absolute conception of God.[159] The paradox is too much for him to compute.

153. Kierkegaard, *Concluding Unscientific Postscript*, 1:485.
154. Kierkegaard, *Concluding Unscientific Postscript*, 1:487.
155. Kierkegaard, *Concluding Unscientific Postscript*, 1:492.
156. Kierkegaard, *Concluding Unscientific Postscript*, 1:493 (italics added).
157. Connell, *To Be One Thing*, 189–90.
158. Kierkegaard, *Concluding Unscientific Postscript*, 1:495.
159. Kierkegaard, *Concluding Unscientific Postscript*, 1:498.

Through Climacus, Kierkegaard shows the challenge of incorporating mature aesthetic existence into Christian living. In a sense, it is a logical impossibility. It is the attempt to unify the absolute and the specific, infinite and finite, divine and human. It is only in the absolute paradox of Christ, through an incarnational understanding of existence that this is possible. Living in Christ, by grace, allows human momentary immediacy to cohere in Christ's eternal being.

In sum, Kierkegaard, in principle, affirms being human and the divine givenness of material reality that it entails. Based on the absolute paradox of Christ, becoming Christian is not merely a spiritual exercise, but is to be played out in the actuality of daily life, amid even the "most trivial of trivialities." Faith formation is here the co-poeticizing of gathering up the concrete moments of incarnate living, while attentively and "harmoniously" aligning these with the work of Christ in oneself, as an act of aesthetic stewardship (while always acknowledging that such alignment does not equate to being Christian—this is merely a penultimate process—being Christian is ultimately a gift of grace by Christ, as divine poet). But even though such everyday discipleship necessarily encompasses sensory immediacy, in practice Kierkegaard appears reluctant to fully endorse even mature aesthetic existence as an aspect of Christian living.

As Climacus illustrated above, Kierkegaard's reticence may be related to the crucial question of how one distinguishes between aesthetic existence as aestheticism, and mature aesthetic existence, which is a valid expression of Christian living. The impetus of Kierkegaard's rhetorical task (reacting to the problematic nature of Romantic sensory immediacy, particularly as it expressed itself in Christendom) clouds his response to this question and the clarity of his affirmation of the material world in general. While his early work displays a strong theology of creation, this is obscured by his later attack on Christendom and the consequent emphasis on imitating the suffering Christ.[160] Possibly, Kierkegaard's attempt to distinguish between aestheticism and mature aesthetic existence, thereby validating a mode of aesthetic existence in Christian life, can be found in his relatively underdeveloped notion of a second immediacy—immediacy after reflection—but this appears to relate to an "inner" immediacy; again, he seems reluctant to fully endorse *sensory* immediacy.

---

160. Pattison, *Quest for Unambiguous Life*, 25n35. See also Pattison, *Kierkegaard and the Theology of the Nineteenth Century*, 80–123.

This leaves us with two questions to take beyond Kierkegaard. First, is it possible to be fully immersed in the humanity of sensory immediacy as an expression of being Christian? For example, *is* it possible for a Christian to enjoy an outing to Deer Park? Or to use another example from Kierkegaard's work, can a Christian delight in aesthetic literary immediacy? In an early journal entry (1837), Kierkegaard reflects,

> Why does the reading of fairy tales provide such fortifying relaxation for the soul? When I am weary of everything and "full of days," fairy tales are always a refreshing, renewing bath for me. *There* all earthly, finite cares vanish; joy, yes, even sorrow, are infinite (and for this reason are so enlarging and beneficial).[161]

Pattison labels this an example of "immediate aesthetic reading," characteristic of how Kierkegaard later suggested we *not* read.[162] Granted, there is resonance in this passage with the Romantic notion of creating a fantastical aesthetic reality. However, does it follow that the experience of aesthetic immediacy in reading is incongruous with Christian living? Does such an aesthetic experience of "fortifying relaxation for the soul" have a place in being Christian?

Second, if it does, what are the implications for the formation of faith? As Climacus notes, this is not an ethical question; it is not a question of permissibility. Rather, the question is related to imitating Christ. Does the celebration of sensory immediacy, in every instance, detract from becoming Christian, or are there times when it contributes to discipleship? If it can offer a positive contribution to faith formation, how do we distinguish between these two modes of sensory immediacy? Here, we will want to recall Kierkegaard's distinction between first and second immediacy, but we will need to move beyond his rudimentary notion of a second immediacy to a more fully developed notion of mature aesthetic existence.

Spotlight on Music:
Music as archetypal sensory immediacy

As explained in the Introduction, in each chapter we will pause to focus the spotlight on music (or, more accurately, a snapshot from the world of music) as a practical example of everyday aesthetic experience, a point of

---

161. Kierkegaard, *Journals and Papers*, 5:112.
162. Pattison, *Kierkegaard and the Theology of the Nineteenth Century*, 224–25.

concretion serving to elucidate the salient points of the broader argument that otherwise might remain somewhat opaque. Kierkegaard points out why music in particular, as archetypal sensory immediacy, is helpful for this purpose.

In *Either/Or I*, Kierkegaard's pseudonym, the aesthete "A," offers a lengthy exposition on music in the form of an essay titled "The Immediate Erotic Stages or the Musical-Erotic." The focus of the essay is Mozart's opera *Don Giovanni*, wherein the character Don Giovanni (based on the legend of Don Juan) is portrayed as the ultimate aesthete, the pinnacle of sensory-erotic immediacy. As is always the case with his pseudonymous work, interpretations abound as to Kierkegaard's intention with this essay. While we will briefly consider the significance of these perspectives below in linking the aesthetic and religious, the fundamental premise of the essay itself is of interest: A's observation that the aesthetic medium of music best represents sensory immediacy.

"A" holds that no other art form exhibits sensory immediacy to the extent that music does. This is because, on the one hand, the literary arts are too closely related to language, thereby associating them with conscious reflection.[163] On the other hand, the visual, plastic, and spatial arts (painting, sculpture and architecture, for example) are manifest as continuity over time. Our engagement with them is, therefore, not strictly "momentary," as is the case with a note or chord of music.[164] While these notes strung together provide an aesthetic experience of "epic character," music is not truly epic, because it nevertheless represents temporal impermanence.[165] While music itself "has an element of time . . . it cannot express the historical in time."[166] Hence the connection to the erotic, since "sensuous love is disappearance in time . . . [and] the medium that expresses this is indeed music."[167] It is therefore "only through music . . . that the sensuous in its elemental originality . . . [is] presented."[168] If music is the ultimate aesthetic medium of sensory immediacy, then the crystallizing question, which we will periodically return to in the

---

163. Kierkegaard, *Either/Or*, 1:56.
164. Kierkegaard, *Either/Or*, 1:56–57.
165. Kierkegaard, *Either/Or*, 1:57.
166. Kierkegaard, *Either/Or*, 1:57.
167. Kierkegaard, *Either/Or*, 1:95.
168. Kierkegaard, *Either/Or*, 1:56.

coming chapters, is the relation of music to being human and becoming Christian. We begin here by putting this question to Kierkegaard.

The key to interpreting this pseudonymous essay is acknowledging Kierkegaard's rhetorical method and intent: By locating his discussion of music within the context of Mozart's *Don Giovanni,* "A" combines both the ideal medium of immediacy and the ideal character of immediacy. He is therefore, "dealing with the immediate in its total immediacy."[169] In fact, his rhetorical emphasis is so clearly on exploring musical sensory immediacy as aesthetic existence that he deliberately misrepresents Mozart's opera. His characterization of *Don Giovanni* as the archetypal aesthete does indeed resonate with Mozart's intention. But "A" further accentuates and glorifies Don Giovanni by removing him from any ethical and religious relation, rendering the archetypal aesthete in isolation, devoid of the intended broader aesthetic-religious context, both in relation to Mozart's other works, as well as within the narrative arc of *Don Giovanni*.[170] "A" deliberately marginalizes the religious Commendatore figure in the opera—the character who is, by A's own admission, the only character over whom Don Giovanni "cannot exercise any power."[171] A's exaggerated heroic framing of the aesthete Don Giovanni, void of any connection to the religious, is clearly intended to be jarring for the reader.

By severing the aesthetic from the religious in dramatic fashion, Kierkegaard is using "A" to provoke the question of the relationship between the two modes of existence. Exactly what *is* the relationship between music, as archetypal sensory immediacy, and religious existence? A narrow reading of Kierkegaard suggests that through "A," he is rhetorically presenting Don Giovanni, and the aesthetic stage of life, as incongruous with and in stark contrast to religious existence. Again, he appears to be driving a wedge between the religious and aesthetic, "excluding the sensuous from religious embodiment."[172] At best, such readings suggest that musical sensory immediacy is not moral or religious but pre-ethical and morally neutral.[173] But these readings do not account sufficiently for Kierkegaard's musical literacy and the Romantic milieu to which he is responding.

169. Kierkegaard, *Either/Or,* 1:74.
170. Zelechow, "Kierkegaard, the Aesthetic," 67.
171. Tseng, "Kierkegaard and Music in Paradox?," 420; Kierkegaard, *Either/Or I,* 125.
172. Zelechow, "Kierkegaard, the Aesthetic," 64.
173. Osolsobe, "Kierkegaard's Aesthetics of Music," 106.

Arguably, the essay is best understood as a work of satire, precisely pointing out the problematic disjunction between Romantic music and religious existence. Shao Kai Tseng shows that Kierkegaard's deliberate misrepresentation of *Don Giovanni* is both musically and culturally informed, intentionally offering a musical treatment of *Don Giovanni* consonant with Romantic composition (in the work of Hector Berlioz, Franz Liszt, and Richard Wagner, for example).[174] The omission of the significant religious theme in A's reading of the opera should be startlingly obvious to a musically literate reader, a satirical tool provoking the reader to consider the role of the religious in not only the opera *Don Giovanni* but in music more generally and sensory immediacy as a whole. Rather than endorsing the severance of the aesthetic from the religious, Kierkegaard is highlighting the problem of aestheticism—the idolatrous Romantic placebo of the infinite, sought through sensory immediacy. It is this specific mode of engaging music, of sensory immediacy, that he wishes to reject in religious existence, not music as a whole, or immediacy per se.

Shao Kai Tseng's suggestion is that Kierkegaard may here be alluding to the fact that there are two types of immediacy, and that an immature "first immediacy" does not have a monopoly on music.[175] "A" himself refers to these two types of immediacy in relation to music: sensuous, erotic immediacy on the one hand, and the Christian embrace of immediacy "qualified by spirit" on the other.[176] For "A," that which is excluded from immediacy, as "qualified by the spirit," is sensuous immediacy, as represented by music in its purest form. Tseng posits that Kierkegaard makes "A"'s argument intentionally weak here in order to show that there is no valid reason for excluding music from immediacy within religious life. Whether this is indeed Kierkegaard's intention, or whether Kierkegaard's distinction between a first and second immediacy is simply insufficiently developed matters little for our purposes. The relevant point is that Kierkegaard's critique in this essay is directed at a particular mode of sensory immediacy—as manifest in momentary musical experience as absolute. But he appears to be suggesting that another mode of immediacy, another way of engaging music, can indeed cohere with religious existence. Perhaps it is this mode of engaging music that he has in mind

---

174. Tseng, "Kierkegaard and Music in Paradox?"
175. Tseng, "Kierkegaard and Music in Paradox?," 422.
176. Kierkegaard, *Either/Or*, 1:70–71.

when connecting musical experience to the religious ideal in his journals, suggesting that "the next life is ... represented as pure music, as a great harmony—would that the dissonance of my life would soon be resolved in it."[177] To further develop the distinction between these two modes of immediacy we will need to move beyond Kierkegaard.

In this chapter, Kierkegaard helped us to see that everyday aesthetic experience is not an insignificant and tangential aspect of life, but plays a vital role in self-development. This formative impact can either be positive or negative, Kierkegaard's own rhetorical emphasis focused on highlighting the danger of the latter. For Kierkegaard, Romantic aestheticism and Danish Christendom provided a fertile context within which a pseudoreality could be created through the fantastical creation of the self. Such an illusory self-creation feeds off the immediacy and reflectivity of unqualified aesthetic existence, as an immature life stage—hence his rejection of this mode of living aesthetically in religious existence. Since both aestheticism and Christendom continue to flourish today, Kierkegaard's warning here remains all too relevant. This is particularly notable in relation to postmodern deconstruction, which, as Walsh suggests, "bears a close resemblance to the early German Romantic mode of living poetically ... in the assertion of an endless process of experimentation and play with a multiplicity of interpretations and roles in language, or writing."[178] But it is the application in the everyday, amid contemporary expressions of politicized Christendom alongside consumer-driven, technology-fueled sensory-immediacy-on-tap that particularly calls for further attention. Impelled by these forces, contemporary construction of pseudorealities and the creation of self therein is even more of a danger than in Kierkegaard's time. Certainly his warning regarding the deformative impact of immature aesthetic existence remains relevant today.

On the positive side, Kierkegaard highlights that the aesthetic contributes to the life of faith through his recovery of poetic living. This points to the integral role that the imagination plays in the relationship between aesthetic existence and self-development, a relationship we will explore more deeply. Self-development as discipleship imitates the absolute paradox of Christ in one's life, embracing life in Christ as both finite, material givenness and, through the grace of God, the infinite. This

---

177. Kierkegaard, *Journals and Papers from Prison*, 5: 74.
178. Walsh, *Living Poetically*, 245.

entails an embrace of faith as a passion to be exercised in embodied actuality, amid the everyday. There is, therefore, a sense of immediacy and embodiment inextricably bound up within Christian living.

As helpful as Kierkegaard's contribution is to an understanding of the aesthetics of discipleship, it is also limited. Even though a close reading provides evidence of Kierkegaard's embrace of the aesthetic in Christian living, he does not explicitly endorse sensory immediacy as a fundamental aspect of becoming Christian. While it is difficult to discern the extent to which his reticence is a genuine reservation he held, a result of his method of indirect communication, or the consequence of the rhetoric he employed in response to his context, it has produced scholarly dissonance regarding the interpretation of Kierkegaard's stance on the matter. Even in arguing that Kierkegaard held a qualified and limited endorsement of aesthetic existence in Christian living, it is clear that we will need to move beyond Kierkegaard to further clarify the relation and the implications for discipleship.

3

The Celebration of Aesthetic Existence in Christian Life

AESTHETIC EXISTENCE IS NOT to be rejected in the Christian life, as a mode of living to be jettisoned when one matures to the point of ethico-religious existence. It is not even to be tolerated, as harmless, peripheral, and inconsequential enjoyment within the discipled life. Rather, it is to be embraced as a fundamental aspect of being Christian, following after Christ incarnate, in all the fullness of embodied this-worldliness. In other words, a robust understanding of the aesthetics of discipleship is founded upon a fully developed Christology. Which in turn reveals an understanding of being fully human that necessarily encompasses both aesthetic and ethico-religious existence.

To some this may seem counterintuitive and incongruent with the Christian life; the obvious objection exclaims: What of relinquishing the pleasures of this world in following Christ? What of entering through the narrow gate? Who better to guide us through these valid questions than Dietrich Bonhoeffer, who famously authored *The Cost of Discipleship*, or as originally named, simply *Discipleship* (*Nachfolge*: literally "following after"). As noted in the previous chapter, Dietrich Bonhoeffer was not only familiar with Kierkegaard's work but drew from and built upon Kierkegaardian concepts that emanated from a mutual concern regarding the nature of true discipleship amid self-seeking Christendom. Bonhoeffer not only further frames the concept of aesthetic existence but will help us to develop an understanding of the positive relation between aesthetic existence and Christian living, grounded in his christological perspective of this-worldliness and his consequent affirmation of penultimate reality.

It may not seem immediately obvious why Bonhoeffer can contribute to the aesthetics of discipleship. After all, his discussion of aesthetics is limited, and he certainly did not develop a systematic perspective of theological aesthetics.[1] However, Bonhoeffer affirms aesthetic existence in the context of his broader theology, in particular his perspective of this-worldly Christ-reality, which makes an important contribution to our understanding by fundamentally connecting everyday aesthetics with lived Christian existence. The contribution that Bonhoeffer explicitly makes primarily affirms the *celebration* of aesthetic existence in being Christian.[2] In addition, there is also an implicit embrace, through the enjoyment of aesthetic existence in his own life, where the *formative* role in becoming Christian is also clear, as can be concretely seen through the way his experience of music influenced his theology.

Bonhoeffer's Call for a Recovery of Aesthetic Existence

The context for Bonhoeffer's reflection on aesthetic existence is particularly significant. It could not be a context more suited to rejection of aesthetic in favor of ethico-religious existence. Confronted by the polarizing brutality of a world war, faced with the atrocities of Nazism and grappling with the ongoing church struggle against complicit German Christendom, Bonhoeffer has not only decided that a moral response demands his active involvement in the resistance (which led to his imprisonment), but is also writing what would become his magnum opus, a systematic account of ethics. In other words, he is living an existence

---

1. For an overview of Bonhoeffer's treatment of aesthetics, see de Gruchy, *Christianity, Art and Transformation*, 147–68.

2. In some ways, rather than speak of the *celebration* of the aesthetic, it would be more accurate to describe *enjoyment* of the aesthetic in the Christian life. *Enjoyment* does indeed capture the holistic sensory and affective nature of aesthetic existence, particularly encompassing the implicit and unintentional. We will, however, be using the word *celebration* for two reasons: First, and most importantly for this chapter, there is an intentionality to the word that accurately communicates the positive and explicit theological affirmation as practiced in the everyday. Second, subtly, and more relevant to the chapters to come, *celebration* can be used in the sacramental sense, as in the celebration of the Eucharist. We will ultimately be moving towards understanding everyday aesthetic existence as everyday liturgy, and the celebration of being human as worship.

saturated with pressing ethical demands and questions, both his ethical action and reflection being impelled by his commitment to follow after Christ. Now, in prison, separated from his friends, family, and fiancée, amid the ongoing bombing raids and facing an uncertain future, he reflects on the unlikely significance of aesthetic existence. Does everyday aesthetic experience have a place in the divine order of how the Christian life is to be lived, even in torrid times such as these?

Surrounded by these pressing societal and personal forces, in a letter written from prison to his close friend Eberhard Bethge, dated 23 January 1944, Bonhoeffer begins his reflection on aesthetic existence with a discussion on the nature and place of friendship. Bonhoeffer considers under which mandate friendship falls: marriage and family, work, state, or church. (Bonhoeffer initially speaks of "communities" or "orders" before finally settling on the term "mandates" to express a divinely imposed task within a particular realm of society.)[3] His response is that it is probably best to consider friendship within the realms of culture and education (*Bildung*). Bonhoeffer's employment here of *Bildung* (translated as "education") is significant; we should recall it as a pivotal concept in Kierkegaard's recovery of poetic living—*Bildung*, as the cultivation and formation of self, holding inherently creative connotations. While friendship is thus best allocated to the realms of culture and *Bildung*, the natures of culture and *Bildung*, however, do not fit neatly within any of the mandates. Where do they then belong? For Bonhoeffer, they belong within the sphere (*Spielraum*) of freedom rather than the domain of obedience. Again, we need to note what is lost in translation here. "*Spielraum* literally means 'room to play' or 'leeway.' The 'sphere of freedom' thus means a space in which one can be creative, take risks, experiment, in other words where 'aesthetic existence' becomes possible."[4] This, too, has a clear relation to Kierkegaard, who framed aesthetic existence as a mode of playful experimentation. Eliminating the *Spielraum* of freedom from human existence is indeed possible—resembling a life lived solely in Kierkegaard's mode of ethical existence—but something of the essence of being human would be lost. As Bonhoeffer puts it, "Someone who doesn't know anything of this sphere [*Spielraum*] of freedom can be a good parent, citizen, and worker, and probably also be a Christian, but whether

---

3. De Gruchy, ed., *Cambridge Companion to Dietrich Bonhoeffer*, 128, 199.
4. Bonhoeffer, *Letters and Papers from Prison*, 268n23.

such a person is a full human being (and thus also a Christian in the fullest sense) is questionable to me."[5]

In fact, Bonhoeffer continues, it is precisely in the Christian life where the *Spielraum* of freedom should flourish most, even in such difficult times.

> I wonder whether—it almost seems so today—it is only from the concept of the church that we can regain the understanding of the sphere [*Spielraum*] of freedom (art, education [*Bildung*], friendship, play). *This means that "aesthetic existence" (Kierkegaard) is not to be banished from the church's sphere; rather, it is precisely within the church that it would be founded anew* . . . Who in our time could, for example, lightheartedly make music, nurture friendship, play, and be happy? Certainly not the "ethical" person, but only the Christian. Precisely because friendship belongs within the scope of this freedom ("of the Christian person"!?), we must defend it confidently against all "ethical" existences that may frown upon it—certainly without claiming for it the "*necessitas*" of a divine command, but by claiming the "*necessitas*" of *freedom*![6]

This important passage provokes a number of points that we will need to further interrogate in order to better understand Bonhoeffer's contribution to the aesthetics of discipleship.

First, and perhaps most fundamentally, why does Bonhoeffer seem so concerned to regain the vitality of aesthetic existence within the church? On the surface it would seem a strange call from a theologian who has become popularly known for his rejection of "cheap grace" and everyday aestheticism, amid the "endless manifold struggle of the spirit against the flesh."[7] It appears that this endorsement of aesthetic existence goes against the essence of what he stood for. Does this represent a reversal of Bonhoeffer's position, or is there more to it than this superficial reading would suggest?

Second, and partly in response to this question, the relationship between the sphere of freedom and the sphere of obedience is critical to our discussion. For the moment, it will suffice to note that for Bonhoeffer, friendship is justified through the "*necessitas*" of freedom. Bonhoeffer's

---

5. Bonhoeffer, *Letters and Papers from Prison*, 268.

6. Bonhoeffer, *Letters and Papers from Prison*, 268 (italics added; italics original on "necessitas" and "freedom").

7. Bonhoeffer, *Discipleship*, 160.

reasoning as to the basis of this "*necessitas*" is anchored in what it means to be fully human, and fully Christian—being "a full human being" or a "Christian in the fullest sense" necessarily requires an existence that encompasses the *Spielraum* of freedom. To understand why Bonhoeffer would claim that the sphere of freedom, and consequently aesthetic existence, plays a humanizing role in life, we need to understand his description of reality, to which we will momentarily turn.

Third, this raises the question of the relationship between aesthetic existence and ethical existence. Bonhoeffer's use of quotation marks regarding "ethical" existences indicates that he is here referring to a caricature of the "ethical" person, as described by Kierkegaard's life stages. We need to explore Bonhoeffer's perspective on the truly integrated aesthetic-*ethical*-religious person, as opposed to an ethical caricature based on a reductionist reading of Kierkegaard, in order to outline the contribution of aesthetic existence to ethical life. Again, starting with Bonhoeffer's description of reality will help us to do this.

Finally, Bonhoeffer's description of aesthetic existence is helpful for more concretely framing the concept and its relationship to discipleship. Locating aesthetic existence within the *Spielraum* of freedom is an important contribution, with expressions of aesthetic existence being play, friendship, art and *Bildung*. If Kierkegaard refers to aesthetic existence in relation to enjoying life, the "play of unending freedom," and sensory existence purely in the moment, then Bonhoeffer is suggesting that such immediacy should be taken up into Christian living.[8] A narrow reading of Kierkegaard (in which aesthetic existence is rejected by the more mature stages of ethical and then religious existence) is therefore at odds with Bonhoeffer's position here. As we have seen, even though a more accurate and nuanced reading of Kierkegaard shows that he does indeed embrace the aesthetic and poetic in religious existence, it is a qualified and limited affirmation of aesthetic existence in Christian living, wherein he appears particularly reticent to explicitly suggest that sensory immediacy can play a role in becoming Christian. Thus, while Bonhoeffer is not directly contradicting this nuanced Kierkegaardian reading, he is more positive about sensory immediacy in the life of faith. Further, by connecting aesthetic existence with not only play and art, but also with friendship and *Bildung*, Bonhoeffer positively connects sensory immediacy with relational poetic categories—in the sense of Kierkegaard's

---

8. Bonhoeffer, *Letters and Papers from Prison*, 268n24.

conception of poetic living—contributing to the imaginative and existentially formative task of divine-human co-creation. In doing so, he challenges Kierkegaard's distinction between immature aesthetic existence as a first immediacy (outer) and mature aesthetic existence as a second immediacy (inner). Bonhoeffer is thus highlighting that mature aesthetic existence in the life of faith is not only inner immediacy but also integrates and embraces outer sensory immediacy (recall Kierkegaard's conception of music as the aesthetic experience that most aptly represents sensory immediacy, in conjunction with Bonhoeffer's endorsement here of "lightheartedly making music" as an expression of Christian living). To better understand the grounds for this vital role of aesthetic existence in Christian life, we need to briefly consider Bonhoeffer's conception of reality.

The Christological Affirmation of Worldly Reality

A brief exploration of Bonhoeffer's conception of reality will help us in two ways: First, his framing of this-worldly christological reality foregrounds the role of everyday aesthetic existence in being human and becoming Christian. Second, Bonhoeffer's perspective on the *process* of how we come to understand reality has implications for the formative role of aesthetic existence in discipleship.

In resonance with a motive impelling Kierkegaard's rejection of both Romantic aestheticism and comfortable Christendom, the challenge of overcoming the gulf between idealism and reality underlies much of Bonhoeffer's theology.[9] Like Kierkegaard's, Bonhoeffer's response to this question is fundamentally christological. To Bonhoeffer, any discussion of reality must inevitably begin with ultimate reality—God. Any quest to uncover reality necessarily faces the challenge of distinguishing between reality and appearance, and for Bonhoeffer the ability to discern the difference is the essence of discipleship.[10] Knowing reality is not knowing *about* reality, but rather seeing into the essence of things, seeing ultimate reality.[11] The only way to know ultimate reality is through revelation, in particular, revelation of the Living Word, Jesus Christ. The key point here

---

9. De Gruchy, *Christianity, Art and Transformation*, 163.
10. Bonhoeffer, *Discipleship*, 178.
11. Bonhoeffer, *Ethics*, 81.

is that this revelation is not doctrine *about* God, but is itself the essence of all existence: Jesus's word creates existence anew.[12]

It then follows that all attempts to comprehend reality must necessarily start with recognition of *ultimate* reality. All else is abstraction.[13] This coheres with a common claim in the field of theological aesthetics: If we are to understand the world in light of ultimate reality, it demands a greater appreciation of the aesthetic sphere of existence.[14] This is so because ultimate reality lies beyond the finitude of rational comprehension. In other words, ultimate reality lies beyond the propositional, within the realm of mystery. As Calvin Seerveld puts it, aesthetic experience can offer us allusive pointers to what lies beyond; these aesthetic pointers function as signposts for navigating this world.[15] Such is the nature of the human experience of wonder. While there is indeed value and an important contribution made by such a perspective of theological aesthetics, once again, the challenge lies here with the gulf between idealism (that which lies beyond) and reality (of this world). If ultimate reality is true reality, but somehow removed from us in the pale here and now, how and where do these two worlds, or realities, meet? While Bonhoeffer agrees with the fundamental importance of starting with ultimate reality, his argument for the revelation of ultimate reality is not nearly as Platonic. It is not about creating some sense, or image, of ultimate reality as the ideal, removed, but significant for the way we live. He rejects any notion of idealism as a means of navigating reality. Rather, it is "in Jesus Christ that the reality of God has entered into the reality of the world"; the disparity between "ought" and "is" is eradicated in Christ.[16] Critically, reality can only be known by *participating* in the reality of Christ. Through the incarnation, death, and resurrection of Christ the two worlds have been united, and by participating in the reality of Christ, one participates not only in the ultimate reality of God, but also in the reality of the world. In this understanding of reality, reality and goodness are inextricably intertwined. This is the basis of Bonhoeffer's ethics, "The question of the

---

12. Bonhoeffer, *Ethics*, 62.
13. Bonhoeffer, *Ethics*, 54.
14. As argued, for instance, in Avis, *God and the Creative Imagination*.
15. See Begbie's discussion of Seerveld's concept of allusiveness in Begbie, *Voicing Creation's Praise*, 135.
16. Bonhoeffer, *Ethics*, 54.

good becomes the question of participating in God's reality revealed in Christ."[17]

Participation in becoming fully human, as Christ became human, provides the impetus behind Bonhoeffer's encouragement to embrace "this-worldliness." The Christian life is not defined by religion but rather by a mature worldliness. It is "living fully in the midst of life's tasks, questions, successes and failures, experiences, and perplexities."[18] It is only here, participating with God in this-worldly, incarnational experiences, located within a particular time and a particular place that true faith is learned. "This is how one becomes a human being, a Christian."[19] To Bonhoeffer, faith, and how this is lived out in the world, is not a matter of systematic doctrine, which is first and foremost articulated through a conceptual framework. Rather, faith takes seriously the finitude and fragility of being human within this world. Claiming that action is always in response to a carefully considered principle, conceptual ideal, or ultimate duty

> is a misjudgement of historical human existence in which everything has its time (Ecclesiastes 3)—eating, drinking, sleeping, as well as conscious decision making and acting, working and resting, serving a purpose and just being without purpose, meeting obligations and following inclinations, striving and playing, abstaining and rejoicing.[20]

It is particularly important for us to note here the value that Bonhoeffer places on the nonutilitarian expressions of human life. For Bonhoeffer, moments of rest, play, enjoyment, and "just being without purpose" are an important part of what it means to be human, and therefore a fundamental aspect of being Christian. Aesthetic existence is thus not distinguished from religious existence; rather, they cohere in the life of the Christian. The life of the world matters because there is simply no dichotomy between the reality of God and the reality of the world, which come together in the reality of Christ; thus Bonhoeffer's comment, for example, that the best "christological" interpretation of the Song of Solomon is to "read it as a song about earthly love."[21]

17. Bonhoeffer, *Ethics*, 50.
18. Bonhoeffer, *Letters and Papers from Prison*, 486.
19. Bonhoeffer, *Letters and Papers from Prison*, 486.
20. Bonhoeffer, *Ethics*, 365.
21. Bonhoeffer, *Letters and Papers from Prison*, 410.

Embracing Both Aesthetic Existence and Costly Discipleship

The objection may be raised at this point that there seems to be a lack of consistency in Bonhoeffer's thinking regarding the value of aesthetic existence. While he clearly does embrace the aesthetic in his later writings (particularly his *Letters and Papers from Prison*), in some of his earlier writing he appears to be distinctly opposed to the aesthetic life. For example, in *Discipleship* there is an apparent dichotomy between the Christian and the world. Christians are "to engage the world in a frontal assault ... in order that their 'unworldliness' might become fully visible."[22] "The world celebrates, and they stand apart. The world shrieks 'Enjoy life', and they grieve."[23] It would seem difficult to integrate Bonhoeffer's later embrace of aesthetic existence with this apparent rejection of the life of the world. However, a more careful examination will show that there is continuity in Bonhoeffer's thought, even while there is indeed a significant theological development. This can be illustrated by briefly considering: the consistency of his personal aesthetic appreciation across his lifetime; the context and style of the respective writings; and the trajectory of his theology.

While it does indeed appear that Bonhoeffer, through his later writing, *expressed* greater appreciation for the aesthetic, Bonhoeffer always embraced an implicit sense of aesthetic appreciation. From a young age, as part of a family with significant social standing, Bonhoeffer was exposed to the arts. In particular, Bonhoeffer flourished as a musician, his father hoping that Bonhoeffer would choose the career path of concert pianist.[24] Throughout Bonhoeffer's life, his love for music never waned, as evidenced by his regular references to music, and his discovery and adoption of African American spirituals. While the earlier years of Bonhoeffer's life did not include theological reflection on the aesthetic, the aesthetic was constantly present as an important part of Bonhoeffer's life, and references to art and aesthetics are scattered throughout his writings.[25] De Gruchy therefore suggests that "aesthetic existence was an essential part of [Bonhoeffer's] own education and cultural formation (*Bildung*)."[26] Eberhard Bethge remembers that even during the years of

---

22. Bonhoeffer, *Discipleship*, 244.
23. Bonhoeffer, *Discipleship*, 103.
24. Bethge, *Dietrich Bonhoeffer*, 25.
25. De Gruchy, *Christianity, Art and Transformation*, 138.
26. De Gruchy, *Christianity, Art and Transformation*, 150.

the Finkenwalde Seminary (which provided much of the impetus for the writing of *Discipleship*), Bonhoeffer loved playing games—he permitted no classes on Sundays but was at the forefront of organizing games—and "nobody in Finkenwalde was more eager for plays and music than he."[27] The point is confirmed by Bonhoeffer's niece, Renate Bethge, who recalls that it "was so normal for us and for him, as we played music often, even games sometimes, that I did not see that there was much new like a 'turn to the aesthetic.'"[28] There is no doubt that during his time in prison Bonhoeffer explored the aesthetic more intentionally than before, writing a novel and a play and expressing himself through poetry. Nevertheless, there is no discontinuity in Bonhoeffer's lifelong appreciation of the aesthetic, but rather, towards the end of his life, explicit reflection and engagement with that which had hitherto been largely implicit.

Second, it is helpful to identify differences in the style of Bonhoeffer's writing, as dictated by context. The context of prison (and all that accompanied this phase of Bonhoeffer's life: separation from fiancée, friends and family; the failed assassination attempt; the war drawing to a close; etc.) proved catalytic for a reflective, even at times effusive style. This is accentuated by the more informal genre of writing that we are dealing with in *Letters and Papers from Prison*. By contrast, the rhetoric that Bonhoeffer employs in *Discipleship* makes it clear that he is here concerned with "struggle" writing. At the time of its writing, Bonhoeffer would not have identified himself with the broader German resistance struggle, but he is writing as an *ecclesial* activist, working to challenge the church to greater faithfulness. The urgency of the task at hand—the health of the church amid the destructive turmoil of Nazi Germany—demanded a stark, binary description of the options moving forward. Resonating with the task that befell Kierkegaard in his "attack on Christendom," this was a matter of ultimate concern, with no room for compromise.

Third, theologically, we find both a consistent trajectory as well as a significant new development. Bonhoeffer's close friend Eberhard Bethge has insightfully shown that Bonhoeffer's action and thought can be organized around three phases of his life.[29] Popular works in the middle period, such as *Discipleship* and *Life Together*, have been contrasted (as we did above) with writing from his final phase, thereby arguing for an

---

27. Bethge, "The Challenge of Dietrich Bonhoeffer's Life," 24; Bethge, *Dietrich Bonhoeffer*, 429.

28. De Gruchy, *Christianity, Art and Transformation*, 150n59.

29. Bethge, "The Challenge of Dietrich Bonhoeffer's Life."

aesthetic turn.³⁰ However, Bethge shows that there is clear continuity between the first and third phases, the second phase being a reaction necessitated by the Church Struggle, as noted above. Bethge points out that right from the start, as a student, Bonhoeffer was immersed in the antirationalistic trend of the German Youth Movement with its terminology of the philosophy of life.³¹ "This-worldliness" was therefore not a late discovery for Bonhoeffer, even though he may not have used the term at this point. Right from the first phase a driving concern was the "concrete nature of the message."³²

If Christology is the consistent core of Bonhoeffer's theology, then the incarnation is at the heart of this from the start.³³ To illustrate Bonhoeffer's this-worldly Christology, even in this early phase, Bethge quotes Bonhoeffer,

> The community of Christ is not the meeting place of those apart from life, but the center of life; the center of men "who persevere together in the midst of the world, in the depths of it, in its trivialities and bondages." This reads like a quotation from one of the prisoner letters, but it was said [more than ten years prior to his imprisonment] in November, 1932.³⁴

It is for this reason that the second phase, a necessary response to Nazism, is sometimes considered an interruption, a detour from the trajectory of Bonhoeffer's this-worldly theology. Amid the horrors of the time, "the world becomes the threatening jungle which must be passed through."³⁵ While his thought and writing is still christological in focus, the circumstances demanded exposition through the lens of eschatology rather than creation theology.

Bethge shows that in the third phase it is not Bonhoeffer's Christology that changes, but again, that to which he is responding: "the world come of age."³⁶ This leads to Bonhoeffer's critique of religion, since it is religion that separates the practice of Christianity from the world in four ways.

---

30. For examples arguing for an aesthetic turn, see Holland, "First We Take Manhattan," 377; Jones, "Dietrich Bonhoeffer's *Letters and Papers.*"
31. Bethge, "The Challenge of Dietrich Bonhoeffer's Life," 4.
32. Bethge, "The Challenge of Dietrich Bonhoeffer's Life," 7.
33. Bethge, "The Challenge of Dietrich Bonhoeffer's Life," 8.
34. Bethge, "The Challenge of Dietrich Bonhoeffer's Life," 13.
35. Bethge, "The Challenge of Dietrich Bonhoeffer's Life," 18.
36. Bethge, "The Challenge of Dietrich Bonhoeffer's Life," 32.

First, the chasm is due to the individualistic inwardness of religion (a critique that lies at the heart of Bonhoeffer's rejection of Kierkegaard's distinction between an "inner" second immediacy in the life of faith and an "outer" first immediacy of the aesthete). Second, the metaphysical nature of religion necessarily creates two realms of existence, which consequently devalues sensory existence. Third, religion as a "province of life" is relegated to an increasingly isolated and disconnected sphere of life. Finally, religion is entrenched in the *deus ex machina* concept: "God must be there for providing answers, solutions, protection, and help."[37] In this final phase, Bonhoeffer is therefore concerned with recovering the worldliness of Christianity, a trajectory established in the first phase with its incarnational focus. Or to put it differently, in *Discipleship* Bonhoeffer is confronting the issue of how to be a Christian in the world, in light of being a Christian *against* the world, while in *Letters and Papers* he is dealing with the issue of being a Christian *in* and *for* the world.

In sum, there is consistency throughout Bonhoeffer's treatment of this-worldliness, once we take into account his personal aesthetic appreciation across his lifetime, the context and style of the respective writings and the christological thread that runs through his theology. In this sense it is not accurate to describe the third phase as a turn to the aesthetic. However, there is indeed an important shift in this final phase.

For the first time in this third phase, Bonhoeffer begins to *explicitly* explore theology through the lens of aesthetic reflection. In other words, while there is consistency in his thought throughout the three phases, here he approaches the Christian life from a slightly different perspective, using different terminology. Whether he was consciously aware of this development is not clear. While it is difficult to predict exactly how this exploration would have unfolded had his life not been cut short, it seems reasonable to surmise that it would have gone on to play a significant role in his work from this point onwards.

The value of identifying these three phases is not simply apologetic, as a defense of Bonhoeffer's later explicit embrace of the aesthetic. Rather, it is precisely the richness of these three phases, taken together, as they mutually inform one another, that best contributes to the aesthetics of discipleship. As Bethge points out, the christological expansiveness of Bonhoeffer's first and third phases is most helpfully perceived alongside

---

37. Bethge, "The Challenge of Dietrich Bonhoeffer's Life," 34.

the exclusiveness of the second phase.[38] In his *Ethics*, Bonhoeffer makes the same point: "The more exclusively we recognize and confess Christ as our Lord, the more will be disclosed to us the breadth of Christ's lordship."[39] Even amid the exclusive and binary context of the second phase, a close reading of *Discipleship* makes it clear that behind the rhetoric lies continuity in Bonhoeffer's thinking about the christological, this-worldly nature of reality. Discipleship *is* this-worldly, but it is a mature, disciplined this-worldliness, as opposed to a self-seeking worldliness. This explains oxymorons such as "The 'unworldliness' of the Christian life is meant to take place in the midst of this world." It is in "daily life" amidst "secular vocation" that the Christian life is to be played out.[40] The quotation given earlier, encouraging Christians "to engage the world in a frontal assault," goes on to explain that this needs to happen *in* the world, "The world must be contradicted within the world."[41] In other words, an accurate vision of christological, this-worldly reality needs to be lived out amid distorted, self-seeking visions of reality. This is consistent with Bonhoeffer's description of this-worldliness in *Letters and Papers from Prison*. Here, he contrasts the two senses of this-worldliness: "I do not mean the shallow and banal this-worldliness of the enlightened, the bustling, the comfortable, or the lascivious, but the profound this-worldliness that shows discipline and includes the ever-present knowledge of death and resurrection."[42]

Bonhoeffer's two senses of this-worldliness are vital to understanding not only his endorsement of aesthetic existence but also consequently an accurate portrayal of the aesthetics of discipleship. He is clearly arguing for the fact that everyday life in the world is a fundamental part of being human, yet he is also qualifying the claim. It is a *disciplined* life in the world, or mature worldliness, that he is presenting as a vision of the Christian life, in contrast to a self-seeking worldliness. This is Bonhoeffer's distinction between mature aesthetic existence and aestheticism. Rather than aesthetic existence being ultimate reality itself, mature aesthetic existence is lived in light of ultimate reality. A question follows: How does this distinction play out in practice, in the everyday? What does mature

---

38. Bethge, "The Challenge of Dietrich Bonhoeffer's Life," 28–29.
39. Bonhoeffer, *Ethics*, 344.
40. Bonhoeffer, *Discipleship*, 245.
41. Bonhoeffer, *Discipleship*, 244.
42. Bonhoeffer, *Letters and Papers from Prison*, 485.

aesthetic existence look like? We will return to this shortly. In order to respond, first we need to further delineate Bonhoeffer's distinction between the "ultimate" and "penultimate."

Ultimate and Penultimate Reality

As we have seen, although there is continuity in Bonhoeffer's thinking around worldliness, there is also a maturing process, cultivated by changing circumstances, which leads to a significant shift in his approach. We can see this in the very same letter from prison we referred to above, discussing "this-worldliness." Here, while standing by the essential message of *Discipleship*, Bonhoeffer reflects on the "dangers" of the book, intimating that he would have written it differently had he to write it again. He explains that for a long time he thought he "could learn to have faith by trying to live something like a saintly life," writing "*Discipleship* at the end of this path." Later he discovered that "one only learns to have faith by living in the full this-worldliness of life."[43] Prior to writing *Discipleship*, Bonhoeffer had spent much of his energy working within the realm of the church. Following the book, he spent more time collaborating with others, outside of the church, in the resistance movement. Here he engaged with non-Christians committed to the fight for human dignity. This appears to have stimulated his thinking around what it means to be fully human in the world. As noted, his focus was shifting from the binary struggle of being a Christian amid the war to envisioning the future of Christianity after the war. Or, using Bonhoeffer's terminology, it is helpful to consider *Discipleship* as a work dealing primarily with the "ultimate," while later, particularly when exploring the "*Spielraum* of freedom," Bonhoeffer spends more time on the "penultimate."

Bonhoeffer describes the "ultimate" as "justification of the sinner by grace alone."[44] God's mercy to a sinner is God's final word. It is ultimate in two senses. First, it is qualitatively ultimate: "There is no word of God that goes beyond God's grace." Second, it is temporally ultimate: "Something penultimate always precedes it, some action, suffering, movement, intention, defeat, recovery, pleading, hoping—in short, quite literally a span of time at whose end it stands."[45] Bonhoeffer explores the question of what

---

43. Bonhoeffer, *Letters and Papers from Prison*, 486.
44. Bonhoeffer, *Ethics*, 146.
45. Bonhoeffer, *Ethics*, 150.

THE CELEBRATION OF AESTHETIC EXISTENCE IN CHRISTIAN LIFE 77

the relationship is between the ultimate and penultimate. He points to two unhelpful responses: First, a radical response can see only the ultimate of value, the ultimate and penultimate being "in mutually exclusive opposition."[46] From this perspective "everything penultimate in human behavior is sin and denial."[47] Second, the compromise response, which asserts that since the ultimate and penultimate are distinct, "The penultimate retains its inherent rights, but it is not threatened or endangered by the ultimate."[48] These are both problematic responses because "they make the penultimate and the ultimate mutually exclusive . . . One absolutizes the end, the other absolutizes what exists."[49]

It is helpful to illustrate how this concept has been applied to a theological perspective on politics, and then to draw a parallel to aesthetics. Robin Lovin applies Bonhoeffer's description of the penultimate in articulating the approach of a Christian realist, a political strategy which acknowledges that it is often more helpful to focus on "limitation and balance" than "final victory."[50]

> Concentration on the penultimate requires, according to Bonhoeffer, a rejection both of the radical politics that is willing to destroy anything and everything for the sake of ultimate truth and of the compromises that, by suspending judgement until ultimate truth is fully present, slip by degrees into relativism. The Christian realist shares the radical's dissatisfaction with injustice, but focuses on responsible choices among the concrete possibilities now available.[51]

Lovin is here echoing Reinhold Niebuhr's suggestion (amid the context of social and political action in Nazi Germany) that "an adequate religion is always an ultimate optimism which has entertained all the facts that lead to pessimism."[52] Politically then, hope is found by embracing the penultimate in light of the ultimate. The same applies to aesthetics. The ultimate (beauty, as the vision of God) informs the penultimate (aesthetic existence).

46. Bonhoeffer, *Ethics*, 153.
47. Bonhoeffer, *Ethics*, 153.
48. Bonhoeffer, *Ethics*, 154.
49. Bonhoeffer, *Ethics*, 154.
50. Lovin, *Christian Realism*, 5.
51. Lovin, *Christian Realism*, 5.
52. Niebuhr, *Christianity and Power Politics*, 182.

If the ultimate and penultimate are both important, Bonhoeffer suggests that the key to their integration is a christological understanding of reality, incorporating the incarnation, death, and resurrection of Christ. "A Christian ethic built only on the incarnation would lead easily to the compromise solution; an ethic built only on the crucifixion or only on the resurrection of Jesus Christ would fall into radicalism and enthusiasm. The conflict is resolved only in their unity."[53] Jesus Christ, the human being, "lets human reality exist as penultimate, neither making it self-sufficient nor destroying it."[54] The penultimate matters because it is in Christ that "the reality of God encounters the reality of the world and allows us to take part in this real encounter."[55] Bonhoeffer points out that logically nothing can be self-referentially penultimate; it is always penultimate in relation to the ultimate. In other words, while the penultimate precedes the ultimate, it "does not determine the ultimate; the ultimate determines the penultimate."[56] Concretely, from the perspective of the ultimate, "two things are addressed as penultimate: *being human and being good*."[57] A critical assertion necessarily follows this claim: "the penultimate must be preserved for the sake of the ultimate. Arbitrary destruction of the penultimate seriously harms the ultimate. When, for example, a human life is deprived of the conditions that are part of being human, the justification of such a life by grace and faith is at least seriously hindered, if not made impossible."[58] This does not mean that anything done in the penultimate can guarantee or even initiate the ultimate, but it does mean that preparation can be made for the reception of the word. Herein lies the importance of this concept for our discussion of the role of aesthetic existence in Christian life.

The *Spielraum* of freedom—encompassing play, friendship, the arts, and so forth—is an expression of the penultimate. While the *Spielraum* of freedom is not the ultimate, it retains significance in light of a christological view of reality; this affirmation of the penultimate means that aesthetic existence is an important aspect of Christian life. However, as we have noted, it is a qualified endorsement of aesthetic existence. The error

---

53. Bonhoeffer, *Ethics*, 157.
54. Bonhoeffer, *Ethics*, 158.
55. Bonhoeffer, *Ethics*, 159.
56. Bonhoeffer, *Ethics*, 159.
57. Bonhoeffer, *Ethics*, 159.
58. Bonhoeffer, *Ethics*, 160.

lies in making aesthetic existence absolute. Or, in other words, allowing the penultimate to become the ultimate. As long as aesthetic existence is considered penultimate, Bonhoeffer not only tolerates it, but calls for its recovery, because it is a celebration of what it means to be human. It is an embodiment of christological this-worldliness.

If this is Bonhoeffer's explicit affirmation of aesthetic existence, by implication he also further affirms that everyday aesthetic existence is an agent in the process of formation [*Bildung*]. The penultimate prepares the way for the ultimate. We cannot control the ultimate, for we engage reality in the penultimate. We cannot bring in the kingdom, but we can act in anticipation of it. We cannot initiate the word of grace, but we can either nurture a receptive environment or hinder it. In Bonhoeffer's words, "There are conditions of the heart, of life, and in the world that especially hinder the receiving of grace, that is, which make it infinitely difficult to believe."[59] Which gives rise to a core question for the aesthetics of discipleship: Does everyday aesthetic existence create "conditions of the heart" that nurture or hinder belief? Even from what we have covered thus far, it should be apparent that this is a complex question. Beyond a simple yes or no, a robust account of the aesthetics of discipleship needs to show *how* this may or may not happen. In subsequent chapters, we will engage the mechanics of the *how*, as we move beyond Bonhoeffer. For the moment, we will limit our focus to the *possibility* of aesthetic existence affecting belief. In order to explore Bonhoeffer's contribution to this question, we will shift from discussing his description of reality to his view on the process whereby we comprehend christological reality and participate in it, in other words, discipleship.

Discipleship as Seeing and Partaking in Reality

While *Discipleship* is hardly the first work one would think to turn to in order to consider Bonhoeffer's validation of aesthetic existence, it contains an implicit understanding of the fundamental role that the aesthetic plays in being human and becoming Christian. We will initially consider this in relation to the book as it stands, before exploring how this may have been developed had Bonhoeffer had the opportunity to elaborate further on his thinking regarding aesthetic existence.

59. Bonhoeffer, *Ethics*, 162.

As we have discussed, Bonhoeffer suggests that reality should be *seen* in light of the ultimate. In other words, when confronted by identical this-worldly stimuli, a christological perception of worldly reality differs from a nonchristological perception. Bonhoeffer describes this as seeing into the essence, or the depth of things, *seeing* reality in God.[60] This is significant because what Bonhoeffer is describing here is an imaginative act—the human ability to "see as." In the chapters to come, we will explore the nature and workings of this productive function of the imagination in greater detail, but here it is simply important to acknowledge the imagination as a way of seeing. In *Discipleship*, a repeated theme is sight, image, vision, the eye, and so forth. For Bonhoeffer, discipleship is the ability to *see* reality in light of Christ, to see beyond appearances, to see the kingdom, which is the real. "The disciples always see only Christ. They do not see Christ *and* the law, Christ *and* piety, Christ *and* the world . . . so their vision is simple . . . If the eye sees something other than what is real, then the whole body is deceived. If the heart clings to the appearances of the world, to the creatures instead of the creator, then the disciple is lost"[61] The path of costly discipleship is understanding reality in light of Christ, "no longer seeing oneself, only him who is going ahead."[62] Earlier we quoted Bonhoeffer speaking of the world celebrating life, while Christians stand apart, as a potential example of Bonhoeffer's rejection of this-worldliness. But in that passage, Bonhoeffer goes on to illustrate that it is the two senses of this-worldliness that he is contrasting.

> The world celebrates, and they stand apart. The world shrieks 'Enjoy life,' and they grieve. They *see* that the ship, on which there are festive cheers and celebrating, is already leaking. While the world *imagines* progress, strength, and a grand future, the disciples know about the end, judgment, and the arrival of the kingdom of heaven, for which the world is not at all ready."[63]

Faced with the same sensory stimuli, Bonhoeffer is presenting two ways of imagining the world, two ways of "seeing as."

However, Bonhoeffer wants to make it clear that these are not simply two equally valid perspectives on the way things are; he is contrasting an illusory understanding of the world, which is nothing but appearances,

---

60. Bonhoeffer, *Ethics*, 81.
61. Bonhoeffer, *Discipleship*, 161.
62. Bonhoeffer, *Discipleship*, 86.
63. Bonhoeffer, *Discipleship*, 103 (italics added).

with a perception of the real. Discipleship is learning how to tell the difference.[64] In other words, echoing Kierkegaard, the imagination is a human faculty that can either aid our perception of reality or distort it. As we have seen, Bonhoeffer is highly critical of the fantastical use of the imagination when it comes to perception of reality. Even with the noblest intentions of living a good life, if this is not grounded in reality it is the "craziest Don Quixotry."[65] It is the equivalent of Don Quixote riding into battle with imaginary armor for "the chosen lady of his heart who doesn't even exist."[66] It is mere fantasy. It is important to note, again in resonance with Kierkegaard, that the church is not immune to such fantastical illusions of reality, which is exactly the point of Bonhoeffer's critique of German Christendom. Whether under the guise of Christendom or not, disconnecting goodness from christological reality leads to a distorted vision of what it means to live the good life. Severed from its christological mooring, aesthetic experience easily becomes everyday aestheticism, the absolute measure of goodness, with faith relegated to the "spiritual" realm of existence.

If then, on the one hand, the distortion of reality by a fantastical use of the imagination is problematic, on the other, the productive imagination plays an important role in discipleship: Seeing christological reality requires this paradigmatic function of the imagination.[67] To see the kingdom of God is to see reality through the paradigm of Christ. Seeing this-worldly reality in light of ultimate reality requires a way of seeing that is not limited to finite, rational proposition. In other words, imaginative constructs such as metaphor, symbol, and story become indispensable tools for perception of reality. Hence Jesus's use of parables for envisioning the kingdom of God; Bonhoeffer drawing on the metaphors of the hidden treasure in the field and the pearl of great price to communicate the reality of costly grace, for instance.[68] In essence, Bonhoeffer's description of discipleship is founded on the importance of a new way of seeing reality, in which the imagination plays a critical role. It is a vision of reality, fueled by aesthetic phenomena such as story, metaphor and symbol, encompassing both this-worldly and divine reality.

64. Bonhoeffer, *Discipleship*, 177.
65. Bonhoeffer, *Ethics*, 51.
66. Bonhoeffer, *Ethics*, 80.
67. Garret Green offers a helpful articulation of the paradigmatic imagination in Green, *Imagining God*, 61–82.
68. Bonhoeffer, *Discipleship*, 44.

Yet, if Bonhoeffer is arguing for an imaginative way of seeing the world, it would be a mistake to equate this with a conceptual, idealist image disconnected from the earthiness of reality. He is not suggesting that discipleship is the process of moving from idea to action. As previously noted, engaging christological reality is not a question of proceeding from ideal to realization, but is about *participation* in such reality.[69] This participation is, first and foremost, a question of obedience. It is in the act of obedience that perception of reality is shifted. In the act of obedience, as Peter steps out of the boat into the waves—a this-worldly, bodily experience—Peter's reality changes (see Matt 14:28–31). Just as Kierkegaard rejected the notion that disciples can be "admirers" but rather need to be "imitators" of Christ, Bonhoeffer proclaims that, "Any intended discipleship without this step [of obedience] to which Jesus calls becomes deceptive enthusiasts' illusion."[70] In other words, obedience is not the consequence of seeing rightly but the precursor. This is not to say that perception of reality cannot change without literal obedience. Bonhoeffer explains this through the story of the rich young man Jesus commands to give away all his possessions as an expression of faith. The point here is not the giving of possessions but rather seeing reality through Christ so that even if we have the possessions, "we have them as if we did not have them."[71] As long as we understand that "it would be the infinitely easier way to understand Jesus' commandment simply and obey it literally," there is room for a christological conversion of the imagination that does not entail literal obedience (while acknowledging that such a conversion of the imagination will necessarily involve a consistent form of action in the world). Bonhoeffer therefore describes an organic, symbiotic, and two-way relationship between obedience and perception of reality, action and imagination. Just as any exercise of the imagination (perception of the kingdom) without obedience is illusion, so too aesthetics disconnected from the ethico-religious is mere aestheticism, having lost all reference to reality.

During this brief excursus into Bonhoeffer's description of discipleship as a process of coming to perceive christological reality, we have not yet explicitly considered the role of everyday aesthetic existence. If a

---

69. Bonhoeffer rejects any distinction between inward and outward life, arguing that such a distinction is not biblical (Bonhoeffer, *Letters and Papers from Prison*, 457).

70. Bonhoeffer, *Discipleship*, 62.

71. Bonhoeffer, *Discipleship*, 80.

conversion of the imagination grounded in this-worldly obedience is at the core of discipleship, we can return to the question of whether aesthetic existence hinders or nurtures this process. Bonhoeffer does not answer this question. He was just beginning to explore the concept when his life was cut short. What would it have looked like if he had further developed his thinking around aesthetic existence? Of course we cannot know with certainty, but it is helpful to further extrapolate the trajectories we have uncovered thus far.

We can start with what is clear: Bonhoeffer affirmed aesthetic existence because he argued for the christological nature of reality. Jesus Christ, as human, calls us to take our this-worldly humanity seriously. Celebration of being fully human is an important task in the penultimate, as it paves the way for the ultimate. Bonhoeffer argued that aesthetic existence—friendship, play, art, *Bildung*—has a role to play in the affirmation of human dignity.

However, Bonhoeffer is not endorsing this-worldliness unreservedly. As we have seen, it is a mature, disciplined sense of this-worldliness for which he is arguing. It follows that this should therefore apply to aesthetic existence—Bonhoeffer calling for a mature, disciplined aesthetic existence as opposed to mere aestheticism. It is tempting to borrow a phrase from Calvin Seerveld and propose that "aesthetic obedience" is what Bonhoeffer is suggesting.[72] After all, Bonhoeffer's emphasis on obedience is grounded in a distinct sense of this-worldliness. This means that embodiment and the senses are an integral part of this obedience.[73] But this would be to misrepresent what Bonhoeffer is calling for in a recovery of aesthetic existence. It would be to impose Kierkegaard's ethical life-attitude of permissibility onto a category that should be more fully understood in terms of the relational interactions of becoming and being Christian. It is not the "*necessitas*" of obedience or divine command that drives Bonhoeffer's embrace of aesthetic existence, but the "*necessitas*" of freedom. He specifically contrasts this realm of freedom with the realm of obedience. The latter is marked by the response to a command or mandate, while the former is an expression of human freedom, not engaged for a particular purpose, outcome, or utility, but for its own sake, purely for the gift of "being in the moment."[74]

72. Seerveld, *Rainbows for the Fallen World*, 42.

73. Bonhoeffer, *Discipleship*, 225–26, 232.

74. This is not to say that aesthetic existence does not have purpose or utility. To the contrary, the coming chapters will argue that this is an unavoidable by-product

Bonhoeffer's qualification of aesthetic existence is, therefore, rooted in his relational understanding of freedom.

> Freedom is not a quality that can be uncovered; it is not a possession, something to hand, an object . . . instead it is a relation and nothing else . . . Being free means 'being-free-for-the-other', because I am bound to the other. Only by being in relation with the other am I free.[75]

If relationship provides the conceptual framework within which we should understand the realm of freedom, and consequently aesthetic existence, then it follows that a christological basis of relationship should guide this understanding. The Christian life is a participation in Jesus's "being-for-others."[76] If aestheticism is the end result of self-centered aesthetic existence, Bonhoeffer's relational paradigm suggests that mature aesthetic existence is guided by love. A kenotic approach to aesthetic existence may appear to be an oxymoron, but it is worth considering whether a selfless approach to aesthetic experience is not more likely to lead to wonder (and an accurate vision of reality) rather than the self-centered titillation of aestheticism (and an illusory perception of the real). In this sense, not only is aesthetic existence a celebration of being human, but it also plays a fundamental role in the revelation of reality. Bonhoeffer suggests that if love is the compass that orients action in the world, such action provides a new vision of reality: "love makes the disciple able to see."[77] Drawing from Bonhoeffer's musical metaphors, we could say that love of Christ is the *cantus firmus* grounding the polyphony of mature aesthetic existence in christological reality. To explore this more fully we need to turn to Bonhoeffer's engagement with music and the way this influenced his own personal and theological formation.

Spotlight on Music: Sensory Immediacy Generates "Living" Metaphors

Bonhoeffer's love for music provides fertile ground for an investigation into the relationship between music, as the archetypal aesthetic

---

(whether intentional or not) and is an important reason for taking aesthetic existence seriously.

75. Bonhoeffer, *Creation and Fall*, 63.
76. Bonhoeffer, *Letters and Papers from Prison*, 501.
77. Bonhoeffer, *Discipleship*, 140.

experience of sensory immediacy, and Christian living. (Our spotlight on music will therefore be more substantial in this chapter than in the others, in order to do justice to the richness at hand.) There are two particular aspects in focus here, again as in the last chapter, using the lens of music to crystallize and substantiate key points for our understanding of the aesthetics of discipleship. First, based on his musical experience, Bonhoeffer draws on musical metaphors, which elucidate his argument, thereby offering further clarity on his embrace of mature aesthetic existence. Not only are these metaphors insightful, but they imply that the realm of free play, being in the moment musically, contributed to his explicit theology. Second, therefore, we need to consider the nature of this aesthetic contribution to Bonhoeffer's theology. The suggestion here is that the metaphors which he employs are not merely the consequence of theological reflection on aesthetic existence (music, here), but the inverse—that his theology may be, at least partially, the consequence of formative paradigms created through his musical experience.

To fully appreciate the impact of music on Bonhoeffer's life and thought, we should recall that he was a proficient musician whose practice and enjoyment of music remained a lifelong passion. As already noted, music was a constant presence in the Bonhoeffer home throughout his formative years, and at one stage it appeared to both him and his parents that he might pursue a career as a concert pianist. By the age of ten he was performing Mozart sonatas, and not long after, began composing cantatas and trios. Saturday evenings were spent accompanying his mother and sister in "songs by Schubert, Schumann, Brahms and Hugo Wolf."[78] At seventeen, he was accompanying his sister on the lute as they performed at parties. This musically saturated existence continued throughout his life, references to music appearing regularly in his work. His time in Harlem expanded his musical appreciation, where he collected gramophone recordings of spirituals that he would later use to introduce students at Finkenwalde to the musical genre.[79] At Finkenwalde, the "two Bechstein grand pianos . . . were in constant use," while Bonhoeffer's extensive "collection of gramophone records, remarkable for those days, was at everyone's disposal," often playing the little-known spirituals.[80] The designation of a "music room" in itself is

78. Bethge, *Dietrich Bonhoeffer*, 25.
79. Bethge, *Dietrich Bonhoeffer*, 150.
80. Bethge, *Dietrich Bonhoeffer*, 427.

significant, since the underground seminary at Finkenwalde represented Bonhoeffer's practical template of what discipleship looks like as "life together." In Bonhoeffer's 1936 report, he writes, "Now as before, we spend a great deal of time and derive great joy from our music making ... in general, I can hardly imagine our life together here without our daily music making. We have driven out many an evil spirit in this way."[81] Bonhoeffer's Bechstein grand piano as well as the gramophone collection had previously traveled with him to England for his time there as a parish minister. Again, England was a new cultural context in which Bonhoeffer did not hesitate to expand his musical appreciation, adding to his gramophone collection, prompted by his enthusiasm for "the quality of the English choirs."[82] His rooms there too were bustling with musical activity, as he was "playing trios and quartets" or listening to music.[83] On occasion, notably, it was through music that he developed friendships here (recall Bonhoeffer's alliance of music and friendship as modes of aesthetic existence).[84]

Later, in prison, as Bonhoeffer begins to think about music and aesthetic existence explicitly, in theological terms; it is important to therefore remember that it is a reflection built on a lifetime of implicit existential embrace. This lifelong love of music fundamentally integrated Bonhoeffer's vision of the good life with music.[85] For instance, in a prison letter sending his best wishes to the Bethges for a blessed Pentecost, music is a natural component of Bonhoeffer's vision for a season of goodness, "I wish you fine weather, much pleasure with little Dietrich, and many nice and quiet hours and good music!"[86]

In an important sense, even in prison, deprived of musical instruments and recordings, music continued to pervade Bonhoeffer's existence. His letters are scattered with musical notation as he imaginatively re-experienced these pieces "inwardly." Hearing music "from within," gave him "an existential appreciation of Beethoven's music from when he was deaf," and helped him to more clearly attune himself to the beauty of

---

81. Bonhoeffer, *Theological Education at Finkenwalde*, 278–79.
82. Bethge, *Dietrich Bonhoeffer*, 328.
83. Bethge, *Dietrich Bonhoeffer*, 328.
84. Bethge, *Dietrich Bonhoeffer*, 328.
85. Smith, "Bonhoeffer and Musical Metaphor," 197.
86. Bonhoeffer, *Letters and Papers from Prison*, 401.

a piece.⁸⁷ One particular instance of such an imaginative re-experiencing points to the impact of music as aesthetic existence in his life. It is a portrait that exemplifies the experience of music as sensory immediacy. Bonhoeffer recalls leaving a seminar, in which the highly respected Adolf von Harnack lauded his work. He admits to still being "full with this" as he entered the Philharmonic Hall for a performance of Bach's Mass in B Minor. "Then the great 'Kyrie eleison' began, and *at that moment everything else sank away completely*. It was an indescribable impression. Today I am moving through it by memory, section by section . . . [It] is for me Bach's most beautiful music."⁸⁸

His time in prison, therefore, offers us a valuable opportunity to explore the interplay between Bonhoeffer's aesthetic existence, imagination, and theological reflection. Not only is Bonhoeffer here without instruments and recordings, necessitating the inward re-experiencing of music, but the nature of his informal and reflective letter writing offers us a unique window onto his processing of the experience.

Bonhoeffer's Musical Metaphors

Bonhoeffer's explicit reflection on music produces a handful of overlapping musical metaphors that he uses theologically in his prison letters. The way Bonhoeffer employs these metaphors—fugue, *Grundton*, polyphony, and the related notions of cantus firmus and counterpoint—resonates with Kierkegaard's description of poetic living, clarifying that mature aesthetic existence operates in "harmony" with Christ as divine poet.

The Metaphor of Fugue in Response to Fragmentation

Both Kierkegaard and Bonhoeffer lament the fragmentary nature of existence. For Kierkegaard, as we have seen, Romantic existential aesthetics merely accentuates the fragmentary nature of life by locating the self in discrete and disconnected sensory moments. His call to "be one thing" is ultimately only to be actualized in Christ, as manifestation of both the finite and infinite. For Bonhoeffer, it is particularly the context of war—and the intensification of human finitude, mortality, and brokenness

---

87. Bonhoeffer, *Letters and Papers from Prison*, 332.
88. Bonhoeffer, *Letters and Papers from Prison*, 177 (italics added).

that war brings—which provokes his concern. In a reflection that mirrors Kierkegaard's observation of the radical vacillation of Romantic "moods," Bonhoeffer laments the behavior of his fellow prisoners in a letter to Bethge, noting that, "When bombers come, they are nothing but fear itself; when there's something good to eat, nothing but greed itself ... They are missing out on the fullness of life and on the wholeness of their own existence. Everything ... disintegrates into fragments."[89] In a sense, Bonhoeffer is here describing everyday aestheticism, the devolution of life into the absolutization of sensory immediacy, along with the concomitant fragmentation that ensues. The timeless nature of this observation should be immediately apparent. While the nature of the "bombers" may change (a global pandemic, for instance), and the allure of "something good to eat" take different forms (something good to listen to, watch, touch, and so forth—whatever may be pleasing to the senses in the moment), the vacillation of "moods" are marks of the fragmentation wrought by everyday aestheticism (a reality further exacerbated by contemporary consumerism and the amplified broadcast of these existential moods via social media).

While being confronted by the fragmentation of life is a timeless reality of a fallen world, in a letter to his parents, Bonhoeffer mourns the exacerbated brokenness that war brings "both professionally and personally," and the feeling this arouses of "how unfinished and fragmentary our lives are."[90] However, further in the same letter, he adds a pivotal reflection that emanates from his Christology: "But precisely that which is fragmentary may point to a higher fulfillment, which can no longer be achieved by human effort."[91] In a letter written just two days later, with these thoughts obviously still in his mind, he turns to his love of Bach's music to convey the sentiment to Bethge. Again, he bemoans that "we experience ... our professional and personal lives ... as fragmented," but here he notes that it is not merely the consequence of the war but extends the experience of fragmentation to the demise of the polymath and concomitant rise of the "specialist" in intellectual life, producing mere siloed "technicians," even in the arts.[92]

---

89. Bonhoeffer, *Letters and Papers from Prison*, 405.
90. Bonhoeffer, *Letters and Papers from Prison*, 301.
91. Bonhoeffer, *Letters and Papers from Prison*, 301.
92. Bonhoeffer, *Letters and Papers from Prison*, 305.

> What matters, it seems to me, is whether one still sees, in this fragment of life that we have, what the whole was intended and designed to be ... After all, there are such things as fragments that are only fit for the garbage ... and others which remain meaningful for hundreds of years, because only God could perfect them, so they must remain fragments—I'm thinking, for example, of the *Art of the Fugue*. If our life is only the most remote reflection of such a fragment, in which, even for a short time, the various themes gradually accumulate and harmonize with one another and in which the great counterpoint is sustained from beginning to end—so that finally, when they cease, all one can do is sing the chorale "Vor Deinem Thron tret' ich allhier"[*I come before thy throne*][93]—then it is not for us, either, to complain about this fragmentary life of ours, but rather even to be glad of it.[94]

Bonhoeffer is here using the musical concept of fugue, and in particular Bach's *Art of Fugue*, in an attempt to capture the theological assertion that the fragmentary nature of human finitude only has meaning within the larger divine composition of life. It is not only that a fugue, which weaves multiple voices into a musical tapestry, is a metaphor that captures this integration well, but this is particularly so in the famed fugues of Bach, and here, significantly, the *Art of Fugue*, which remained unfinished at the time of Bach's death, and therefore, fragmentary.[95] Amid the limitations of human finitude, "The fragments do not fly apart but find their coherence in Christ, in whom the broken themes of praise are restored."[96] In contrast to those overcome by the fragmented immediacy of fear, greed, or desperation amid the bombing raids Bonhoeffer observed above, he goes on in that letter to assert that, "Christianity, on the other hand, puts us into many different dimensions of life at the same time; in a way we accommodate God and the whole world within us."[97] To try to capture

---

93. "The chorale traditionally associated with Bach's *Art of Fugue*" (Bonhoeffer, *Letters and Papers from Prison*, 306n22).

94. Bonhoeffer, *Letters and Papers from Prison*, 306.

95. Bonhoeffer also likened the resistance movement, and the Hitler assassination plot in particular, to a performance of the *Art of Fugue*. It proved to be a prescient metaphor, not only because of the unfinished and therefore fragmentary nature of the plot, but also because this alludes to the selfsame theological point regarding the fragments of finite human endeavor not being sufficient in and of themselves, but taken up and ordered by God. See Pangritz, "Point and Counterpoint," 40.

96. De Gruchy, *Christianity, Art and Transformation*, 167.

97. Bonhoeffer, *Letters and Papers from Prison*, 405.

what he means by this, he refers to another musical metaphor, describing it as multidimensional polyphony.

Polyphony, Cantus Firmus and Counterpoint

Bonhoeffer introduces his well-known metaphor of polyphony in a letter concerning the rightful place of erotic love. Amid his own loneliness in prison, and in response to Eberhard Bethge's longing and love for his wife, Renate (particularly when separated due to military service), Bonhoeffer considers the right orientation of these worldly desires. As we have seen, being founded in the love of Christ distinguishes mature aesthetic existence from aestheticism, and this is best explained through Bonhoeffer's framing of Christian living as polyphony (the coherence of multiple independent melodies in a single, textured composition).

Mature aesthetic existence, marked by a commitment to loving relationships (with creation, God, and humankind), could be described as a polyphonous celebration of christological reality. There is perhaps no more powerful aesthetic experience than sensual love. As Bonhoeffer considers how to respond well to earthly, erotic love, he describes the polyphony of life, anchored in the cantus firmus (the base melody in a polyphonic composition) of love for God.

> What I mean is that God, the Eternal, wants to be loved with our whole heart, not to the detriment of earthly love or to diminish it, but as a sort of cantus firmus to which the other voices of life resound in counterpoint . . . Even in the Bible there is the Song of Solomon, and you really can't imagine a hotter, more sensual, and glowing love than the one spoken of here (cf. 7:6!). It's really good that this is in the Bible, contradicting all those who think being Christian is about tempering one's passions . . . Where the cantus firmus is clear and distinct, a counterpoint can develop as mightily as it wants.[98]

"God, the Eternal" is the cantus firmus, and love of God does not negate, or obliterate the earthly sensory-erotic (to use a term from Kierkegaard). Recall Kierkegaard's challenge of an outing to the amusements of Deer Park. Climacus could not conceive how one could be consumed by "God, the Eternal," and at the same time be present in the "trivial" of this-worldly existence. Bonhoeffer's response here is that God-given, earthly

---

98. Bonhoeffer, *Letters and Papers from Prison*, 394.

aesthetic existence does not need to be controlled by the *"necessitas"* of obedience (Kierkegaard's ethical sphere of permissibility) but can freely flourish "as mightily as it wants" in counterpoint to the cantus firmus of love of God. Bonhoeffer reads these two—the divine cantus firmus and the earthly counterpoint—as reflecting the nature of Christ.[99]

> The two are "undivided and yet distinct," as the Definition of Chalcedon says, like the divine and human natures in Christ. Is that perhaps why we are so at home with polyphony in music, why it is important to us, because it is the musical image of this christological fact and thus also our *vita christiana*?[100]

As disciples of Christ then, in "following-after," incarnational Christian life also embraces these "undivided and yet distinct" aspects of *cantus firmus* and counterpoint. Therefore, the disciple should not draw back from engagement with earthly reality, but as the cantus firmus is given wholehearted expression, the counterpoint of this-worldly existence is not only validated, but maintains its own identity and integrity, thereby providing the existential unity to which Kierkegaard aspired in his call "to be one thing." Bonhoeffer continues,

> I wanted to ask you to let the cantus firmus be heard clearly in your being together; only then will it sound complete and full, and the counterpoint will always know that it is being carried and can't get out of tune or be cut adrift, while remaining itself and complete in itself. Only this polyphony gives your life wholeness.[101]

In a sense then, we could say that Bonhoeffer is here building upon and expanding Kierkegaard's notion of poetic living as harmonious co-creation with Christ. A mature approach to aesthetic existence is one anchored, first and foremost, in love for God, as the cantus firmus, which enables celebration of the sphere [*Spierlraum*] of freedom, within the bounds of harmony and resonance. Such an embrace of aesthetic existence is an affirmation of all that is good and human in the penultimate, preparing the way for the ultimate.

---

99. Begbie, *Music, Modernity, and God*, 209.
100. Bonhoeffer, *Letters and Papers from Prison*, 394.
101. Bonhoeffer, *Letters and Papers from Prison*, 394.

Music as Paradigm-Forming

While the *Art of Fugue* and polyphony elucidate Bonhoeffer's argument for this-worldly Christian existence, a third musical metaphor, the German term *Grundton*, speaks to the paradigmatic nature of these metaphors. In other words, up until this point we have been considering the illustrative value of these metaphors, helpful linguistic tools to clarify the argument. However, while this is valid, the question we need to engage at this point is whether these metaphors function solely as ornamental tropes—useful for painting a vivid mental picture, but not fundamentally a necessary aspect of the argument—or whether these musical experiences shaped Bonhoeffer's imagination, being paradigmatically formative, and thereby contributing to his perception of reality.

Grundton and Formation through Music

In a letter to Eberhard and Renate Bethge, Bonhoeffer offers thoughts for the day of the baptism of their son (Bonhoeffer's godson, also named Dietrich, who would intriguingly go on to become a professional musician). Amid his reflections, prayers, and blessings, Bonhoeffer affirms, "Music, as your parents understand and practice it, will bring you back from confusion to your clearest and purest self and perceptions, and from cares and sorrows to the *Grundton* [translated 'underlying note'] of joy."[102]

There are three observations we can make here: First, Bonhoeffer ties music to self-formation and perception. The suggestion here is that music in and of itself, as archetypal sensory immediacy, has the ability to influence the way we see reality and our sense of self therein. Second, Bonhoeffer carefully qualifies that it is specifically music, "as your parents understand and practice it," which offers this positive influence. This alludes, once again, to the fact that it is *mature* aesthetic existence that offers a positive formative influence, as a celebration of aesthetic this-worldliness in polyphonous counterpoint to the divine cantus firmus. Third, Bonhoeffer refers to the musical metaphor of a "*Grundton*" of joy. Translated here as "the underlying note," it refers to the English "tonic" or "key note" ("the 'first degree of a major or minor scale' or 'the main note

---

102. Bonhoeffer, *Letters and Papers from Prison*, 385.

of a key . . . after which a key is named'").[103] While this metaphor resonates with Bonhoeffer's description of the cantus firmus in polyphony, the significant point to note here is that the existential "*Grundton* of joy" is experienced by way of music itself. It is precisely through mature aesthetic existence, through a rightly ordered, christologically "polyphonic" experience of music, that young Dietrich will be able to see reality for what it is (*seeing as*—aesthetic existence feeding the productive imagination), facilitating a clear understanding of self, and the essence of peace and joy in a tumultuous world.

Bonhoeffer's use of *Grundton*, therefore, raises the question of whether his musical metaphors are only illustrative cognitive concepts, the consequence of theological reflection distinct from sensory experience, or whether, in an important sense, the lived experience of these musical metaphors (his personal, sensory experience of fugue, polyphony, *Grundton*, etc.) were formative for his own perception of reality, being catalytic for the creation of conceptual paradigms. The limited evidence we have to work with eliminates the possibility of a simplistic answer, and in any case, such a response would also offer a flawed and inadequate portrayal of human formation and existence. As we will further explore in the coming chapters, it is reductionist and therefore inaccurate to describe this as a simple, linear relationship: aesthetic experience informing the imagination, which in turn shapes conceptualization. Rather, there is a complex and symbiotic relationship between aesthetic experience, the imagination and conceptualization, which together, holistically contribute toward human perception and existence. The crux of the issue at this point, however, is that abstract conceptualization neither functions independently of aesthetic experience, nor is it sufficient, in and of itself, for capturing and communicating the totality of human existence. An allusion to this can be seen as Bonhoeffer attempts to draw from these living musical metaphors in order to capture implicit truth, and his consequent struggle to capture their meaning in the abstraction of language. Both here in this letter (he says "It hasn't turned out the way it should have"),[104] and in the polyphony letter (where he says, "Do you understand what I mean?" and "I don't know whether I have said this clearly"),[105] he appears

---

103. Smith, "Bonhoeffer and Musical Metaphor," 199.
104. Bonhoeffer, *Letters and Papers from Prison*, 382.
105. Bonhoeffer, *Letters and Papers from Prison*, 395.

to be drawing on these metaphors in an effort to express a lived truth that lies beyond the limitations of language.

Music as Formative for Bonhoeffer's Theology

Bonhoeffer's musical experience and reflection while in prison occurs very much in tandem with his theological thinking and development in this period.[106] The chronology here is particularly worth noting; most of Bonhoeffer's allusions to music in his letters precede his pivotal theological question of what Christianity really is, "or who is Christ actually for us today?" penned on April 30 1944.[107] In other words, Bonhoeffer's musical reflections begin prior to what Bethge describes as Bonhoeffer's "new theology."[108] The intriguing question is whether they contributed to this theological development, and thus whether this points toward his mature aesthetic existence playing a formative role in his perspective of reality.

Although there are a number of musical references in Bonhoeffer's letters prior to April 1944, three in particular are worth noting for our purposes here. We have already discussed one, Bonhoeffer's reflection on Bach's *Art of Fugue*, in a letter on February 23, 1944. Here Bonhoeffer for the first time introduces his thoughts on the multidimensionality of life, as reflected in contrapuntal music, which he would later expand upon as the polyphony of life, amid his "new theology." The two other references are significant because in both of them Bonhoeffer offers us a window onto his existential processing of the music, as he experiences it "inwardly," physically writing out the musical notation in these letters. On March 27, 1944, Bonhoeffer describes his "listening" to Beethoven's opus 111 with his "inner ear," and being existentially struck by how beautiful and pure the experience was: "all the dross falls away, and it seems to take on a 'new body.'"[109] It is an existential experience clearly intertwined with (perhaps even catalytic for) his reflections on Easter, and the importance of living in light of the resurrection, as the letter goes on to explore.

However, the first reference, his reflection on a Heinrich Schütz composition in a letter from December 1943, is perhaps most interesting,

---

106. For a detailed account, see Pangritz, *The Polyphony of Life*.

107. Pangritz, "Point and Counterpoint," 29; Bonhoeffer, *Letters and Papers from Prison*, 362.

108. Bethge, *Dietrich Bonhoeffer*, 853–92.

109. Bonhoeffer, *Letters and Papers from Prison*, 332.

THE CELEBRATION OF AESTHETIC EXISTENCE IN CHRISTIAN LIFE   95

both because it is the earliest, and also because we have here the clearest depiction of the connection between his existential experience of music and his consequent theological reflection. Before looking specifically at this letter, it is helpful to understand it in the context of Bonhoeffer's long-standing appreciation Schütz's music.

Many of the musical references in Bonhoeffer's earlier prison letters relate to Heinrich Schütz, "the 'father of German music' in the seventeenth century."[110] Bonhoeffer's embrace of Schütz stemmed from the latter's ability to unite music and word, in the liturgical settings of the Psalms, for example. In earlier years, this is precisely what Bonhoeffer found to be lacking in music from the Romantic tradition. On the one hand, Bonhoeffer's love for music in the Romantic tradition remained constant throughout his life. During the time at Finkenwalde, for example, Bethge notes that Bonhoeffer's "Romantic heritage was strongly evident in his playing of Chopin, Brahms, and excerpts from the delightfully stylish *Rosenkavalier*."[111] But on the other hand, he initially rejected the place of such Romantic music, Beethoven in particular, in the church. As he notes, some ten years prior to his prison letters, Beethoven's music "seems to be nothing but the eternal expression of human suffering and passion," a glorification of visceral human existence not suited for church use.[112] In other words, Bonhoeffer initially had reservations regarding the place of musical sensory immediacy in becoming Christian, like Kierkegaard, limiting this to a "second immediacy," or the immediacy after reflection, wherein word and music unite.

Yet, ironically, it is precisely through Schütz, in this December 1943 letter, that Bonhoeffer finds himself grappling with the unity of this-worldly desire and divine reality.[113] Here, months before engaging the question of who Christ is for us today, Bonhoeffer writes to Bethge reflecting on a Schütz composition, the Augustinian "O bone Jesu."[114] In particular, he imaginatively re-experiences the music of the line, "O how my soul longs for you," writing out the musical notation of the seven notes for the singing of the "O." This is significant because in the context of a hymn "colored by erotic associations," as Pangritz explains,

110. Pangritz, "Point and Counterpoint," 30.
111. Bethge, *Dietrich Bonhoeffer*, 429.
112. Bonhoeffer, *London, 1933–1935*, 356.
113. See also de Gruchy, "The Search for Transcendence."
114. Bonhoeffer, *Letters and Papers from Prison*, 30–31.

"In Schütz's setting the melismatic figure on 'o' is repeated four times, each time a fifth higher (e flat-b flat, b flat-f, f-c, c-g) so that the musical expression is intensified in an extraordinary measure . . . By means of transposed repetition of the melismatic motif, the 'ecstatic cry of longing' forms the 'center and climax' of the composition."[115] Bonhoeffer enters into the visceral passion of the music as he experiences it inwardly, then comments, "Doesn't this passage in its ecstatic longing combined with pure devotion, suggest the restoration of all earthly desire?"[116]

Here, Bonhoeffer's sensory-erotic experience of music appears to be informing his theology, perhaps contributing to his later, more explicit reflections on christological this-worldliness, thereby enhancing a christological trajectory that would ultimately lead Bonhoeffer to affirm that relationship with God is not "religious" and otherworldly. Rather, "genuine transcendence" and relationship with God is a new life in "'being there for others,' through participation in the being of Jesus. The transcendent is not the infinite, unattainable tasks, but the neighbor within reach in any given situation. God in human form!"[117] Consequently, Bonhoeffer's this-worldly aesthetics (in the form of his embrace of mature aesthetic existence) proves distinctive from a theological aesthetics that harnesses the aesthetic primarily as a means of engaging the (otherworldly) transcendent. In contrast to his earlier rejection of Romantic music in the church, his renewed appreciation for Beethoven during this period may well point toward a fuller understanding of mature aesthetic existence in the life of this-worldly Christianity, the selfsame pure passion that he initially ejected from ecclesial life now informing his thoughts on the resurrection, as we saw above.[118]

It is worth also noting that in the same Schütz letter, in fact, in the very next paragraph, Bonhoeffer offers an example of the impotence of music which is *not* "polyphonous," in contrast to the formative musical experience of "O bone Jesu." Bonhoeffer describes how "a sweet old man" comes to the prison on Christmas Eve to play carols on his trumpet. Clearly, he has good intentions, but the effect on the prisoners is only "demoralizing" and they try to drown out his playing with whistles and noise. Bonhoeffer notes that in "*this* misery" (his italics) of prison

---

115. Pangritz, "Point and Counterpoint," 32.
116. Pangritz's own translation. Pangritz, "Point and Counterpoint," 33.
117. Bonhoeffer, *Letters and Papers from Prison*, 501.
118. De Gruchy, "The Search for Transcendence."

life, such music is only "playfully sentimental" and therefore unhelpful. Bonhoeffer appears to be suggesting through these contrasting examples that music, as mature aesthetic existence, should be in harmony with both the ultimate hope of God (the cantus firmus) as well as a sober acknowledgement of the penultimate temporal context (whether that be prison or a more joyful context). Failure to account for both of these in aesthetic expression simply produces sensory stimuli that titillate, while being disconnected from the christological vitality of both life incarnate and life divine.

While these three inward musical experiences in Bonhoeffer's earlier letters—Bach's *Art of Fugue*, Beethoven's opus 111 and Schütz's "O bone Jesu"—each appear to provoke his theological reflection, taken together they also offer theological cohesion suggestive of Bonhoeffer's broader conceptual perspective. Bonhoeffer's Beethoven-inspired Easter reflections on "the new body" dovetail with his response to fragmentation through the *Art of Fugue* and ultimate christological hope, both mutually driven by his longing for the "restoration" of earthly desire through his existential experience of Schütz's composition. In short, collectively these reflections suggest Bonhoeffer's eschatology in musical terms.[119]

The question this poses is, therefore, whether Bonhoeffer's embrace of mature aesthetic existence is not only a consequence of his this-worldly Christology (which it is), but whether his christological this-worldliness is also informed by his mature aesthetic existence. Friedrich Schleiermacher affirms the latter, the fundamentally formational aspect of aesthetic existence: "Music is one great whole; it is a special, self-contained revelation of the world."[120] He argues that even though a multitude of cultural and individual musical expressions are possible, great music is akin to a religious a priori, moving musicians and hearers beyond the particular, beyond the systems of music (or religion), toward a common essential reality. Whether we embrace Schleiermacher's thesis or not, it is clear that Bonhoeffer's experience of music, and his consequent reflection on music while in prison, at the very least, had an organically symbiotic relationship with his theological development. But it may well also have provided categories of thought that he would not otherwise have had access to.[121] As Jeremy Begbie argues, it is "con-

---

119. Pangritz, *The Polyphony of Life*, 51.
120. Schleiermacher, *On Religion*, 51.
121. De Gruchy, *Christianity, Art and Transformation*, 145.

ceptuality arising from music [which] enables him to elucidate critical fields of doctrine."[122] It is a conceptuality that does not draw from music as an illustrative tool, but music is the very constitutive means through which the concepts are formed. Bonhoeffer is not drawing on music, he is thinking musically. "Bonhoeffer's musical experience, specifically his aural experience of simultaneously sounding and mutually resonating tones... extended in time and woven around a cantus firmus... is 'made available' to the theological conceptuality and language concerned with the multidimensionality of the Christian life."[123] Begbie is here rejecting the understanding of concepts as "isolated mental units" that provide a bridge between words and "things-in-the-world."[124] Rather than three discrete elements—words, concepts and things-in-the-world—Begbie draws on Kathleen Callow in describing concepts as "'habitual events', habits of thought that order human experience in various configurations. Concepts are 'thought-in-action'. We do not attend thoughtfully *to* them; we attend *with* them, by means of them."[125] An example clarifies the point: The concept of vacation draws from "a huge variety of direct sensory experiences of holidays, as well as a complex of associations garnered from elsewhere—sun, time to read, family reunions, and so on ... The concept is not a mental picture of a tidily bounded object but pertains to the world-as-experienced."[126] With Begbie, we can conclude that there is "every reason to believe" that this paradigmatic conceptual formation is happening through our sensory experience of music.[127] It is therefore erroneous to limit theological formation to the realm of mental units, but, as with the entirety of ethico-religious existence, theological development is inseparable from embodied life, including our everyday aesthetic experiences.[128]

In summary, Bonhoeffer's engagement with music elucidates two important contributions that he makes to our understanding of the aesthetics of discipleship. Firstly, his musical metaphors themselves, particularly polyphony, articulate a helpful model for distinguishing

---

122. Begbie, *Music, Modernity, and God*, 208.
123. Begbie, *Music, Modernity, and God*, 210.
124. Begbie, *Music, Modernity, and God*, 206.
125. Begbie, *Music, Modernity, and God*, 206.
126. Begbie, *Music, Modernity, and God*, 206.
127. Begbie, *Music, Modernity, and God*, 207.
128. Begbie, *Music, Modernity, and God*, 207.

between self-centered everyday aestheticism (an impediment to discipleship) and mature aesthetic existence (as integral to becoming Christian). Mature aesthetic existence operates in the realm of free play, not in the Kierkegaardian sphere of ethical obedience. A counterpoint can "develop as mightily as it wants" if grounded in the existential cantus firmus of love for God.

Bonhoeffer's point is affirmed by Karl Barth's perception of Mozart's music, the essence of which Barth described as play. Barth's description is significant in light of Kierkegaard's choice of Mozart to illustrate that music is fundamentally sensory immediacy. Karl Barth, however, suggests that such play is integral to Christian life,

> Our daily bread must also include playing. I hear Mozart . . . at play. But play is something so lofty and demanding that it requires mastery. And in Mozart I hear an art of playing as I hear it in no one else. Beautiful playing presupposes an intuitive, childlike awareness of the essence or center—as also the beginning and the end—of all things. It is from this center, from this beginning and end, that I hear Mozart create his music.[129]

Rather than binding word to music, Mozart's music is a playful expression, a "free counterpart" to the word.[130] As such, Barth perceives "Mozart's music as 'parables of the kingdom' . . . as 'theology' . . . 'mediating' the praise of the cosmos . . . witness[ing] to the theonomous *perichoresis* of the triune life."[131] For Barth, this mastered playfulness carries significant theological weight: "the golden sounds and melodies of Mozart's music have from early times spoken to me not as gospel but as parables of the realm of God's free grace as revealed in the gospel—and they do so again and again with great spontaneity and directness."[132] Free play, everyday existence within the *Spielraum* of freedom, is therefore not peripheral to the Christian life but at its "essence or center," as Barth puts it. It is to be wholeheartedly embraced as a voice, in all its fullness, within the polyphonic composition of a life lived in worship of God.

Sensory immediacy only becomes problematic when this voice is pursued in isolation, as a means to the absolute, rejecting the cantus firmus. Whether such absolute aesthetic existence is approached via the

---

129. Barth, *Wolfgang Amadeus Mozart*, 16.
130. Barth, *Wolfgang Amadeus Mozart*, 38.
131. Moseley, "'Parables' and 'Polyphony,'" 264.
132. Barth, *How I Changed My Mind*, 71.

aestheticism of Kierkegaard's Don Juan, the reflection of his Seducer (or Nietzsche's Dionysian movement "beyond good and evil" for that matter, which we will turn to in the next chapter), the common deficiency here is the attempt to turn fragmentary finitude into the infinite absolute. By contrast, in mature aesthetic existence, "the mystery of the ultimate is glimpsed not grasped," for it is always mediated in the penultimate polyphony of life.[133] The fragmentary nature of human finitude, therefore, is not to be rejected but embraced, as it offers grounding bounds and limits to mature aesthetic existence amid the restlessness for the ultimate, which drives powerful aesthetic expression. Within the frame of this christological polyphony, aesthetic existence can, and should, freely flourish in the Christian life.

The first contribution of Bonhoeffer's musical metaphors is, therefore, that they offer a model for distinguishing *mature* aesthetic existence. The second contribution is important for our trajectory going forward in the coming chapters: These metaphors are not merely illustrative, but Bonhoeffer's very aesthetic experience of music informed his theological conceptualization. This challenges Kierkegaard's distinction between a first and second immediacy. Kierkegaard distinguishes a second immediacy as being "after reflection," thus an engagement with the aesthetic consequent to conceptualization. However, if conceptualization is organically and symbiotically in relation to sensory experience in the world, then such a distinction is not valid. Not only is mature aesthetic existence polyphonous celebration of christological this-worldliness, but it nurtures paradigms for perceiving such reality.

Bonhoeffer then, leaves us with both a theological affirmation of everyday aesthetic existence, grounded in Christology, as well as further questions we need to answer regarding the relationship between aesthetics, ethics and faith. What relationship does aesthetic existence have to the shaping of the imagination, and consequently the way we see reality, even when these aesthetic experiences are not engaged for

---

133. De Gruchy, "The Search for Transcendence," 204. De Gruchy notes that, "As deafness increased and death approached, Beethoven delved deeper into his subconscious, not just for his own sake, but also for the sake of universal harmony. But as he is about to experience transcendence—towards the end of his final piano sonata (Op. 111)—there is a moment of pregnant silence. He has entered holy ground and, overtaken by awe, he draws back from grasping the ultimate." The question Beethoven poses here for us is whether silence has an important role to play in mature aesthetic existence, not only in music, but amid the frenetic consumerism and grasping materialism which marks contemporary aesthetic experience.

utilitarian purposes? Do everyday aesthetic experiences—celebrations of the *Spielraum* of freedom such as play, friendship, music, a crafted meal, and so forth—affect the way we see the world, and consequently how we act in it? If they do, then everyday aesthetic existence is not only something to be celebrated in the penultimate, as an expression of goodness in fully-human, this-worldly existence; it is also fundamental to meaning and action, ethics and faith.

At the beginning of this chapter, we noted Bonhoeffer's association of aesthetic existence with art, play, friendship, and *Bildung*. As relatively obvious expressions of aesthetic existence, it is not difficult to understand why he connected art and play with the sensory immediacy of Christian living, as illustrated by our discussion on music. "Friendship," here, is interesting, since it affirms that aesthetic existence is best understood and lived out in the context of relationality, guided by love. Friendship is, at times, an expression of sensory immediacy, but there is more to it than that, and including it here, within the category of aesthetic existence, is illustrative of the guiding cantus firmus of love for mature aesthetic existence. However, it is *Bildung* that we need to probe further. As noted, this resonates with Kierkegaard's description of poetic living, being the outworking of mature aesthetic existence. If we understand *Bildung* as cultural formation, the process (engaging all the faculties) whereby a person is educated to maturity, then what is the role of everyday aesthetic existence in personal formation? To assert that there is a connection here is not only an observation regarding the aesthetics of discipleship, but a broader anthropological reality: Aesthetic existence plays an essential role in being human, specifically in our development and formation. It is the nature and mechanics of this relationship to which we need now turn.

4

Aesthetic Existence as Fundamental in Being Human

THE TEMPTATION TO DISMISS aesthetic existence as peripheral—a pleasant diversion, yet ultimately inconsequential to the serious business of life—not only fails to reflect a christological vision for life, but also does not account for the pivotal role it plays in human perception and formation. This should be an obvious connection to make, which logically follows if one presupposes that a christological vision for life coheres with being fully human. That it needs to be explicitly articulated is an indication of the problematic schism that too often exists between religious existence and existence as embodied this-worldliness. An integrated theological vision of being human should necessarily accord with a this-worldly account of human existence that is universally applicable. By exploring such a this-worldly account, it becomes clear that everyday aesthetic experience is not only a pleasurable aspect of being human, but that it is fundamental to being human and the creation of meaning. In other words, aesthetic existence plays an important role not only in discipleship but in *all* human formation (or malformation), whether labeled religious or otherwise. The aim of this chapter is to describe this significant contribution that aesthetic existence makes to human perception and formation through the imaginative construction of ways of seeing, or world-making paradigms.

In the span of human history, it is not a new phenomenon to dismiss the contribution of aesthetic existence to human flourishing as insignificant at worst, or secondary at best. Even if we reject von Balthasar's accusation that Kierkegaard contributed to the wedge driven between aesthetic and ethico-religious existence, such a wedge undeniably exists. Although these modes of existence have taken on various guises over the centuries, they are invariably pitted against each other, whether it be Enlightenment rationality versus Romantic sensibility or the classical Apollonian in opposition to the Dionysian. More often than not, it is the Apollonian mode of existence that is endorsed as preeminent, embraced as fundamental to human progress and flourishing. And while there is no question that scientific and instrumental rationality has contributed immensely to modern human existence, this has also come at the cost of dispensing with the critical role that aesthetic existence has to play in being human. Being fully human demands that these two modes of existence cohere, that they interact with each other, challenge and serve each other, and thereby offer a holistic vision of human existence in the world. Yet, as Iain McGilchrist has argued, the Apollonian mode has become the master, to the catastrophic detriment of the world today.[1]

McGilchrist is one of the more erudite commentators on helping us better understand and navigate the interrelationship between the Apollonian and Dionysian modes of human existence. McGilchrist is a psychiatrist, but it is his broader interdisciplinary nous that makes his contribution so insightful, as he draws from a range of fields, including his work as a literary scholar to inform a broader philosophical, perhaps fundamentally anthropological argument for holistic human engagement with the world. Both Bonhoeffer and McGilchrist endorse aesthetic existence on the basis of our relationship to reality. In this regard, one way to describe their respective contributions would be that Bonhoeffer's is primarily ontological while McGilchrist's is essentially epistemological. Bonhoeffer embraces aesthetic existence because the nature of reality is christological, thereby validating the penultimate as incarnational, embodied existence. McGilchrist's focus is not on the nature of reality, but on how we know it. He suggests that if we look closely at this process, we cannot but acknowledge that a ratiocentric approach to reality provides a distorted view of the world. McGilchrist helps us to see that aesthetic existence plays a pivotal role in our perception of the world, and thereby our self-understanding in relation to reality. Consequently, the nature of our everyday aesthetic existence affects our formation as human beings.

---

1. McGilchrist, *The Master and His Emissary*.

Apollonian and Dionysian Perception of Reality

Although Bonhoeffer and McGilchrist may seem worlds apart, a mutual catalyst for their work is Friedrich Nietzsche's insightful critique of the modern world in relation to aesthetics, best crystallized by Nietzsche's exploration of the classical tension between an Apollonian and a Dionysian approach to life. Much has been written in Western thought on the archetypal pair of ancient Greek gods, Apollo and Dionysus (also known as Bacchus), largely because they capture so well the two fundamental, seemingly contradictory, ways of being human in the world. As John de Gruchy succinctly explains,

> Apollo . . . was the god of wisdom whose prophetic oracle at Delphi encouraged the virtues of civilised living, harmony, self-knowledge, rhetoric, and moral earnestness, amongst all who sought counsel . . . Apollo represented human rationality and denigrated the world of passion . . . If Apollo represented "masculine" virtues of rationality and order, the Dionysian cult had its roots in the more ancient cult of the Divine Mother with its emphasis on the power of nature, the instincts and the non-rational. Dionysian worship or bacchanalia, as the dramatist Euripides described it, was characterised by its devotees "in ecstasy flinging back the head in the dewy air." Induced by wine and usually sexually promiscuous, it gained an enthusiastic following even if only on the fringes of decent society, the society of Apollo. Such was its attraction that the Roman senate passed a decree against bacchanalia as a serious threat to the well being of society. Yet Euripides discerned that inspired religious emotion cannot be ignored, for while it may menace the good order of the *polis* and dissolve the bonds of society, it is an elemental force that has to be taken into account.[2]

The relation to our discussion thus far should be immediately apparent. Certainly, at face value, Kierkegaard's perception of aesthetic existence was largely if not completely Dionysian, as existence purely in the moment, reveling in the "play of unending freedom."[3] The critical question is whether the Dionysian is to be equated with a superficial reading

---

2. De Gruchy, *Christianity, Art and Transformation*, 14.

3. Ultimately, even such a reading of Kierkegaard's aesthetics must acknowledge that the "indeterminacy" of such a Dionysian sensory immediacy has a fundamental relationship to the "determinacy" of the imagination. See Smyth's discussion of Kierkegaard's "eros aesthetics" in Smyth, *A Question of Eros*.

of Kierkegaard's aesthetic stage of life, and therefore to be discarded as soon as one has matured sufficiently to embrace the Apollonian. Or, is the Dionysian an important aspect of being human, just as important as the Apollonian, and could it possibly play a role, perhaps even a crucial role, in our personal formation? These are the questions before us in this chapter. Nietzsche's critique of modernity and Christianity, through this mythological lens, is a helpful starting point.

Nietzsche's Modern Cult of Dionysus

To Nietzsche, the modern Western world, largely at the behest of centuries of Christian dominance, suffered from Apollonian hegemony. While we may ascribe some of Nietzsche's critique to his limited and particular experience of Lutheran Christianity, it would be a mistake to therefore dismiss his observations out of hand.[4] There is indeed truth to the fact that from its early history, Christianity has tended to align itself with the Apollonian rather than Dionysian. Perhaps "an inbred Christian sensing of the risk of releasing uncontrollable, even demonic, energies has generally preferred the values of Apollo to those of Dionysus."[5] Much of this tone was set early on, through the likes of the asceticism of the desert fathers, with their renunciation of the body and this-worldliness, and Augustine's suspicion of the senses and their ability to rouse fleshly passions.[6] For Nietzsche, this rejection of the Dionysian is a rejection of life itself, and Augustine therefore epitomizes all that is problematic about Christianity, Nietzsche naming him a "monster of morality,"[7] whose filth you could "smell" by reading him.[8] By contrast, Nietzsche himself has no desire to be a "saint," but rather a "disciple of the philosopher Dionysus."[9]

Duncan Forrester echoes the evaluation that the root of this early Christian Apollonian emphasis was a consequence of the need for control over "dangerous" feelings and emotions, particularly with regard to sexuality. He quotes from Gregory of Nyssa to illustrate the point, "Any action, thought or word which involves passion is out of harmony with

---

4. Williams, *The Shadow of the Antichrist*, 104.
5. De Gruchy, *Christianity, Art and Transformation*, 16.
6. De Gruchy, *Christianity, Art and Transformation*, 16.
7. Nietzsche, *The Gay Science*, 224.
8. Nietzsche, "The Anti-Christ," 63.
9. Nietzsche, "Ecce Homo," 71.

Christ and bears the mark of the devil, who makes muddy the pearl of the soul with passions and mars that precious jewel."[10] The irony is that for a religion built upon the bedrock of the doctrine of creation and with the incarnation at its core, celebration of the material, of the body and the senses is notable by its absence, or at least as a somewhat muted presence, in the history of Christianity. As the faith aligned itself with the Roman ideals of a harmonious, moral and orderly society (indeed, Nietzsche called Christianity "the last Roman construction"),[11] a trajectory was established that owes more to a classical heritage than it does the biblical text.[12]

Nietzsche offered a scathing critique of what he saw to be the Christian rejection of the Dionysian. To Nietzsche, Christian "slave morality" simply represents the rationalization of weakness by justifying and making noble the state of inescapable inferiority.[13] He saw this type of moralizing as a mere coping mechanism, which inhibits engagement with fullness of life. Nietzsche proposes that "art—and *not* morality—is the true *metaphysical* activity of man . . . the existence of the world is *justified* only as an aesthetic phenomenon."[14] By contrast, Christianity leaves no space for the aesthetic, condemning it as illusory in contradistinction to the absolutes of morality. To which Nietzsche responds,

> Behind this mode of thought and valuation, which must be hostile to art if it is at all genuine, I have never failed to sense a hostility to life—a furious, vengeful antipathy to life itself: for all of life is based on semblance, art, deception, points of view . . . Christianity was from the beginning, essentially and fundamentally, life's nausea and disgust with life, merely concealed behind, masked by, dressed up as, faith in "another" or "better" life. Hatred of "the world," condemnation of the passions, fear of beauty and sensuality, a beyond invented the better to slander this life, at bottom a craving for the nothing, for the end.[15]

Nietzsche concludes that for the Christian, "The body is an object of hatred, hygiene is rejected as sensuousness . . . [on the Christian closure

---

10. Forrester, *Truthful Action*, 11.
11. Nietzsche, *The Gay Science*, 221.
12. De Gruchy, *Christianity, Art and Transformation*, 16–17.
13. Nietzsche, *Beyond Good and Evil*, 151–58. He expands further in Nietzsche, "On the Genealogy of Morality."
14. Nietzsche, "The Birth of Tragedy" (trans. Speirs), 8 (italics original).
15. Nietzsche, *The Birth of Tragedy* (trans. Kaufmann), 22–24.

of public baths] . . . It is Christian to hate spirit . . . it is Christian to hate the senses, to hate enjoyment of the senses, to hate joy in general."[16] Thus his call to reject this insipid morality, to move "beyond good and evil," severing aesthetics from ethics, a vision impelled by the momentum of Romanticism and shared with the composer Richard Wagner and the philosopher Arthur Schopenhauer, among others.[17]

Nietzsche's insightful critique provoked reaction from Bonhoeffer and McGilchrist alike, whose responses we will turn to in a moment. But before we do so, it is important to take a moment to acknowledge that at the heart of Nietzsche's argument is a significant warning about the dangers of modern idolatry: making God in our own image.[18] While a safe, controlled faith that fits neatly within the bounds of an ordered life may seem appealing, the question needs to be asked as to whether such a faith is fundamentally able to allow for genuine otherness, and thus whether such a Christian faith is indeed biblical. Do the bounds of an exclusively rational faith not necessarily limit it to the finite? Is the aesthetic not a gateway, perhaps even the sole gateway, to the mystery that is an inevitable consequence of engaging the divine? Does the Christian rejection of the Dionysian usher in Apollonian idolatry—Jesus made in Apollo's image? These are some of the important questions that Nietzsche raises, and they have direct bearing on understanding the aesthetics of discipleship. We will return to them at the end of the chapter, but they lie in the background throughout. As we work toward resolving them, we would do well to note that the unhinging of the aesthetic from ethics is clearly not the solution, as Nietzsche's role in the rise of Nazism, and even South Africa's apartheid, makes evident. "Nietzsche's Romanticism remains a constant reminder of the inevitably horrendous and tragic political consequences of placing the mythologically inspired interests of 'blood and soil' over the constraints of reason and morality."[19]

---

16. Nietzsche, "The Anti-Christ," 18.

17. De Gruchy, *Christianity, Art and Transformation*, 15, 65–66. De Gruchy exposits the danger of such a Romantic aesthetic in de Gruchy, "The Search for Transcendence."

18. Benson, *Graven Ideologies*.

19. De Gruchy, *Christianity, Art and Transformation*, 66.

Bonhoeffer's Response to Nietzsche

While it should be apparent that our exploration of Bonhoeffer's work in the previous chapter is directly applicable here, a few brief comments are in order, which highlight his specific reaction to Nietzsche, providing a helpful platform for our engagement with McGilchrist's response.

In a sense, the whole corpus of Bonhoeffer's work is a reaction to Nietzsche's critique, since at the core of Bonhoeffer's theology is an incarnational Christology, "His response to Nietzsche, with whom he shared a 'lust for life', was to show how life in its fullness was to be found in Jesus Christ."[20] Bonhoeffer acknowledges that Lutheranism's rejection of the natural is cause for valid Nietzschean critique. But through the themes that pervade his work, Bonhoeffer clearly shows Christianity's this-worldliness, affirming the body and the earth, the "celebration of human freedom and life," even while allied to "his 'theology of the cross' in which joy is only discovered through struggle and suffering."[21] Bonhoeffer challenges Nietzsche's claim that Christianity rejects the Dionysian celebration of life by showing that aesthetic existence is fundamentally a part of living incarnationally in the penultimate as a Christian.

As we have seen, Bonhoeffer's direct reflections on aesthetic existence take place toward the end of his life, in his letters from prison. It is here too that he responds to the duality of Nietzsche's mythological lens,

> We go along too easily with Nietzsche's primitive alternatives, as if the "Apollonian" concept of beauty, and the "Dionysian," the one we call demonic nowadays, are the only ones. But that isn't the case at all. Take, for example, Brueghel or Velázquez, or even Hans Thoma, Leopold Kalckreuth, or the French Impressionists. They have a beauty that is neither classic nor demonic, but simply earthly in its own right; and I must say that this is the only sort of beauty that speaks to me personally.[22]

Bonhoeffer is making a significant point here, one that is central to a robust understanding of the aesthetics of discipleship. The "primitive alternatives" of Apollo and Dionysus represent two typical, contrasting approaches to the aesthetic. The Apolline represents the otherworldly pursuit of the Platonic ideal of beauty. This is marked by an emphasis on form, harmony, and unity, attributes that are, if not quantifiable, at the

---

20. De Gruchy, *Christianity, Art and Transformation*, 165.
21. De Gruchy, *Christianity, Art and Transformation*, 152.
22. Bonhoeffer, *Letters and Papers from Prison*, 331.

very least, rationally comprehensible and are worthy of the reasonable ideal. While the appeal of such an ordered aesthetic lies in escape from the pain and brokenness of life, ultimately such a perfect ideal can seem disconnected from tangible, earthly existence and consequently prove impotent, as Bonhoeffer himself personally expressed.

> Presumably we are made in such a way that perfection is boring to us; I do not know whether that was always the case. But I have no other way to explain the fact that Raphael remains as distant and indifferent to me as Dante's paradise. Likewise, neither eternal ice nor eternal blue sky appeals to me. I seek "perfection" in what is human, living, earthly, that is, neither in the Apollonian nor in the Dionysian or Faustian.[23]

In contrast to the Apolline, the Dionysiac represents earthy celebration of the sensory, that which is out of control, visceral, in the moment, which can be transcendental in its own right, but through ecstatic experience rather than ordered form. At worst, approaching aesthetics through the lens of this "primitive alternative" creates a binary wherein the one is pitted against the other, with a single approach preeminent. At best, it offers a duality to be navigated by holding these two approaches to life in healthy tension. Bonhoeffer is suggesting that we reject the polarity in favor of an incarnational approach to life, which is integrative in its own right. This exactly why he is able to call for a recovery of aesthetic existence from a prison cell, amid Hitler's atrocities. What he is presenting is not a Dionysian hedonism or an Apollonian escape from this world to an otherworldly, utopian ideal of beauty, but rather a celebration of this-worldly, christological reality; "a 'worldly Christianity' rooted in God's revelation in Christ yet able to celebrate the polyphony of life amidst the tragedies of our time."[24]

The challenge that lies before us is to articulate what this incarnational approach to everyday aesthetic existence entails. Everyday aesthetic existence is largely dismissed by an Apollonian approach as insignificant. Play, or reveling in an aesthetically pleasing moment, for example, only has value to the extent that it is rationally comprehensible as a pointer to an otherworldly, Platonic ideal. By contrast, a Dionysian approach makes the aesthetic experience absolute, resulting in an aestheticism, which, while appearing to validate everyday aesthetic

---

23. Bonhoeffer, *Letters and Papers from Prison*, 494–95.
24. De Gruchy, *Christianity, Art and Transformation*, 137.

existence, ironically devalues it by disconnecting it from ethics and personal formation. The question lying before us, which Bonhoeffer raises in response to Nietzsche, is whether an incarnational approach to aesthetic existence is fundamentally integrative, encapsulating both an Apollonian and Dionysian approach to life, while also superseding the polarity.

Bonhoeffer could only take us to a certain point in this exploration, both because his life and work were cut short, and also because of the milieu within which he thought and wrote. We have to remember that although Bonhoeffer had a profound intuitive appreciation for the aesthetic, his *explicit* approach was fundamentally scientific. With his father being a nationally renowned psychiatrist, both his familial and formal education embedded him in a scientific approach to engaging the world. Little wonder then that his brother Karl Friedrich became a leading chemist while Bonhoeffer himself would go on to grapple with Christ amid the modern progress of "a world come of age." In other words, even while acknowledging the revelatory role music played, alongside his criticism of an Apollonian approach to life, in many respects the modern, ratiocentric tools with which Bonhoeffer worked could only take him so far in his attempt to validate the role of aesthetic existence in the Christian life.

If Bonhoeffer's claim regarding the this-worldly nature of incarnational reality is accurate, thereby validating the senses and the body, then the human body itself should offer insight into the nature and workings of formation. In other words, in order to explore the relationship between aesthetic existence and formation, the connection between embodiment and the development of meaning is an important link to probe. Western society has long valued a largely Apollonian approach to the formation of moral citizens of the *polis*, built on the ancient Greek embrace of *paideia*. Over the centuries this approach has become increasingly ratiocentric, which led to Nietzsche challenging this artificial perception of reality and the subsequent insipid morality that ensues. Here, Iain McGilchrist's voice is helpful, as he offers a fundamentally embodied response to Nietzsche's critique. Through his work we can ask what the human body, and the brain in particular, tells us about the formation of meaning, and better understand the role the Dionysian plays.

The Human (Brain) as Both Apollonian and Dionysian

While Bonhoeffer suggests (founded in the incarnation) that the Christian life not only brings together a Dionysian and an Apollonian

AESTHETIC EXISTENCE AS FUNDAMENTAL IN BEING HUMAN

approach to life but supersedes them, McGilchrist argues (we could say, from a creational perspective) for a universal and foundational anthropological truth: The Dionysian and the Apollonian are both indispensable aspects of human being. Consequently, aesthetic existence is fundamental to being human in the world, to the creation of meaning and personal formation. If Bonhoeffer encourages us to reject the "primitive alternative" of Apollo and Dionysus in favor of an incarnational approach to reality, McGilchrist endeavors to show that this mythological dichotomy is actually a helpful tool for understanding human perception, even if ultimately the ideal is to overcome the dichotomy and cultivate integration. He suggests that these two modes of engaging the world are evident in the workings of our bodies, specifically, according with the lateralization of the human brain.

Valid research into the hemispheric differences of brain function is clouded by popular misconceptions that need to be rejected. It is neither helpful nor accurate to suggest that "the left hemisphere is . . . gritty, rational, realistic but dull, and the right hemisphere airy-fairy and impressionistic, but creative and exciting." Or even worse, "that the left hemisphere, hard-nosed and logical, is somehow male, and the right hemisphere, dreamy and sensitive, is somehow female."[25] Hemispheric difference is much more complex than these crude, stereotypical generalizations. However, there *are* indeed important distinctions between the hemispheres, and we should not lose sight of these valid differences amid the inaccurate oversimplifications.[26]

McGilchrist argues that the hemispheric differences are best understood through noting the distinctive attention each gives to the world.

> The right hemisphere underwrites breadth and flexibility of attention, where the left hemisphere brings to bear focussed attention. This has the related consequence that the right hemisphere sees things whole, and in their context, where the left hemisphere sees things abstracted from context, and broken into parts, from which it then reconstructs a "whole": something very different.[27]

Echoing Nietzsche's mythological dichotomy, these two distinct modes of existence create two ways of perceiving our environment, mutually contributing to an accurate perception of reality, subsequent creation

---

25. McGilchrist, *The Master and His Emissary*, 2.
26. Güntürkün et al., "Brain Lateralization."
27. McGilchrist, *The Master and His Emissary*, 27.

of meaning, and then action in the world.[28] As an entry point into McGilchrist's work, we could say that the left hemisphere offers a largely Apollonian perception of reality while the right presents a Dionysian. The very title of his book, *The Master and His Emissary*, is taken from a Nietzschean parable.[29] The essential idea is that the human mind functions best when the left hemisphere (the emissary, with its attention to detail) serves the right hemisphere (the master, which offers context and a sense of the whole). McGilchrist's central thesis, following Nietzsche, is that in recent history this has been inverted: the emissary has assumed the role of master, with dire consequences.

> We have now reached a point where . . . the balance has swung too far—perhaps irretrievably far—towards the Apollonian left hemisphere, which now appears to believe that it can do anything, make anything, on its own. Like the emissary in the fable, it has grown tired of its subservience to the Master, and as a result the survival of the domain they share is, in my view, in the balance.[30]

Contrary to the popular belief that "the right hemisphere may add a bit of colour to life [but] the left hemisphere . . . does the *serious* business," McGilchrist argues that the right hemisphere, and the Dionysian tendencies associated with it, is vital to an accurate perception of reality, and our subsequent formation as human beings.[31]

Excursus: Handling McGilchrist's Work Well

Before we can proceed, we need to pause to better understand the nature of McGilchrist's unique work, noting its strengths and weaknesses. McGilchrist is indeed a psychiatrist, known for his work on brain lateralization, but to draw on his work solely or even primarily as brain science is both to misunderstand his most valuable contribution and also to deflect from that core contribution to controversial scientific debate on lateralized brain function. Make no mistake: while directly engaging the relevant neuroscience will not be our focus, McGilchrist's research on brain lateralization is meticulous, and he is adamant that the

---

28. McGilchrist, *The Master and His Emissary*, 3.
29. McGilchrist, *The Master and His Emissary*, 14.
30. McGilchrist, *The Master and His Emissary*, 240.
31. McGilchrist, *The Master and His Emissary*, 92.

science underlying his work is robust.[32] However, McGilchrist's work is thoroughly interdisciplinary, and his most valuable contribution cannot be confined to the realm of neuroscience but is better understood as a philosophical and psychiatric commentary on the nature of human apprehension of the world.[33] The philosopher John Cottingham describes his work as "humane philosophizing," moving beyond the bounds of "the austerely technical, science-based methodology that dominates so much contemporary philosophy" to draw on "a wealth of material from literature, art, music and cultural history."[34] In this sense, McGilchrist's argument is best understood not as a neurological one but as "psycho-ethical or spiritual."[35] McGilchrist's concern is broader than brain science, which is why our reading of his work cannot be constrained to interpreting it solely through that narrow lens.

While on the one hand, McGilchrist's interdisciplinary approach is sorely needed, providing a cohesive and holistic perspective of the nature of human interaction with the world, on the other, in doing so he stretches the methodological bounds of the respective disciplines he draws from, neuroscience in particular. In one sense, McGilchrist's findings on lateralization are controversial, critics suggesting that his conclusions are generalized and reductionist, failing to account for the complexity of brain modularity.[36] However, in another sense, as Michael Spezio has

32. McGilchrist's position on brain lateralization is extensively researched, drawing from around 2 500 papers. Leading neuroscientists have endorsed his work, including "the Marco Polo of neuroscience," V. S. Ramachandran, Jaak Panksepp (who defined the field of affective neuroscience), Colwyn Trevarthen, James Wright (both Trevarthen and Wright worked alongside the famed brain lateralization expert and Nobel laureate, Roger Sperry), Michael Trimble, Alwyn Lishman, Jurg Kesselring and Todd Feinberg. See Rowson and McGilchrist, "Divided Brain, Divided World," 25–27; McGilchrist, "Split Brain, Split Views"; Ramachandran et al., "Comments: Some Responses To The Master And His Emissary."

33. For a robust critique and interdisciplinary evaluation of his contribution, see Wildman and Coakley, eds., "Engaging Iain McGilchrist."

34. Cottingham, "Brain Laterality and Religious Awareness," 363; Cottingham, "What Is Humane Philosophy?"

35. Cottingham, "Brain Laterality and Religious Awareness," 364.

36. See for instance Corballis, "The Evolution of Lateralized Brain Circuits"; Spezio, "McGilchrist and Hemisphere Lateralization." It is important to point out that McGilchrist himself repeatedly acknowledges the nuances and complexities regarding lateralization; brain modularity can become reductionist if it does not first acknowledge the variability and plasticity in brain function. It is clear that there are other brain modularities in operation (not merely right/left hemisphere modularity). In responding to Kosslyn and Miller's *Top Brain, Bottom Brain*, McGilchrist points out

pointed out, they are not controversial at all; this is because McGilchrist defies many of the categories and conventions dictated by the field.[37] In other words, he approaches brain lateralization with a set of questions, and methods to resolving those questions, that fall outside the bounds of empirical neuroscience.[38]

A core question for McGilchrist is *why* the brain is divided. He asks this question for the purpose of better understanding the nature of being human and our relationship to the world. Contrary to the recognized neuroscientific quest, McGilchrist is "not interested at all in 'localising' *functions* in the brain (something of which he is often accused), but in asking more speculatively, but again historically and evolutionarily, '*Why* is the brain divided? Is this *because* [the hemispheres] are engaged in different aspects of human experience?'"[39] Both the question and its purpose go beyond neuroscience. While exploring the merits of lateralized brain function hypotheses is within the gambit of neuroscience, as Cottingham puts it,

> the question of how we are to *interpret* these different modes of awareness, and what is disclosed by them, necessarily takes us outside science. There is nothing mysterious or "spooky" about this: we are biological creatures, and all that we do and think is mediated by the way in which our biological equipment, including our brains, is structured; but the *meaning* of what we do or think necessarily outstrips such mediation.[40]

For McGilchrist, any attempt to answer the question of why the brain is divided, and its impact on phenomenology, must necessarily operate from the paradigm of understanding the human as person, not the human

---

that "The existence of one doesn't in any way suggest the absence of the others: they are not independent, but interconnected in such a way that each is, in fact, implied in the others." Ellis and Solms argue that these modularities and networks are more complex and variable than previously allowed for, some being "hard-wired" while others are "soft-wired," as determined through environmental factors. The key point to note here (apart from the observation that neuroscience has hardly reached consensus on these matters, and that it remains a rapidly developing field) is to heed McGilchrist's encouragement not to be reductionist in our application of the hemispheric lateralization of brain function. See McGilchrist, "Exchange of Views"; Ellis and Solms, *Beyond Evolutionary Psychology*.

37. Spezio, "McGilchrist and Hemisphere Lateralization," 388.
38. Kundu and Smith, "The Relationship of Lateralization," 385.
39. Coakley, "Concluding Eirenic (and Mostly 'Unscientific') Postscript," 424.
40. Cottingham, "Brain Laterality and Religious Awareness," 366.

as machine.[41] His contention is that the very mechanistic lens through which neuroscience operates limits its contribution to the broader anthropological question. He rejects mechanistic "neurospeak"—"'circuitry,' 'modules,' 'functions' and 'mechanisms' of every conceivable (and many inconceivable) kinds"—for this reason, arguing that approaching the brain as a machine necessarily already locks findings and interpretation of findings into an unhelpful paradigm.[42]

> This goes back to the matter of which questions one asks. If I were engaged in localizing, say, a "reward circuit," it would be important for me to use the same categories and definitions as other researchers, in order to make my results comparable. But I am starting without preconceptions about any such thing as a "reward circuit," and instead asking "what is it like for human experience when this brain region is active or ceases to function?" That may show up in all sorts of human ways that we recognize in life, rather than in a list of functions drawn up by neuroscientists themselves. Let me be clear: my aim is *not* to find "centers for," e.g., certainty or optimism. My aim is the humanistic one of relating the brain to phenomenology, and understanding the overall difference between the hemispheres.[43]

McGilchrist's humanistic approach thus opens him up to the charge of anthropomorphizing his discussion of the hemispheres.[44] It is a charge to which he pleads guilty, but his approach is intentional.[45] Attempting to understand the distinction between the hemispheres of the brain mechanically is akin to explaining the "difference between Fox News and CNN by focussing on the mechanics of studio lighting, TV signal transmission, cathode ray tubes, plasma/LED screens, etc."[46] A single hemisphere of the brain is neither a machine nor a person on its own, but each hemisphere can sustain consciousness (appearing "to have not just different cognitive strategies, but different goals, values, opinions and emotional timbre, a fact which becomes apparent as soon as one hemisphere, for whatever reason, loses function"), which prompts McGilchrist

---

41. McGilchrist, "A Response to Commentators," 400–404.
42. McGilchrist, "A Response to Commentators," 403.
43. McGilchrist, "A Response to Commentators," 409.
44. Trimble, "Book Review."
45. McGilchrist, "Author Response to Trimble Book Review," 287.
46. McGilchrist, "Cerebral Lateralization and Religion," 320.

to argue that understanding hemispheric difference through the model of a person is more helpful to his task than the model of machine.[47]

The anthropomorphic charge assumes that such an approach projects partiality, and inversely, a mechanistic study is scientific and thus offers an objective account, but if McGilchrist's thesis is accurate, then the abstraction of science only offers a partial account of the nature of being human. In other words, approaching lateralization anthropomorphically may well upset the boundaries of science; however, it is not in the interest of rejecting it but of grounding it and humanizing it. The critical point here is that McGilchrist is not pitting himself against science. To the contrary, McGilchrist suggests that brain science has much to teach us about the two distinct yet complimentary modes of human existence, and he maintains that his findings are scientifically robust. But he is also unafraid to challenge convention. In this sense, Coakley is right in making a connection between Kierkegaard and McGilchrist, the latter being "unscientific" in the same sense of the former's "unscientific postscript," both challenging "science" not as a valid epistemological discipline, but as hegemonic, narrow paradigms and epistemological norms governing the modern age that bow before abstraction unfettered.[48] McGilchrist is thus best read as a provocateur and cultural prophet. He does indeed take science extremely seriously, and he would balk at any suggestion otherwise, but his core contribution lies in his insightful analysis of two age-old modes of human existence (not only reflected in classical Apollonian and Dionysian mythology, but echoing similar articulations in Goethe's *Faust*, Schopenhauer, Henri Bergson, and Max Scheler's *Die Formen des Wissens und die Bildung*) and the implications for life in the world should one dominate the other.[49]

McGilchrist's scientific findings are, therefore, used here fittingly rather than foundationally. The argument for these two modes of human apprehension does not ultimately rest on neuroscience, but the science nevertheless contributes to a holistic understanding of human apprehension. Science is not the basis for the argument, but appears to resonate with a broader perspective from humane philosophy, thereby further enhancing our understanding. It goes without saying that should the neuroscientific conclusions ultimately prove dissonant to the broader argument, this

---

47. McGilchrist, "Cerebral Lateralization and Religion," 320.
48. Coakley, "Concluding Eirenic (and Mostly 'Unscientific') Postscript," 423–24.
49. Coakley, "Concluding Eirenic (and Mostly 'Unscientific') Postscript," 430.

will have to be revisited. But the point is that the core of what McGilchrist contributes to our understanding of the aesthetics of discipleship does not rest on the minutiae of his account of brain lateralization (notably because McGilchrist is suggesting a correlative, not causative relation between lateralization and the respective modes of apprehension—he is not addressing the mind-body problem).[50] Neuroscience is a complex and dynamic field. McGilchrist acknowledges this, and although he makes a compelling case for the science supporting his thesis, whether or not our understanding of the brain ultimately affirms or challenges McGilchrist's depiction of brain lateralization, his fundamental argument for the two modes of existence remains important.[51] Therefore, neuroscience is but one gateway into this discussion. It is, however, a particularly intriguing and helpful one, as we seek to better understand the connection between sensate embodiment and human formation. McGilchrist makes a strong case that this gateway offers an avenue to better understanding these two modes of existence via a literal truth (the two ways of apprehending the world accord with the respective hemispheres of the brain), but even if this gateway eventually turns out to be metaphorical (the operation of the hemispheres as "only" a metaphor for these two modes of existence), it would still have value. As McGilchrist himself has put it, even if it is ultimately shown to be "just" a metaphor, it is a metaphor well worth engaging, as it is precisely through metaphor that we come to understand the world.[52]

Brain Lateralization and the Hemispheric Differences in Attention

As already noted, brain lateralization is complex, so the danger of a brief summary here is reductionism, reflecting an inaccurate representation of brain function. In order to mitigate this danger, right at the outset, it is important to point out that aesthetic existence is not only to

50. McGilchrist, *The Master and His Emissary*, xiv–xv.

51. Evidence of this can be seen from the broad range of fields (including scientific disciplines) that have endorsed McGilchrist's thesis, applying it to their own contexts, including medical general practice and psychotherapy. See Goldie, "The Implications of Brain Lateralisation"; Tweedy, *The Divided Therapist*; Evans, "Gestalt."

52. McGilchrist, *The Master and His Emissary*, 462. McGilchrist again reaffirms this in the preface to the second edition, McGilchrist, *Master and His Emissary* (new expanded ed.), xxi.

be associated with the right hemisphere; it is more nuanced than that. While many aspects of aesthetic existence are related predominantly to right hemispheric brain function, there are aspects also related to the left hemisphere. A healthy approach to aesthetic existence should necessarily involve both hemispheres. In fact, it appears that aesthetic existence becomes unhinged from ethics and faith precisely when it is dominated by the *left* hemisphere, as self-seeking titillation in a closed system of sensory stimulation. As we will see, this is the type of immature aesthetic existence that Kierkegaard sought to discard and is contrary to the aesthetic existence Bonhoeffer embraced.

McGilchrist describes a range of hemispheric distinctives, based on the respective roles that the two hemispheres play in our engagement with the world. These binary roles, even though they often seem contradictory, ideally function as complementary, held in tension with each other. While the right hemisphere's attention is *broad and flexible* (as in a bird scanning the environment, predominantly with their left eye, for a mate or a predator), the left is *focused and grasping* (as in a bird identifying and pecking at seed, predominantly using their right eye).[53] The left largely deals with what is *already known* while the right deals with the *new*. Significantly, "it follows that in almost every case what is new must first be present in the right hemisphere, before it can come into focus for the left."[54] Thus, the right is stronger in dealing with *possibility* (hence its connection with creativity, being more capable of a "frame shift"), while the left deals largely with *predictability*.[55] While the left is responsible for *division*, unpacking sensory data into meaningful information, the right brings *integration*, synthesizing experience with broader reality.[56] Consequently, the left deals primarily with the *abstract*, while the right connects this with *context*.[57] The left then, *organizes and categorizes*, while the right allows for *individuality*.[58] Hence, the right "sees individual entities . . . as belonging in a contextual whole . . . from which they are not divided. By contrast the left sees parts" as belonging to a category.[59] Little

---

53. McGilchrist, *The Master and His Emissary*, 37.
54. McGilchrist, *The Master and His Emissary*, 40.
55. McGilchrist, *The Master and His Emissary*, 40.
56. McGilchrist, *The Master and His Emissary*, 42.
57. McGilchrist, *The Master and His Emissary*, 49.
58. McGilchrist, *The Master and His Emissary*, 51.
59. McGilchrist, *The Master and His Emissary*, 54.

wonder then that the left can be described as *impersonal* versus the right as *personal*;[60] the strength of the left dealing with the *nonliving*, versus the *living* of the right.[61] Although the left is also involved in emotion, it is the right that deals with emotional recognition and expression, and consequently empathy.[62] It should already be apparent that aesthetic existence, as embodied and emotive engagement with reality, draws heavily on the nature of the often preconscious attention that the right hemisphere offers the world.

Before we look at the implications for everyday aesthetic existence, we need to further explore this right-hemisphere connection by taking a closer look at three specific hemispheric distinctives, with direct connection to aesthetic existence: the temporal hierarchy of attention; explicit certainty versus implicit fluidity, and embodiment versus abstraction.

The (Temporal) Hierarchy of Attention

A key theme in McGilchrist's argument, particularly relevant to the aesthetics of discipleship, is the temporal, and thus ontological hierarchy of attention between the two hemispheres of the brain. That which is new is first presented in the right hemisphere of the brain before being passed over to the left hemisphere for processing, following which it returns to the right again for contextual application: "the right → left → right progression."[63] This means that "conscious awareness lags behind unconscious apprehension by nearly half a second."[64] The implication of this is that the right hemisphere does not only have temporal primacy but also "ontological supremacy. Whatever the left hemisphere may add—and it adds enormously much—it needs to return what it sees to the world that is grounded by the right hemisphere."[65] In other words, the left hemisphere takes what is presented by the right, organizes and categorizes it, making sense of it, before re-presenting it to the right for integration with the world. This vital process enables the brain to cope with the changing, fluid nature of reality. McGilchrist articulately describes the ideal

60. McGilchrist, *The Master and His Emissary*, 54.
61. McGilchrist, *The Master and His Emissary*, 55.
62. McGilchrist, *The Master and His Emissary*, 66.
63. McGilchrist, *The Master and His Emissary*, 46.
64. McGilchrist, *The Master and His Emissary*, 164.
65. McGilchrist, *The Master and His Emissary*, 195.

interaction between the hemispheres, which has significant implications for the formative role of aesthetic existence,

> One can never step into the same river twice—Heraclitus's phrase is, I believe, a brilliant evocation of the core reality of the right hemisphere's world—one will always be taken unawares by experience, since nothing being ever repeated, nothing can ever be known. We have to find a way of fixing it as it flies, stepping back from the immediacy of experience, stepping outside the flow. Hence the brain has to attend to the world in two completely different ways, and in so doing to bring two different worlds into being. In the one, we experience—the live, complex, embodied, world of individual, always unique beings, forever in flux, a net of interdependencies, forming and reforming wholes, a world with which we are deeply connected. In the other we "experience" our experience in a special way: a "re-presented" version of it, containing now static, separable, bounded, but essentially fragmented entities, grouped into classes, on which predictions can be based. This kind of attention isolates, fixes and makes each thing explicit by bringing it under the spotlight of attention. In doing so it renders things inert, mechanical, lifeless. But it also enables us for the first time to know, and consequently to learn and to make things. This gives us power.[66]

To the extent that the ontological primacy of the right hemisphere is maintained, this power is subject to the context of a person's lived reality, their existence in the world. In other words, the right hemisphere offers the critical sense of "betweenness," or relationality, which both enables the power and control that the attention of the left hemisphere offers, but also limits it, as it is tested in the context of the Other. Initially, in the right hemisphere "we experience the world pre-reflectively, before we have had a chance to 'view' it at all, or divide it up into bits," thus offering a sense of "togetherness," which precedes even the left-hemisphere awareness of subject and object.[67] This provides a vital context for the abstract, analytical work of the left hemisphere.

> The right hemisphere needs the left hemisphere in order to be able to "unpack" experience. Without its distance and structure, certainly, there could be, for example, no art, only experience... But, just as importantly, if the process ends with the left hemisphere, one has only concepts—abstractions and conceptions,

66. McGilchrist, *The Master and His Emissary*, 30–31.
67. McGilchrist, *The Master and His Emissary*, 31.

not art at all. Similarly the immediate pre-conceptual sense of awe can evolve into religion only with the help of the left hemisphere: though, if the process stops there, all one has is theology, or sociology, or empty ritual: something else. It seems that, the work of division having been done by the left hemisphere, a new union must be sought, and for this to happen the process needs to be returned to the right hemisphere, so that it can live.[68]

The respective roles of the hemispheres point toward the vital connections between prereflective, embodied, sensory, lived experience (right hemisphere), which is then consciously processed and systematized (left hemisphere) before being applied to contextual reality (right hemisphere). It is too reductionist to suggest that this right → left → right progression equates to aesthetic existence → rational reflection (belief) → action in the world (ethics), for it is more complex and nuanced than such a neat formula allows.[69] Nevertheless, based on McGilchrist's work, it is difficult to deny the pivotal formative role of aesthetic existence in this process.[70]

If this progression is the ideal, then as Nietzsche's Apollonian critique of modernity points out, the modern orientation to the world is decidedly imbalanced, originating not in right-hemisphere concretion, but left-hemisphere abstraction.

> What if the left hemisphere were able to externalise and make concrete its own workings—so that the realm of actually existing things apart from the mind consisted to a large extent of its own projections? Then the ontological primacy of right-hemisphere experience would be outflanked, since it would be delivering—not 'the Other', but what was already the world as processed by the left hemisphere. It would make it hard, and perhaps in time impossible, for the right hemisphere to escape from the hall of mirrors, to reach out to something that truly was 'Other' than,

---

68. McGilchrist, *The Master and His Emissary*, 199.

69. Here, we can recall Kierkegaard's distinction between a first and second immediacy, his articulation of a first immediacy lacking left-hemispheric processing.

70. We will at times refer back to this right → left → right hemispheric progression. The point here is not strictly the hemispheric progression itself, but the principle that underlies it. Other neuroscientists have argued for the same point, without referring to hemispheric progression. Panksepp, for instance, has shown that affect is primal, while Ellis and Solms draw from the latest research to argue that the cognitive is "soft-wired," built upon the sensory which is "hard-wired" in neurological development. See Panksepp, *Affective Neuroscience*; Ellis and Solms, *Beyond Evolutionary Psychology*.

beyond, the human mind. In essence this was the achievement of the Industrial Revolution.[71]

The evidence of this externalization of the left hemisphere's artificial categories is evident in our "rectilinear urban environments"; our mechanistic, grasping engagement with the natural world (and consequent "despoliation, exploitation and pollution"); the isolation of individuals and the increasing virtualization of all of life, including leisure, often enjoyed by an immersion into "a largely insubstantial replica of life," through a plethora of visual and social media, the formation of online worlds in various guises, such as gaming.[72] This serves as a reminder, once again, that all aesthetic existence is not equal—the pivotal point being that such an overreliance on left hemisphere attention to the world (and consequent creation of pseudoworlds) is dangerous because it becomes entirely self-referential.

It has long been acknowledged in the field of theological aesthetics that this is exactly why engagement with the aesthetic is vital to comprehension of reality: the aesthetic draws one beyond oneself (outside the left hemisphere's self-referential system of signs) into wonder, mystery, awe and the acknowledgement of the divine Other. While McGilchrist's research confirms such an argument as neuropsychologically valid, it goes beyond this, pointing to significant implications for *everyday* aesthetic existence. It is not only aesthetic experiences marked by wonder and awe that offer a sense of contextual reality. *All* everyday sensory existence is presented initially to the right hemisphere, offering a paradigmatic sense of the whole. In other words, while it is accurate to say that the role of the right hemisphere is to draw one outside oneself into relationship with the Other, this is a fundamentally incarnational process. It is not merely a divine Other that one occasionally encounters through wondrous aesthetic experience, but the this-worldly Other of neighbor and nature, Creator and created world encountered through everyday aesthetic existence.[73] This echoes Bonhoeffer's incarnational rejection of the binary between the real and ideal, which in turn is a response to Nietzsche's critique of Christianity's rejection of this-worldly life. The this-worldly

---

71. McGilchrist, *The Master and His Emissary*, 386.

72. McGilchrist, *The Master and His Emissary*, 387.

73. Here it is worth considering the work of neuroanatomist Raymond Tallis, who exposits the embodied nature of transcendence, our use of a forefinger for pointing being one such example, illustrating "everyday transcendence." See Tallis, *Michelangelo's Finger*.

transcendence that everyday aesthetic existence can potentially provide plays an important role in contextualizing existence in relation to the Other, thereby countering the development of a pseudoworld centered on the self.

Explicit Certainty versus Implicit Fluidity

Ultimately, the question this raises is the role of everyday aesthetic existence in the process of how we come to know reality. As we have seen, both hemispheres have a role to play in this epistemological process, which is compromised if undue reliance is placed on one of the modes of attention. While the right hemisphere engages directly with the fluidity and changing nature of everyday life, sensitive to all that is implicit in this experience, the left seeks to make this explicit through abstract conceptualization, which can be linguistically expressed as certainty. While the system of signs that is language (the domain of the left hemisphere) is crucial for expressing meaning, not all meaning is reducible to explicit language. The right hemisphere, responding to implicit meaning, governs many of our unconscious responses. It deals with nonverbal communication, for example, responding unconsciously to facial expressions and body language, at the level of milliseconds.[74] While the right hemisphere reads the whole, which is implicit, the left builds toward meaning by piecing together explicit parts.

> Using the familiar information-processing terminology, the left hemisphere favours analytic, sequential "processing" [incrementally constructing "certainty"], where the right hemisphere favours parallel "processing" of different streams of "information" simultaneously . . . there is an "aha!" moment when the whole suddenly breaks free and comes to life before us. For it, though, knowledge comes through a relationship, a betweenness, a back and forth reverberative process between itself and the Other, and is therefore never finished, never certain.[75]

As helpful as the right-hemisphere process may be for perceiving a holistic sense of reality (including the divine, and all that is bound to remain implicit), the challenge is that this way of knowing the world can never

---

74. McGilchrist, *The Master and His Emissary*, 71.
75. McGilchrist, *The Master and His Emissary*, 228.

be transferred to another via explicit language, hence the reticence of the modern, left-hemisphere-dominated world to acknowledge it.

To make matters worse, the left hemisphere will claim certainty, even if the information available from the right is inconclusive or absent altogether. Startling research illustrates the point. In split-brain patients (where the two hemispheres are not connected as they should be, via the corpus callosum), experimenters present an image to the right hemisphere—a snow scene, for instance. The right hemisphere cannot articulate what it has seen (language being the domain of the left hemisphere), but when asked to select an image from a range of cards, with the left hand the right hemisphere selects a snow shovel (while the left hemisphere, with the right hand, selects a random image, bearing no relation). Next, the experimenters flash a different image concurrently to each of the hemispheres; each hemisphere thus only has knowledge of its own image. Again, the right hemisphere is presented with the image of a snow scene while the left hemisphere is presented with the image of a chicken claw. When asked to select cards, the right hemisphere and left hand again selects the shovel, while the left hemisphere and right hand selects a chicken. Remarkably, when the subject is asked to explain the choices, even though the left hemisphere cannot possibly know the reason for the selection of the shovel, it logically explains that a shovel is needed to clean out a chicken shed. In other words, as the experimenters put it, the left hemisphere "without batting an eye" offers an explanation, with certainty, as to the cause of the reaction "as a statement of fact," even though it clearly could not know the (implicit) reasoning involved by the right hemisphere.[76] While the left hemisphere's ability to extract explicit meaning is crucial to human understanding and communication, it is merely an intermediate step; it should neither be the starting point nor the end point in healthy engagement with reality, and subsequent formation of knowledge.

As previously noted, both hemispheres have a role to play in aesthetic existence, but unquestionably, engaging the world through everyday aesthetic existence is, at the very least, significantly prereflective, intuitively engaging the implicit. Aesthetic existence then, with its Dionysian tendencies, plays a role in formation since it offers a way of knowing the world that the Apollonian does not have access to. Further,

---

76. McGilchrist, *The Master and His Emissary*, 81.

if an attempt is made to reduce its implicit knowledge of the world to the explicit certainty of the left hemisphere, much of its value is lost.

> Many important aspects of experience, those that the right hemisphere is particularly well equipped to deal with—our passions, our sense of humour, all metaphoric and symbolic understanding (and with it the metaphoric and symbolic nature of art), all religious sense, all imaginative and intuitive processes—are denatured by becoming the object of focussed attention, which renders them explicit, therefore mechanical, lifeless.[77]

Ideally, "the implicit grounds the explicit," which has the interesting implication that feelings are not the consequence of cognitive assessment, rather affect comes first and thinking follows, as research shows.[78] The question then, is how the formative value of right-hemisphere attention influences conscious knowledge. In essence, the answer to this is found in the connections between embodied, aesthetic engagement with reality, the formation of living metaphors and the subsequent paradigmatic shaping of the imagination, a process we will explore shortly. In order to do so, we need to look briefly at the connection between embodiment and the right hemisphere.

Embodiment versus Disembodied Abstraction

Aesthetic existence is fundamentally sensory and embodied. For the abstract processing of the left hemisphere, this is marginal to knowing reality; sensory experience is processed as data for systematic categorization, explicit certainty being the goal. That which does not contribute to this goal is discarded. By contrast, for the right hemisphere, the body is inextricably bound up in a sense of self and our existence in the world; our body is "something we 'live.'"[79] Of course, it is true that each hemisphere is connected to the contralateral half of the body when it comes to motor and sensory function, but it is only the right hemisphere that has a sense of the whole body in relation to self. The left hemisphere knows only of the existence of the right side of the body. If the right hemisphere does not function, the left side of the body ceases to exist to the individual

---

77. McGilchrist, *The Master and His Emissary*, 209.
78. McGilchrist, *The Master and His Emissary*, 184.
79. McGilchrist, *The Master and His Emissary*, 67.

involved.[80] While the right hemisphere perceives the body to be that through which we live, a part of our identity, the left is detached from the body, seeing it as a thing among other things, "devitalised, a corpse."[81] "If the right hemisphere is not functioning properly, the left hemisphere may actually deny having anything to do with a body part that does not seem to be working according to the left hemisphere's instructions. Patients will report that the hand 'doesn't belong to me' or even that it belongs to the person in the next bed, or speak of it as if made of plastic."[82] Further, since the right hemisphere is attuned to the body, it makes sense that it also "is far more closely linked to the physiological changes that occur in the body when we experience emotion," thereby contributing to the superiority of the right regarding affect.[83]

Again, if the hemispheres work harmoniously, complementing one another, these respective strengths allow for: bodily engagement with lived reality (as temporally and ontologically primal) as well as subsequent disinterested contemplation, which ideally then converges in wise action in the world. However, if the left hemisphere rejects the ontological primacy of the right, thereby rejecting embodiment as foundational to knowing reality, meaning is locked within hermetic abstraction, the body simply being a means through which this meaning is imposed on the world. Nevertheless, it is difficult to argue with the fact that we are fundamentally connected to reality through our body, which the mediated awareness of the left hemisphere is utterly reliant on for engagement with the world (whether the left hemisphere acknowledges this or not cannot change this necessary connection). Existence is rooted in the body and senses. Consequently, this is the nexus of a primal awareness of the world, which both temporally and ontologically precedes conscious engagement, contributing to a way of knowing reality that cannot be reduced to the explicit certainty of the left hemisphere. McGilchrist draws from Heidegger to articulate this point:

> We do not inhabit the body like some alien Cartesian piece of machine wizardry, but live it . . . In trying to convey the "otherness" of a particular building, its sheer existence or *essent* prior to any one act of cognition by which it is partially apprehended,

---

80. McGilchrist, *The Master and His Emissary*, 66.
81. McGilchrist, *The Master and His Emissary*, 67.
82. McGilchrist, *The Master and His Emissary*, 67.
83. McGilchrist, *The Master and His Emissary*, 69.

> Heidegger speaks of the primal fact of its existence being made present to us in the very smell of it, more immediately communicated in this way than by any description or inspection. The senses are crucial to the "presence" of being, "to our apprehension of an *is* in things that no analytic dissection or verbal account can isolate."[84]

As fundamental as this embodied sense of being is, and despite its temporal and ontological primacy, the fact that it remains largely implicit means that it can be undervalued since it is a somewhat "transparent" contribution. "It is the most essential characteristic of the body that it disappears as an independent thing the more it fulfils its service . . . In this the body performs like a work of art. Just as Merleau-Ponty says that we do not see works of art, but see according to them, so that although they are vital for what we see, it is equally vital that they become transparent in the process, we live in the world according to the body, which needs its transparency, too, if it is to allow us to be fully alive."[85] If the left hemisphere predominates, treating the body merely as an assemblage of parts, the body loses this transparency, becoming explicit, and thus functioning merely as a tool for utilitarian purposes. In the realm of sexuality, for example, pornography is a manifestation of this left-hemisphere explicitness.[86] This once again highlights the fact that aesthetic existence can become hijacked by the left hemisphere, which is arguably no less formative, although it merely reinforces, through embodiment, the closed system of signs that the left hemisphere has labeled reality.

In summary then, the right hemisphere offers a primal account of reality, grounded in embodied, affective and implicit knowledge of the world. It should be apparent from this brief survey that aesthetic existence plays a role in this paradigmatic attention that the right hemisphere gives to the world. It should also be clear that both hemispheres, both modes of attending to the world offer indispensable contributions to an accurate understanding of reality, highlighting the danger of acknowledging only the Apollonian in the epistemological process. In other words, while these complementary ways of attending to the world both offer vital components of the epistemological process, when either one dominates, the net result is a distorted apprehension of reality, if not a completely artificial

---

84. McGilchrist, *The Master and His Emissary*, 153.
85. McGilchrist, *The Master and His Emissary*, 439.
86. McGilchrist, *The Master and His Emissary*, 439.

one. McGilchrist's concern is ultimately to show that a left-hemisphere, self-referential, hyper-self-conscious manner of attending to the world marks modernity. However, there are "points of weakness" to break out of this "hall of mirrors," which has become a culturally engrained mode of being in the world. These "points of weakness" are

> the body, the soul and art (which relies on body and soul coming together) . . . The "lived" body, the spiritual sense, and the experience of emotional resonance and aesthetic appreciation are all principally right-hemisphere-mediated. What is more *they each have an immediacy which bypasses the rational* and the explicitness of language, and therefore leads directly to territory potentially outside of the left hemisphere's sphere of control.[87]

This nexus of body, soul, and the aesthetic is precisely the realm of aesthetic existence. In order to elucidate the formative role of everyday aesthetic existence, we need to take a closer look at the epistemological implications of this right-hemispheric manner of attending to the world.

The Formative Nature of Aesthetic Existence

To recap, Nietzsche's critique of modernity—targeting the artificial construction of Apollonian reality and the rejection of a Dionysian embrace of life itself—is important for us to attend to, as it highlights that a fundamental aspect of being human is lost with the dismissal and denigration of aesthetic existence. To Nietzsche, Christianity is at the heart of this distortion, which he sees as spurning, or at the very least undermining, the value of aesthetic existence. While this is, unfortunately, an accurate assessment of certain expressions of "Christianity," this should not be the case. As Bonhoeffer shows, Christianity is fundamentally incarnational—thus his call for an embrace of aesthetic existence as a penultimate expression of faith, amid the goodness of this-worldly life. In the process, Bonhoeffer points out an essential connection between formation (*Bildung*) and aesthetic existence. Thus our turn to McGilchrist, who in sharing Nietzsche's critique of modernity, reveals that the Dionysian tendencies of right-hemisphere attention are vital to human formation and perception of the world. Within the process of apprehending reality, there are unconscious, implicit, affective, and embodied elements, all of which are aspects of aesthetic existence. Therefore, as both Bonhoeffer and McGilchrist foreground in response to Nietzsche's critique of Apollonian

---

87. McGilchrist, *The Master and His Emissary*, 438 (italics added).

modernity, reality is fundamentally embodied, and thus of the senses. Bonhoeffer helps us to see that rejection of this is rejection of christological life itself, while McGilchrist shows us that devaluing the Dionysian tendencies of the right hemisphere creates a circular, self-referential, and artificial knowledge of the world. The way out of this hall of mirrors is to recover the value of body and soul and their engagement with the aesthetic, in which everyday aesthetic existence plays a significant part. Doing so will demand an appreciation of the formative role of metaphor and the imagination. Everyday aesthetic existence is bound up with the implicit and unconscious formation of meaning-making metaphors and the shaping of the paradigmatic imagination. Before we take a closer look at the significance of metaphor and the imagination for the aesthetics of discipleship, a few introductory comments regarding the apprehension of reality are in order.

Knowing Reality through Everyday Aesthetic Existence

Even though the epistemological process is undeniably conscious, rational, and explicit, as we have seen, it would be erroneous to assert that it is *exclusively* so. Brain lateralization and the nature of right-hemisphere attention clearly shows that unconscious, implicit, affective, and embodied engagement with the world also plays a role. In fact, it is a pivotal role, a grounding one, that provides the context within which the abstract rationality of the left hemisphere can flourish. If knowing reality were merely a question of systematic arrangement of abstract concepts, the organization of information, then aesthetic existence would be irrelevant. It would merely be a bit of fun on the side, the insular and frivolous excitement of the senses, entertainment that has no bearing on knowledge of the world and self. However, if reality is fundamentally relational, as Bonhoeffer asserts, it follows that our embodied experience of being in the world, of engaging the other, is the basis for meaning.

McGilchrist suggests that the abstract, conceptual knowing of facts is a left-hemisphere endeavor, while the right hemisphere knows through experience as a living being in relationship. The former is fixed and certain while the latter is individual and relies on personal engagement with the Other. The former can be commodified and transferred via propositional language, the latter can only be known through experience.[88] Although English is an exception, in many languages these two ways of knowing

---

88. McGilchrist, *The Master and His Emissary*, 95.

"are referred to by different words: the first by, for example, Latin *cognoscere*, French *connaître*, German *kennen*; the second by Latin *sapere*, French *savoir*, German *wissen*."[89] The way we attend to the world leans far too heavily toward the information-harvesting, disembodied *kennen* of the left hemisphere, encroaching even on the way we engage living beings as utilitarian commodities. Rather than *kennen* encroaching on the realm of *wissen*, *kennen* should be grounded in the context of *wissen*. Or, in the words of philosopher Martha Nussbaum, we should embrace a fundamentally relational approach to knowing—"love's knowledge." Nussbaum asserts that at its core, knowledge

> might be a complex form of life . . . Knowledge cannot be gained through intellectual *grasping*—through the greedy, controlling, manipulative employment of intellectual force . . . Knowledge cannot be *merely* intellectual. Intelligence cannot "know" apart from feeling and commitment and ways of being that are consistent with what is known.[90]

To illustrate the problem of apprehension dominated solely by *kennen*, McGilchrist considers the extreme, in which knowledge of reality is gained exclusively via a left-hemisphere mode of attention, and notes that the symptoms are identical to schizophrenia "in all its major predilections—divorce from the body, detachment from human feeling, the separation of thought from action in the world, concern with clarity and fixity, the triumph of representation over what is present to sensory experience, in its reduction of time to a succession of atomistic moments, and in its tendency to reduce the living to the devitalised and mechanical."[91] It is thus important to emphasize that these two ways of attending to the world do *not* merely represent an inconsequential choice of two modes of knowing, as though either will do, the choice simply being a matter of personal preference.

To be clear, there are two senses in which aesthetic existence is significant for our perception of the world. First, since the right hemisphere's sensory and affective engagement with the world is largely unconscious and implicit, it is possible, and highly likely, that we are unaware of the

89. McGilchrist, *The Master and His Emissary*, 96.

90. Nussbaum here is summarized in Dykstra, *Growing in the Life of Faith*, 142 (italics original).

91. Schizophrenia itself, "as John Cutting has shown, appears to be a state in which the sufferer relies excessively on (an abnormally functioning) left hemisphere" (McGilchrist, *The Master and His Emissary*, 335).

extent to which aesthetic existence shapes our apprehension of reality, regardless of whether we consciously embrace an Apollonian or Dionysian approach to life. In this sense, aesthetic existence is formative for all, whether it is acknowledged as such or not. But second, conscious affirmation of the aesthetic creates an avenue to break out of the self-referential system of signs by acknowledging the value of that which cannot be reduced to the explicit, thereby embracing the Other in apprehension of reality. To expand on both of these points we need to look more closely at the meaning-shaping nature of metaphor and the imagination.

Meaning-Making Metaphor

Metaphor is closely related to reason, which only seems paradoxical because we have inherited an Enlightenment view of reason as rationality.[92] While explicit, abstract, linear, and sequential argument is the realm of rationality, McGilchrist suggests that valid, deductive problem solving incorporates a broader range of mental processing, which involves both hemispheres.[93] Clearly, by aligning metaphor with reason, he is not referring here merely to the use of metaphor as a flowery figure of speech. The Enlightenment perspective of metaphor holds that, at best, it is a helpful linguistic tool to convey emotion; at worst, it is an unnecessary ornament, easily discarded should one choose to express the same concept literally. Either way, "metaphor can have nothing directly to do with truth."[94] But the power and necessity of metaphor is that it is a connection to embodied reality, a means of connecting abstract conceptualization with the material world. There is thus a sense in which *all* language is metaphorical.

> Every word, in and of itself, eventually has to lead us out of the web of language, to the lived world, ultimately to something that can only be pointed to, something that relates to our embodied existence. Even words such as 'virtual' or 'immaterial' take us back in their Latin derivation—sometimes by a very circuitous path—to the earthy realities of a man's strength (*vir-tus*), or the feel of a piece of wood (*materia*). Everything has to be expressed

---

92. McGilchrist, *The Master and His Emissary*, 332.
93. McGilchrist, *The Master and His Emissary*, 65.
94. McGilchrist, *The Master and His Emissary*, 332.

in terms of something else, and those something elses eventually have to come back to the body.⁹⁵

In other words, the metaphorical nature of language is evidence of the "betweenness," or relationality, which pervades a right-hemisphere apprehension of the world. However, the vast majority of the metaphors that we use as part of daily language are dead metaphors, their connection to embodied existence in the world lost amid the abstraction of language. But this does not deny the primacy of embodiment in the very formation of these metaphors, and thus language itself. In fact, McGilchrist suggests that poetic use of language (hearkening back to the origin of language in music) is an attempt to recover the living, right-hemisphere connection with reality that abstract language has lost. Here we can turn once again with McGilchrist to music to substantiate his point and illustrate that aesthetic existence is primal in engaging reality.

Spotlight on Music:
Metaphor and the Musical Origins of Language

Kierkegaard helped us to frame music as archetypal sensory immediacy. We then saw, through Bonhoeffer's life and work, that music, as a form of aesthetic existence, is not merely ornamental to life, but formative. His musical metaphors were not simply helpful illustrations but theological concepts formed though his musical experience. McGilchrist argues that this is because music is a primal means of capturing the affective relationality that pervades human life. Music is not peripheral to the serious business of life but can implicitly capture reality in a fuller sense than words can ever do.

> This must be what Mendelssohn meant by his otherwise paradoxical pronouncement that "the thoughts that are expressed to me by music I love are not too indefinite to be put into words, but on the contrary too definite." Language returns us inevitably to the worn currency of re-presentation, in which the unique qualities of everything that exists are reduced to the same set of terms. As Nietzsche put it: "Compared with music all communication by words is shameless; words dilute and brutalise; words depersonalise; words make the uncommon common."⁹⁶

---

95. McGilchrist, *The Master and His Emissary*, 116.
96. McGilchrist, *The Master and His Emissary*, 74.

Further toward capturing the fullness of reality, McGilchrist suggests, contrary to Kierkegaard, that musical sensory immediacy is not the aesthetic moment temporally isolated from other moments but rather a moment saturated with eternity. It is a moment that paradoxically,

> partakes of eternity . . . it does not so much use the physical to transcend physicality, or use particularity to transcend the particular, as bring out the spirituality latent in what we conceive as physical existence, and uncover the universality that is, as Goethe spent a lifetime trying to express, always latent in the particular. It is also a feature of music in every known culture that it is used to communicate with the supernatural, with whatever is by definition above, beyond, "Other than," our selves.[97]

When considering this participatory, affective, and intuitive engagement with reality that music offers, it is hardly surprising that the right hemisphere is crucial for musical engagement. While both hemispheres of the brain are involved in musical performance, in amateur musicians it is associated predominantly with right-hemisphere brain activity. Unsurprisingly, but interestingly, this is not the case with professional musicians wherein the "play" of music demands disciplined abstraction. However, professional musicians playing Bach's polyphonic music produce strong right-hemisphere activity, perhaps pointing to the heightened somatic and affective awareness of the Other in contrapuntal music.[98] Amusia, the condition of being unable to understand, perform, or appreciate music, is associated with damage to the right hemisphere of the brain.[99] Music then, rather than being peripheral to life, is a manifestation of right-hemisphere relationality, an affective and implicit engagement with the "betweenness" of reality.

In fact, McGilchrist's contention is that language itself has its genesis in music.[100] Here he follows the lead not only of contemporary theories

---

97. McGilchrist, *The Master and His Emissary*, 77.
98. McGilchrist, *The Master and His Emissary*, 75.
99. McGilchrist, *The Master and His Emissary*, 74.

100. McGilchrist is less concerned here with the precise nature or chronology of language development, as he is to show that language had a musical and perhaps also gestural origin. Thus, whether language developed from music, or if both developed independently from what has been called "musilanguage" matters little. Likewise, if gesture played a significant role in this development it would only further affirm the embodied nature of language, music being "deeply gestural in nature: dance and the body are everywhere implied in it" (McGilchrist, *The Master and His Emissary*, 102, 119).

of language, such as put forward by Steven Mithen, but points out that the theory has been explored in the last three centuries by Rousseau, von Humboldt, and Jespersen respectively.[101] Archaeological evidence appears to indicate that early humans made music before language existed, since the anterior condylar canal at the base of the skull, as well as the thoracic vertebral canal are essentially the same size in modern humans as in the earliest human skeletons discovered. These canal sizes point to articulatory and respiratory nerve control associated with speech long before humans used language. "The explanation of this sophisticated control and modulation of the production of sound, in the absence of language as we know it, has to be that it was for a sort of non-verbal language, one in which there was intonation and phrasing, but no actual words: and what is that, if not music?"[102] Further, as Salomon Henschen points out, "The musical faculty is phylogenetically older than language; some animals have a musical faculty—birds in a high degree. It is also ontogenetically older, for the child begins to sing earlier than to speak."[103] As human infants learn language, "Intonation, phrasing and rhythm develop first; syntax and vocabulary come only later."[104] Hence the parenting phenomenon of "'baby talk'—which emphasizes what is called prosody, the music of speech."[105]

> Perhaps the most striking evidence, though, is that there are extant tribes in the Amazon basin, such as the Pirahã, a hunter-gatherer tribe in Brazil, whose language is effectively a kind of song, possessing such a complex array of tones, stresses, and syllable lengths that its speakers can dispense with their vowels and consonants altogether and sing, hum or whistle conversations.[106]

The Pirahã are indeed striking, not only because of the musical nature of their language, but also because their language contains no numbers or colors.[107] Daniel Everett is a linguist who has spent much of his life studying the tribe, who are "committed to an existence in which only

---

101. Mithen, *The Singing Neanderthals*; McGilchrist, *The Master and His Emissary*, 104.
102. McGilchrist, *The Master and His Emissary*, 102.
103. McGilchrist, *The Master and His Emissary*, 103.
104. McGilchrist, *The Master and His Emissary*, 103.
105. McGilchrist, *The Master and His Emissary*, 103.
106. McGilchrist, *The Master and His Emissary*, 106.
107. Everett, *Don't Sleep, There Are Snakes*, 115–21.

observable experience is real," so that "the Pirahã do not think, or speak, in abstractions."[108] Intriguingly, in resonance with what appears to be a life dominated by sensory immediacy, he names this the "immediacy of experience principle."[109] The cognitive anthropologist Brent Berlin suggests that Everett's work points to the fact that the "Pirahã may provide a snapshot of language at an earlier stage of syntactic development."[110] Or, to put it in McGilchrist's terms, are the Pirahã an example of a reliance, or even overreliance on right-hemisphere attention, just as modernity subscribes to an overreliance on left-hemisphere attention? This would certainly explain the inextricable unity of language and music for the Pirahã.

These musical origins of language point to the ability of music to facilitate aesthetic attunement to the relational nature of reality. We will discuss the importance of attunement and fittingness more fully in the next two chapters. In anticipation of that discussion, here we can simply note that aesthetic attunement is related to a universal sense of mild synesthesia. This is true of *fitting* music, and traces of it can still be found in language, "in what has become known as the 'kiki/bouba' effect ('kiki' suggesting a spiky-shaped object, where 'bouba' suggests a softly rounded object)."[111] Such word-sounds are residue in language that point toward the deeper and fuller synesthetic nature of all experience; an intuitive, unconscious and embodied sensitivity to relationality that operates prior to cognitive abstraction.

While the left-hemisphere construction of abstract language can become disconnected from embodied life, the somatic and affective nature of music opens the possibility of engaging the fullness of lived reality.[112] Our affinity for music, then, is not merely a craving for insignificant disposable entertainment, or for a tickling of the senses with "auditory cheesecake," (to borrow Stephen Pinker's phrase).[113] Rather, it is deeply embedded in what it means to be human. "Neurological research strongly supports the assumption that 'our love of music reflects the ancestral

108. Colapinto, "The Interpreter."
109. Everett, "What Does Pirahã Grammar," 561.
110. Colapinto, "The Interpreter."
111. McGilchrist, *The Master and His Emissary*, 119.
112. This is not to say that *all* music, by default, attunes one to reality, for this is not the case. Right-hemisphere affective and embodied engagement with the world, if dominated by left-hemisphere grasping, merely becomes self-serving sensationalism.
113. Pinker, *How the Mind Works*, 534.

ability of our mammalian brain to transmit and receive basic emotional sounds,' the prosody and rhythmic motion that emerge intuitively from entrainment of the body in emotional expression: 'music was built upon the prosodic mechanisms of the right hemisphere that allow us affective emotional communications through vocal intonations.'"[114]

The perspective that music is central to being human may seem novel and somewhat foreign, yet this is only so due to the removal of music from communal life in the Western world.[115] Thus, even though music "has a vital way of binding people together, helping them to be aware of shared humanity, shared feelings and experiences, and actively drawing them together," the specialization, compartmentalization, and competition characterizing modern life, as dominated by left-hemisphere engagement with the world, has shifted communal expression of music to the periphery of everyday life.[116] As the neurologist Oliver Sacks notes, today we have a "special class of composers and performers, and the rest of us are often reduced to passive listening. One has to go to a concert or a church or a music festival to recapture the collective excitement and bonding of music. In such a situation, there seems to be an actual binding of nervous systems."[117] Little wonder, then, that many testify, as does Stacy Horn's *Imperfect Harmony*, to the therapeutic marvels of communal singing.[118]

The key point here is that this primal relating happens at a neurological level; it is a sensory engagement with reality prior to critical evaluation. In other words, it is implicit. "The origins of language in music and the body could be seen as part of a bigger picture, part of a primacy of the implicit. Metaphor (subserved by the right hemisphere) comes before denotation (subserved by the left). This is both a historical and an epistemological truth. Metaphorical meaning is in every sense prior to abstraction and explicitness."[119] For language to remain vital, for it to remain connected to lived reality in the sense that music is, its metaphorical nature needs to be nurtured and embraced. Failure to do

---

114. McGilchrist, *The Master and His Emissary*, 103 (quoting Panksepp and Bernatsky, "Emotional Sounds," 136).

115. McGilchrist, *The Master and His Emissary*, 104.

116. McGilchrist, *The Master and His Emissary*, 104.

117. As quoted in McGilchrist, *The Master and His Emissary*, 104.

118. Horn, *Imperfect Harmony*.

119. McGilchrist, *The Master and His Emissary*, 179.

so inevitably results in the virtuality of explicit, symbolic abstraction wherein the depth of implicit meaning is lost.

Metaphor as Rooted in Embodiment

However, this metaphorical nature of language further points to a deeper, elemental truth of human existence. As George Lakoff and Mark Johnson have shown, not only is all language essentially metaphorical, but metaphor, rooted in bodily experience, is the basis for all meaning.[120] The representation of reality within the mind is essentially metaphorical. Research in the field of embodied cognition points to the fact that bodily engagement with the world forms unconscious categories of cognition that guide our conscious thought processes, providing "metaphors we live by."[121] Through our bodily experience of reality from a very early age (even prior to using language), we develop schemata which order our understanding, the paradigms of *in* versus *out*, or *up* versus *down*, for example. "These patterns emerge as meaningful structures for us chiefly at the level of our bodily movements through space, our manipulation of objects, and our perceptual interactions."[122] These schemata are unconsciously formed. Everyday aesthetic existence, therefore, can contribute to the formation of schemata, or metaphors by which we live, since "the very basis of abstract thought, both in its concepts and in the manipulation of those concepts, lies in metaphors drawn from the body."[123]

If this connection between aesthetic engagement → creation of metaphor → shaping of perception holds true, there are significant implications for discipleship, for the relationships between everyday aesthetic existence, faith, and ethics. This connection exists whether one embraces an Apollonian or a Dionysian approach to life. But the former, dominated by the left hemisphere, imposes predefined (concrete, certain, fixed, already-known) categories on aesthetic engagement, thereby simply entrenching the abstract, dead metaphors of conception that allow for the

---

120. Lakoff and Johnson, *Metaphors We Live By*; Lakoff and Johnson, *Philosophy in the Flesh*; Johnson, *The Body in the Mind*.
121. On embodied cognition, see for instance Shapiro, ed., *The Routledge Handbook of Embodied Cognition*; Gallagher, *How the Body Shapes the Mind*.
122. Johnson, *The Body in the Mind*, 29.
123. McGilchrist, *The Master and His Emissary*, 334.

protection of a closed, circular system of artificial reality.[124] This process is dominated by a sense of self-consciousness, and concomitant individualism, utilitarianism and pursuit of self-preservation. By contrast, attending to the material world through a right-hemisphere openness to living metaphor breaks out of self-referential abstraction, engaging the Other, and subsequently nurtures an empathic engagement with the world, which is foundational to ethics and faith.

The church, however, does not by default automatically embrace such right-hemisphere openness to living metaphor. Nietzsche, as we have seen, argued the opposite: the church retreating to the safe certainty of the Apollonian even at the cost of rejecting life itself. Despite the benefits of the Reformation, McGilchrist suggests that aspects of it reflect the dangers of a left-hemisphere-dominated approach to the world, which rejects living metaphor. While the movement is broad, with diverse and complex manifestations, he nevertheless argues that there is a general inclination to the territory of the left hemisphere, including

> the preference for what is clear and certain over what is ambiguous or undecided; the preference for what is single, fixed, static and systematised, over what is multiple, fluid, moving and contingent; the emphasis on the word over the image, on literal meaning in language over metaphorical meaning, and the tendency for language to refer to other written texts or explicit meanings, rather than, through the cracks in language, if one can put it that way, to something Other beyond; the tendency towards abstraction, coupled with a downgrading of the realm of the physical; a concern with re-presentation rather than with presentation . . . In essence the cardinal tenet of Christianity—the Word is made Flesh—becomes reversed, and the Flesh is made Word.[125]

According to McGilchrist's account, the Reformation replaced metaphor and the aesthetic with theory and conceptual abstraction. However, McGilchrist acknowledges that there was indeed an important problem that the Reformation needed to confront, "The problem, as Luther realized, lay not in the statues, the icons, and the rituals themselves, but in the way they were understood. They had lost their transparency as

---

124. C. S. Lewis describes such metaphors as "fossilized," referring to language that has lost its connection with concrete reality and is thus mere abstraction. See Lewis, "Bluspels and Flalansferes."

125. McGilchrist, *The Master and His Emissary*, 323.

metaphors, which are always incarnate and therefore must be left to act on us intuitively—neither just material or just immaterial, but bridges between the two realms."[126]

The support for this bridge between the realms of the material and immaterial is the human faculty of imagination, which enables a living metaphor to have meaning. Again, however, since the ambiguity of the imagination is antithetical to the fixed, certain, and safe world of abstract conceptualization, its epistemological role is not acknowledged by a left-hemisphere approach to reality. "As Schleiermacher put it, the Reformation and the Enlightenment have this in common, that 'everything mysterious and marvellous is proscribed. Imagination is not to be filled with (what are now thought of as) airy images.'"[127]

The Paradigmatic Imagination

Despite the crisis of a world dominated by left-hemisphere attention, the left hemisphere is, of course, vital to functioning well in the world. It is merely focused, left-hemisphere attention, unhinged from the grounding and context of holistic, right-hemisphere perspective, that becomes problematic. The ideal is harmony between the Apollonian and Dionysian, and it is the faculty of the imagination that operates as a bridge between the two ways of attending to the world, enabling "us to take things back from the world of the left hemisphere and make them live again in the right."[128] While the dominance of left-hemisphere attention turns living metaphors into abstract concepts, thereby disconnecting them from embodied reality, the imagination not only returns abstract conceptualization to lived reality but also thereby offers a Gestaltian sense of integration between the explicit and implicit. This is what we will be referring to here, with Garret Green, as the paradigmatic nature of the imagination.[129] Since the imagination cultivates a broad, receptive perspective on reality, guided by the right hemisphere, open to the fluidity and ambiguity of life, it creates space not only for engagement of the Other but for the concomitant integration of the transcendent with embodied, lived reality. In other words, the imagination allows for a paradigmatic perspective of reality

---

126. McGilchrist, *The Master and His Emissary*, 444.
127. McGilchrist, *The Master and His Emissary*, 315.
128. McGilchrist, *The Master and His Emissary*, 199.
129. Green, *Imagining God*, 61–74.

that offers a means of perceiving the whole, not merely the parts. Thus, the parts are not perceived in isolation, but transformed as they are seen according to the whole. Hence, we could simply describe the imagination in terms of "seeing as."[130]

Echoing McGilchrist, James Smith describes the imagination as, "A quasi-faculty whereby we construe the world on a precognitive level, on a register that is fundamentally *aesthetic* precisely because it is so closely tied to the *body*. As embodied creatures, our orientation to the world begins from, and lives off of, the fuel of our bodies, including the 'images' of the world that are absorbed by our bodies."[131] These "images" are not therefore merely ocular; the "imagery" that feeds the imagination emanates from a full-bodied experience of reality. The imagination is thus a powerful epistemological faculty that has the potential to alter perception of reality. Yet, because it is shaped by embodied, affective, and implicit reality, it does not fit the narrow, abstract fact-finding of left-hemisphere processing—hence its rejection by Enlightenment epistemology. But this rejection has two implications. First, the imagination is critical for perception of the divine (extending to all transcendence and everything that remains implicit), which, by definition, cannot be comprehended within the confines of explicit, finite rationality.[132] Second, due to its paradigmatic nature, the imagination plays a role in the formation of *all* meaning (as competing political narratives constructed via social media illustrate all too well—presented with the same scenario, fueled by the imagination, two polarized constituencies will read the world differently, envisaging contrasting realities). In other words, the formative significance of the imagination applies not only to embracing wonder and mystery, but also to our perception and engagement of material, this-worldly reality; the imagination allows for apprehension of right-hemisphere openness while also providing a foundation for left-hemisphere concrete thought and action.

The nature of everyday aesthetic existence is diverse and varied, the broad categories of play, friendship, and art, for example, being easily subdivided into many further subcategories. It would hardly therefore

---

130. Bryant, *Faith and the Play of Imagination*, 89.

131. Smith, *Imagining the Kingdom*, 17.

132. For more on this, see the works already mentioned: Bryant, *Faith and the Play of Imagination*; Green, *Imagining God*; Avis, *God and the Creative Imagination*; Smith, *Imagining the Kingdom*; and Ward, *Unimaginable*, whose work we will engage in the next chapter; see also Brueggemann, *The Prophetic Imagination*.

be helpful, or accurate, to assert that everyday aesthetic existence, as a whole, opens one to the infinite, or provides an imaginative paradigm for engaging reality. In fact, this is not the case in every instance, as we will momentarily discuss. However, it should be clear that everyday aesthetic existence, to the extent that it is embodied and affective and engages the implicit, has the potential both to open one to the Other, as well as to shape the paradigmatic imagination, with implications for this-worldly thought and action.

Formation is a fundamentally imaginative process. If discipleship is the call to imitate Christ, there is an important connection here to the embodied shaping of the imagination as McGilchrist explains,

> We already know from the discovery of the existence of mirror neurons that when we imitate something that we can see, it is as if we are experiencing it. But it goes further than this. Mental representation, in the absence of direct visual or other stimulus—in other words, imagining—brings into play some of the same neurones that are involved in direct perception. It is clear from this that, even when we so much as imagine doing something, never mind actually imitate it, it is, at some level which is far from negligible, as if we are actually doing it ourselves. Imagining something, watching someone else do something, and doing it ourselves share important neural foundations. Imagination, then, is not a neutral projection of images on a screen. We need to be careful of our imagination, since what we imagine is in a sense what we are and who we become.[133]

The implication here is that "discipleship" is a universal human experience. The question is merely what, or who, is doing the "discipling," and to what end? The nature of our attention changes what we find and determines who we become.[134] As the imagination is engaged through friendship, art, and play, for instance, paradigms are created and neural pathways formed that offer a context for understanding reality. The imagination, "seeing as," provides the context for belief, acting "as if" (a point we will explore more fully in the next chapter).[135]

---

133. McGilchrist, *The Master and His Emissary*, 250.
134. McGilchrist, *The Master and His Emissary*, 28.
135. McGilchrist, *The Master and His Emissary*, 170.

Left-Hemisphere "Dionysian" Sensationalism

While everyday aesthetic existence has the potential to draw on right-hemisphere processing, engaging the implicit, shaping the imagination, and opening one to the Other, there is also an expression of aesthetic existence which we could term postmodern aestheticism. If bodily engagement with the world becomes disconnected from a contextual perspective of the whole of reality, which the right hemisphere provides, the body becomes simply a tool to be used for the satisfaction of the left-hemisphere's artificial system of signs. Sensation does not cease to exist, but it is interpreted through this hyper-self-conscious, insular rubric. Rather than jettisoning the senses, the postmodern rejection of Apollonian ideals leaves only the senses to be explored for some feeling of being alive. "The left hemisphere senses that something is wrong, something lacking—nothing less than life, in fact. It tries to make its productions live again by appealing to what it sees as the attributes of a living thing: novelty, excitement, stimulation."[136] In an ironic reconfiguration of aestheticism, it is the senses that absolutely matter, but never with the hope of offering meaning. Disconnected from the whole, all that remains is stimulation and sensation. While the Dionysian is celebrated, it is never towards an end outside the self; rather it is always subservient to the abstract and artificial rules of the game determined by the left hemisphere. "The left hemisphere 'creates' newness by recombining in a novel fashion what is already known, not as imagination does, [but] by allowing something that we thought we knew to be truly revealed for the first time. It is like those children's books with pages split into three, in which you can invent a new animal by putting together the head of a camel, the body of a seal and the legs of a goat."[137] Just like the aesthete's "art for art's" sake, while seemingly a noble elevation of the aesthetic, it is ultimately a devaluation, since it disconnects the aesthetic from life, so the "betweenness" is lost here amid self-reflexive fulfillment.[138]

In other words, "devitalisation leads to boredom, and boredom, in turn, to sensationalism."[139] The end result is a "high stimulus society" that is "represented through advertising as full of vibrancy and vitality," and the concomitant rise of consumerism—all toward the end of "fresh

---

136. McGilchrist, *The Master and His Emissary*, 199.
137. McGilchrist, *The Master and His Emissary*, 408.
138. McGilchrist, *The Master and His Emissary*, 409.
139. McGilchrist, *The Master and His Emissary*, 400.

experience and novel excitement."¹⁴⁰ The consequence is sensation disconnected from right-hemisphere context and the subsequent severance from reality, as "the left hemisphere interposes a simulacrum between reality and our consciousness," leading to the "increasing virtuality" of life.¹⁴¹

It follows then that everyday aesthetic existence, while potentially a life-giving, meaning-shaping embrace of embodied, implicit reality, can become co-opted by left hemisphere processing, thereby simply providing novel excitement within the safe confines of what is already "known." In the realm of friendship, for example, the rise of social media provides the opportunity for a virtual, disembodied re-presentation, which is ultimately not relational, but merely a means of stimulation, safely controlled as a consumerist utility by the click of a button.¹⁴² The rise of gamification in the realm of education provides another example. Gamification provides parameters (rules, objectives, rewards), which are concrete and explicit, celebrating success with novel excitement. The creation of this virtual world, limited to the rational, precludes the formative influence of the implicit. Art, in both the extreme of being highly conceptual, as well as the other extreme of excessively sentimental, can become mere stimulation of the left hemisphere without fundamental connection to lived reality.¹⁴³ In fact, sentimentality is merely a different expression of the same issue we explored regarding pornography. Both stimulate the left hemisphere, offering a placebo of the real, while ultimately disconnected from life, as the writer Flannery O'Connor articulates well: "Pornography . . . is essentially sentimental, for it leaves out the connection of sex with its hard purpose, and so far disconnects it from its meaning in life as to make it simply an experience for its own sake."¹⁴⁴ Significantly, O'Connor suggests that both are an attempt to short-circuit a sense of redemption, a return to innocence, but cannot do so, since they are neither ultimately embedded in embodied, christological reality, nor therefore redemptive in any sense.

Such a left-hemisphere approach to aesthetic existence (perhaps we could call it Apollonian aesthetic existence) is ultimately self-referential.

---

140. McGilchrist, *The Master and His Emissary*, 400.

141. McGilchrist, *The Master and His Emissary*, 402, 407.

142. This is not to say that *all* interaction with social media is marked by such virtual existence, but simply that it provides the opportunity for it.

143. McGilchrist, *The Master and His Emissary*, 410.

144. O'Connor, "The Church and the Fiction Writer," 148.

While it never breaks out of its self-contained system, it offers a virtual experience of the Other. Or, as Nietzsche warned us, we create reality, our perception of the world, including "god," in our own image. Philosophically and theologically, to sustain this system, a left-hemisphere binary is created (the categorizing strength of left-hemisphere attention) between the real and ideal, consequently devaluing the material as merely a manifestation of the abstract, a symbol. As McGilchrist notes, quoting Nietzsche's insightful comment, "'The symbolic replaces that which exists': surely the perfect expression of the triumph of theory and abstraction over experience and incarnation, of re-presentation over 'presencing.'"[145] The problem with binaries such as real-ideal and subject-object are that they are a construction of left-hemisphere attention but are ontologically nonexistent, and thus absent in preconscious, aesthetic engagement with reality.[146] While we cannot deny that they aid our processing and communication about the world, they also challenge what is at the core of right-hemisphere perception of the world: relationality.

In this context, it is best to understand the dichotomy of Apollonian versus Dionysian as exactly that: a mythological binary helpful for our processing and articulation regarding the nature of our engagement with reality, just as we have done with McGilchrist's work in this chapter. Having done so, we need to acknowledge that fundamentally reality (and our engagement thereof) is not found within the dichotomy of Apollo and Dionysis, as Nietzsche suggested, but in the ontological unity of these in Christ, as Bonhoeffer showed. This is important because there are not two ways of attending to Reality. There are two types of attending, but only one provides access to Reality, the other to an artificial system of signs.

Everyday aesthetic existence can therefore either feed modern hyper-self-consciousness or offer a life-giving escape from this hall of mirrors. One the one hand, it can serve to fortify a virtual world created by unhinged, left-hemisphere-dominated attention, thereby entrenching an insular and atomized pseudoreality. On the other, it can contribute to the role right-hemisphere-dominated attention plays in formation, through vital, embodied, implicit engagement with the world, thereby opening one up to relationship with the Other—transcendence in both the otherworldly and this-worldly sense. But it *will* contribute to formation in one

---

145. McGilchrist, *The Master and His Emissary*, 418.
146. McGilchrist, *The Master and His Emissary*, 31, 136–37.

of these two ways, that is quite simply the nature of being human: we live by metaphors that are embodied, which shape our imagination, whether we acknowledge this or not.

As our reading of both Kierkegaard and Bonhoeffer has suggested, that there are two contrasting manifestations of aesthetic existence should come as no surprise since there is a clear distinction between a mature and immature embrace of aesthetic existence. The key question, which we posed at the end of the last chapter, is how we distinguish between the two. At the time, we suggested that Bonhoeffer distinguishes mature aesthetic existence, a polyphonous celebration of christological reality, as being guided by love. McGilchrist concurs, "What ultimately unites the three realms of escape from the left hemisphere's world . . . the body, the spirit and art . . . is that they are all vehicles of love . . . for love is the attractive power of the Other, which the right hemisphere experiences, but which the left hemisphere does not understand and sees as an impediment to its authority."[147]

Everyday aesthetic existence, oriented toward the Other, ordered by love, not only restores, refreshes, and shapes the soul, but does so precisely because experience of the Other opens new vistas, new ways of seeing, of imagining. However, to leave it there, without fully understanding the inextricable relationship with belief and action, is to once again allow a rift to develop between the aesthetic and the ethico-religious. Even to acknowledge a linear and causal relationship between aesthetic existence and consequent belief and action in the world is insufficient. Rather, aesthetic existence, ordered by love, cultivates not only new ways of seeing, but new ways of *being*, a unity of aesthetic-ethical-religious existence. It is to this unity in a life of discipleship that we need now turn.

147. McGilchrist, *The Master and His Emissary*, 445.

5

Aesthetic Existence as Fundamental in Faith Formation

WE ARE ALL BELIEVERS. The fallacy that belief plays a significant existential role solely in those who identify as religious stems from misunderstanding the nature of belief. Just as aesthetic experience plays a formative role in all human existence, so too belief commitments are fundamental to being human, orienting all human choices and behavior. The key point, however, is that belief is not solely the product of rational deliberation, but a relational commitment shaped and formed by the whole gamut of human existence, particularly and notably, that which lies prior to cognition, including aesthetic existence.

As we have seen, influenced by modern ratiocentrism, aesthetic existence is often perceived to be a stage of life that one needs to leave behind as one embraces the serious business of a life of discipleship. However, we dismiss the role of the aesthetic in the Christian life at our peril. Not only is such a stance theologically flawed, as Bonhoeffer's incarnational Christology makes apparent, but it fails to take into account the very nature of being human. Not only is it a sheer impossibility to leave the aesthetic behind in human existence, not only does it contribute to all human perception and formation, for good or ill, but it plays a pivotally catalytic role in the ecosystem of being human, imaginatively and symbiotically feeding on and feeding into belief and action in the world. In other words, any analytical dissection of faith and ethics without due cognizance of the inextricable role that aesthetic experience plays in these domains does not accord with the reality of human existence.

Rather, a life of discipleship, motivated by love of Creator and creation, will necessarily include mature aesthetic existence within a broader mode of relational existence. Faith formation is best understood within such a holistic relational paradigm, requiring an understanding of belief as more than merely a set of rational propositions, but a relational commitment nurtured by mature aesthetic experience and impelled toward practical action.

In the last chapter, McGilchrist helpfully contributed to our understanding of the aesthetics of discipleship. His work highlights that everyday aesthetic existence is fundamental to being human since it plays a preconscious, formative role in the apprehension of reality, doing so through the embodied and affective shaping of the paradigmatic imagination, which determines how we *see as*. McGilchrist proposes that on the basis of such a visceral vision, we consequently "act as if"—we believe. However, in this chapter, we will see that the connection between belief and aesthetic existence is even more fundamental than McGilchrist suggests, and ultimately that aesthetics, belief and ethics cannot be separated. Beliefs operate as relational dispositions, which inform our actions, dispositions that are shaped and formed by our embodied and affective engagement with the world.

Understanding Belief in Relation to Aesthetic Existence

In order to understand the relationship between aesthetic existence and belief we need to take a closer look at the nature of belief, and the distinction between faith and belief. We will begin by considering belief in general (as opposed to *religious* belief), before turning to the implications for a life of faith. McGilchrist's anthropology of belief offers a helpful starting point.

McGilchrist suggests that the nature of belief is misunderstood due to the dominance of left-hemisphere attention that characterizes life in the modern world. The left hemisphere deals with abstraction and categorization, certainty and fixity being the goal, which is to be achieved through ratiocination. This is considered the highest form of knowledge. Consequently, belief is seen to be merely a "feeble form of knowing."[1] According to this way of thinking, if one does not know something with certainty, but one suspects it might be the case, one is said to "believe"

---

1. McGilchrist, *The Master and His Emissary*, 170.

something. For instance, one may say, "'I believe that the train leaves at 6.13', where 'I believe that' simply means that 'I think (but am not certain) that.'" Belief here is merely "absence of certainty."[2]

However, as we have seen, while the left hemisphere indeed has an important role to play in the formation, and particularly communication of knowledge, if it is not submitted to the contextual hierarchy of the right hemisphere → left hemisphere → right hemisphere progression, the result is simulated knowledge disconnected from embodied, material reality. It may well be certain and fixed, but it is a knowledge of *virtual* reality. Embodied and affective engagements with the world, the dominant modes of aesthetic existence, are grounded in the right hemisphere. In other words, while aesthetic existence may have no clear role to play in an epistemological process dominated by abstract ratiocination, the end result of such knowledge is a simulated, and ironically therefore, somewhat feeble form of knowing.

In light of the significance of the right hemisphere → left hemisphere → right hemisphere hierarchy, which necessarily points to the formative and epistemological value of aesthetic existence, we need to reconsider the nature of belief. Right-hemisphere attention has immense and vital (in the full sense of the word) importance. Left-hemisphere certainty disconnected from right-hemisphere context is not the pinnacle of knowledge. Rationality is, therefore, not more dominant than embodied and affective experience in the epistemological process. Consequently, belief is not a weaker form of knowing. Rather, the intuitive, implicit, preconscious, embodied and affective knowing of right hemisphere attention plays an important, perhaps even dominant role in our apprehension of the world and personal formation.

> Belief is a matter of care: it describes a *relationship*, where there is a calling and an answering, the root concept of "responsibility." Thus if I say that "I believe in you," it does not mean that I think that such-and-such things are the case about you, but can't be certain that I am right. It means that I stand is a certain sort of relation of care towards you, that entails me in certain kinds of ways of behaving (acting and being) towards you, and entails on you the responsibility of certain ways of acting and being as well.[3]

---

2. McGilchrist, *The Master and His Emissary*, 170.
3. McGilchrist, *The Master and His Emissary*, 170 (italics original).

Two important points emanate from McGilchrist's stance on belief. First, the description of belief as a relationship has implications for the formative nature of aesthetic existence. If aesthetic existence, through embodied and affective relationship to the world, has the ability to open oneself up to the Other, aesthetic existence is at the heart of the formation of belief, through the creation and sustenance of relationship. It is a gateway to partaking in an ontological reality: the relational nature of the world, or the "betweenness" to which the right hemisphere is receptive. The relationship between the believed and the believer is more complex (even unconscious to a degree), organic, and dynamic than reduction to rational proposition would allow.

Second, the very nature of this relationship entails response-ability; belief is a relation of care. In other words, it is a relation that affects behavior and cannot but do so. This perspective of belief inextricably binds it to ethics. Action then, an ethical response, is not merely an optional consequence of measured ratiocination based on conscious processing of abstract concepts, but the partly preconscious, organic, and necessary relational response to an existential reality.

Notably, belief, as a relation of care, foregrounds desire, just as the left-hemisphere perspective of belief, as a weak form of knowledge, foregrounds the will. If left-hemisphere attention is marked by volitional control, the right is marked by a relational "desire or *longing* towards something, something that lies beyond itself, towards the Other."[4] Once again, this has significant implications for the aesthetics of discipleship. Aesthetic existence is a realm of affective experience, both appealing to and shaping desire, which holds true whether one considers friendship, art, or play, for example. In other words, McGilchrist is arguing that belief is intimately connected with desire. Desire, not the will, functions as the fundamental impetus behind belief. This raises a number of questions: Do we choose our beliefs? To what extent do everyday aesthetic experiences influence our desires, and thus our beliefs? And, if belief is inextricably tied to ethics, what are the implications for the connection between desire and ethical life?

McGilchrist's argument for the integration of aesthetic existence, faith, and ethics rests on his connection between the formation of the imagination (as the faculty that allows us to "see *as*") and the consequent choice to believe (act "as if"). As we have seen, McGilchrist suggests

---

4. McGilchrist, *The Master and His Emissary*, 171 (italics original).

that the imagination is the faculty that bridges left-hemisphere and right-hemisphere attention. Right-hemisphere attention, encompassing preconscious sensory engagement with the world, creates unconscious paradigmatic metaphors, shaping the imagination, which allows us to see the world "*as*" through left hemisphere processing. Drawing from Martin Heidegger, and in reference to Ludwig Wittgenstein's duck-rabbit illustration (which can be *seen as* a duck or a rabbit), McGilchrist affirms that "we see things by seeing them *as* something. In this sense . . . we create the world by attending to it in a particular way."[5] In sum, the imagination (the way we see *as*) is shaped by our embodied and affective relationship with the world, thereby grounding our apprehension of reality.

Based on this embodied and affective relationship with reality, belief is a relational choice, a matter of where one places one's *trust*, despite the impossibility of certainty. The choosing "involves an act of faith, and it involves being faithful to one's intuitions."[6] As one perceives reality through the right hemisphere → left hemisphere → right hemisphere progression, a reality grounded in embodiment and the imagination, one acts on the basis of this reality. One acts *as if*. Belief, therefore, is not optional. Everyone *sees as*, and consequently *acts as if*. Belief is not merely a

---

5. McGilchrist, *The Master and His Emissary*, 151.
6. McGilchrist, *The Master and His Emissary*, 151.

cognitive endorsement of uncertain information, but a holistic relational attitude, a commitment of trust, "a disposition towards the world."[7]

The important question is how the move is made from *seeing as* to *acting as if*. If this is a cognitive choice, are we not simply back where we started with left-hemisphere volition controlling belief? To clarify McGilchrist's position, we can turn to his treatment of belief during the Reformation, particularly in relation to Martin Luther.

The view of belief as a weak form of knowledge is the consequence of a disembodied and abstract epistemology that operates solely in the realm of left-hemisphere rationality. Such an epistemology deals exclusively with signifiers that have lost their connection to reality. Its focus is abstract *re-presentation* rather than embodied *presentation*. As we have seen, *both* right-hemisphere presentation, as well as left-hemisphere re-presentation, are important for healthy perception of the world, through the right hemisphere → left hemisphere → right hemisphere progression. Embodied right-hemisphere presentation shapes the imagination, creating paradigms that function as metaphors, re-presentations for left-hemisphere cognitive processing. This process offers a healthy perception of the world only to the extent that both right-hemisphere presentation and metaphoric, left-hemisphere re-presentation remain in dynamic and vital symbiosis. The Reformation was a reaction to the breakdown of this epistemological homeostasis. The Middle Ages saw "the decline of metaphoric understanding of ceremony and ritual into the inauthentic repetition of empty procedures."[8] One of two responses would have to be pursued: Either the epistemological value of the sensory and affective could be acknowledged, "revitalising metaphoric understanding," or these empty rituals could be discarded, prompting a retreat into left-hemisphere abstraction.[9] Drawing from Joseph Koerner, McGilchrist suggests that while Luther pursued the former, the Reformation as a whole ultimately ushered in the latter.[10]

Luther's concern was not with the use of "images themselves (which he actually endorsed and encouraged) but precisely the *functionalist* abuse of images, images which he thought should be reverenced."[11]

---

7. McGilchrist, *The Master and His Emissary*, 170.
8. McGilchrist, *The Master and His Emissary*, 314.
9. McGilchrist, *The Master and His Emissary*, 314.
10. Koerner, *The Reformation of the Image*.
11. McGilchrist, *The Master and His Emissary*, 314 (italics original).

> Luther perceived that the inner and outer realms, however one expresses it—the realm of the mind/soul and that of the body, the realm of the invisible and the visible—needed to be *as one*, otherwise the outward show had nothing to say about the inward condition. In other words, the visible should be a "presentation," in the literal sense that something "becomes present" to us in all its actuality, as delivered by the right hemisphere. This perception, which is simply part of, and entirely continuous with, the Renaissance insistence on the seamlessness of the incarnate world, inspired Luther to decry the emptiness that results when the outer and inner worlds are divorced. But his followers took it to mean that the outer world was in itself empty, and that therefore the only authenticity lay in the inner world alone. The result of this is that the outer world becomes seen as merely a "show," a "re-presentation" of something elsewhere and nowhere—not an image, since an image is a living fusion of the inner and outer, but a mere signifier, as delivered by the left hemisphere. The transition that is made in this important derailment of Luther's intention is not from belief in outer forms to belief in inner forms, but from a view of outer and inner as essentially fused aspects of one and the same thing to belief that they are separate ("either/or").[12]

The important point that we need to take away from McGilchrist's description here is his affirmation of the integration of inner and outer, body and mind/soul, visible and invisible with regard to belief. The homeostatic relationship between embodied and affective presentation on the one hand, and cognitive re-presentation on the other is an organic whole in which no "either/or" exists. Two points emerge from this with direct relevance to our task at hand.

First, belief as the cognitive choice to *act as if*, operating in the inner realm, is indivisible from embodied and affective formation through the outer. It is the division of this unity into an "either/or," which leads to a functionalist neutering of the true power of metaphor. The icon now needs to be either divine or simply a thing. Rather than being a living metaphor, which partakes in the divine, it can be seen only as a thing, a nondivine representation; a representation that is dispensable since it can be reduced to abstract proposition.[13] "Sacrament becomes

---

12. McGilchrist, *The Master and His Emissary*, 315.
13. McGilchrist, *The Master and His Emissary*, 316.

information-transfer... Its material elements convey not substances, but meanings."[14] As a result of this inward move, following the Reformation "pictures become 'art', moved out of their living context in worship, to an artificial context where they can become allowable and safe."[15] We will return to the implications of this relegation of the aesthetic to disinterested contemplation in the next chapter, but here it is worth noting the association of this move with the "rejection of the body, and of embodied existence in an incarnate world, in favour of an invisible, realm of the mind," resulting in the rise of governing abstraction as "general rules."[16] Belief, as the consequence of inner/outer unity, devolves into a state of inner cognition, a weak form of knowing.

Second, as we have already seen, if the vitality of the outer is lost (here in the functionalist use of ritual and images), it merely reinforces the simulated abstraction of left-hemisphere attention. In other words, a virtual reality is created whereby contrived engagement with the physical world reinforces this simulated perspective of reality. The consequent commitment to *act as if* this reality were true is precisely the devitalized belief that the Reformers were reacting against. Thus, while the connection between aesthetic existence and belief is clear, it comes with a caveat: *If* aesthetic engagement with the world is subservient to and thereby reinforcing a closed, left-hemisphere simulation of the reality, then aesthetic existence in this instance is nurturing the virtualization of belief.

Belief as an Embodied, Relational Disposition

Graham Ward engages McGilchrist's findings regarding belief, further developing the stance that belief is not merely a weak form of knowledge but a relational category.[17] "As such *credo* is not necessarily and immediately linked to a calculus of probabilities and 'causal thinking' (Wolpert), but rather to relational categories like trust, loyalty and empathy."[18] This orientation of "care" is affective and ultimately leads to concrete action. Ward affirms that embodiment, the imagination, and belief are inextricably bound together, thereby acknowledging the role of aesthetic existence

---

14. McGilchrist, *The Master and His Emissary*, 318.
15. McGilchrist, *The Master and His Emissary*, 319.
16. McGilchrist, *The Master and His Emissary*, 319.
17. Ward, *Unbelievable*, 75–83.
18. Ward, *Unbelievable*, 77.

in faith formation. But Ward has one particularly significant critique of McGilchrist's description of belief, which has implications for the aesthetics of discipleship. Ward maintains that McGilchrist's articulation of belief in terms of "acting as if" returns it to the realm of a cognitive choice. If this is so, then the impact of aesthetic existence on belief is peripheral, a secondary influence at best, subservient to conscious choice. For Ward, this is an inaccurate description, since belief is a disposition (involving both conscious and preconscious processes) rather than simply a conscious choice.

Ward suggests that our misunderstanding of belief stems from assessing knowledge through Cartesian and Lockean lenses. Reconsidering Plato may be helpful, which he does through three tropes in "Plato's *Republic*: the simile of the sun, the analogy of the line and the allegory of the cave."[19] The question raised through Plato's exploration of the escalating degrees of knowledge in these tropes is whether belief (*pistis*) is merely a stepping-stone towards true knowledge, to be jettisoned as inferior as soon as a higher form is attained. But this may be something of a Cartesian reading: the journey towards certainty having no utility once certainty itself is achieved; it may be worth taking a closer look at what is going on here. Do primal moves, saturated by desire, intention, and belief, not have a teleological impact on the ultimate destination of clarified, abstract knowledge? A more attentive reading of these tropes seems to indicate that the various levels of knowledge "both refer back to previous levels and ahead to the levels that follow, blurring where the boundaries lie . . . We might say: we come to know that which we believe, trust and are assured to be true. Or even: we believe that we may understand—which seems to be the way Augustine read the Platonic thought available to him in the fourth century CE."[20]

By contrast, the modern perspective of belief as a weak form of knowledge is the consequence of trajectories taken by philosophers such as John Locke. Locke's *Essay Concerning Human Understanding* explores the nature of knowledge and its relationship to belief, in book 4 chapter 15, defining belief as

> being that which makes us presume things to be true, before we know them to be so . . . And herein lies the difference between probability and certainty, faith and knowledge, that . . . each

---

19. Ward, *Unbelievable*, 23–29.
20. Ward, *Unbelievable*, 25.

> immediate idea, each step has its visible and certain connexion; in belief, not so. That which makes me believe, is something extraneous to the thing I believe.[21]

This essentially remains the modern stance on "the epistemology of belief and believing. All cognitive activity takes place in the receiving and receptive mind."[22] A dualism is formed between world and subject, a rift that is only overcome by "certain knowledge." Belief is relegated to speculation about the nature of reality. Thus, "with the association of belief with opinion, fancy and guessing . . . at best faith becomes a Pascalian wager, a leap beyond reason."[23]

We will return to the connection between belief and faith shortly. But the natural consequence of this epistemological perspective is that "we should aspire to knowledge 'altogether clear and bright'—certainty, transparency, daylight forever; a realised eschatology (without God and without judgement) in which there is no shadow of belief or opinion."[24] The irony is that such "certainty" is only achieved by prioritizing left-hemisphere abstraction over right-hemisphere embodied and affective engagement with the world, thereby entrenching the dualism rather than overcoming it.

Ward picks up on McGilchrist's observations of this world-subject dualism, which has interesting implications for the relationship between aesthetic existence and belief. As we have already seen, Lockean epistemology and the dominance of left-hemisphere abstraction has one of two consequences for aesthetic existence. The first possibility is that an I-Thou relationship is encountered through aesthetic experience, which challenges the sufficiency of the left-hemisphere closed system of meaning. By encountering the Other through affective and embodied means, the self-sufficient system of signs is breached, demanding the exploration of reality undiscovered. Belief here, as a relational category, is intertwined with the discovery of the world.

The second possibility is that an immature and self-seeking engagement with aesthetic existence cultivates a sensationalism that merely serves to entrench a simulated reality. Belief here, as a weak form of knowledge, has a potent relationship with aesthetic existence. Since

21. As quoted in Ward, *Unbelievable*, 127.
22. Ward, *Unbelievable*, 127.
23. Ward, *Unbelievable*, 128.
24. Ward, *Unbelievable*, 130.

beliefs, in this instance, are the consequence of a simulated abstraction of meaning, these virtual beliefs can be endorsed by self-seeking aesthetic experience, creating a delusional and therefore dangerous malformation of the left-hemisphere/right-hemisphere symbiosis. We will more fully explore the nature of this simulated belief shortly. Here we need simply note two manifestations of such virtuality: a modern, Lockean naming of such "certainty" as "reality", and the postmodern, Baudrillardian acknowledgement of it as simulacrum, accompanied by pseudovital sensationalism. The similarity here between the modern and postmodern perspectives is in the role immature aesthetic existence plays in validating the virtuality, whether it is named simulacrum in the latter or named reality in the former.

To highlight the role of mature aesthetic existence in a dispositional understanding of belief and its relationship to reality, we need to move beyond the Lockean perspective, delve deeper, and turn to Ward's "architecture of belief."

Dispositional Belief:
Aesthetic Existence Informs "Anticipation" and "Projection"

Ward suggests that belief is a universal human condition, not only to be confined to the realm of *religious* belief.[25] His inquiry leads him to a "biology and neuropsychology of believing," plotting an "architecture" of belief.[26] Like McGilchrist, Ward suggests that an anthropological fallacy—humans are volitional agents prioritizing the rational above the affective and imaginative—lies at the root of our misunderstanding of the place of belief, the imagination, and desire.[27]

In challenging this ratiocentric anthropology, Ward shows that "beliefs inform perception, interpretation and action prior to rationalisation."[28] The important point here is the preconscious, dispositional nature of belief. While there may be flaws in Plato's articulation, what he does rightly point toward is the interrelated and dynamic nature of the levels of knowing, and ultimate action; action at times even preceding conscious volition, which implies that "we are examining not a linear

---

25. Ward, *Unbelievable*, 14.
26. Ward, *Unbelievable*, 14.
27. Ward, *Unbelievable*, 122.
28. Ward, *Unbelievable*, 12.

process but a complex set of feedback and feedforward loops in which believing is deeply implicated."[29]

Ward explores the relationship between belief and "what lies beneath"—that which "is prior to interpretation and the impact it has on the way we think and behave."[30] In 1987 cognitive scientist, John F. Kihlstrom published a seminal article, "The Cognitive Unconscious," in which he argues that we arrive at "judgements and impressions prior to conscious attentiveness."[31] Since the publication of Kihlstrom's article, neuroscientists have probed each aspect of nonconscious activity that he proposed, among other findings, confirming the "time lag" that resonates with McGilchrist's right hemisphere → left hemisphere → right hemisphere progression. In an alternative to McGilchrist's progression, Ward describes the same principle by arguing that the imagination "fills the gaps" in this time lag between sensation and consciousness.[32] "There is a mode of liminal processing, related to embodiment and affectivity, which 'thinks' more quickly and reacts more instinctively than our conscious rational deliberation."[33] Social anthropologists such as Pierre Bourdieu have picked up on this, pointing out that the way we make sense of the world is tightly bound up with a partly preconscious "'habitus'—encultured dispositions, socialised mindsets and biases."[34] We will return to Bourdieu and "habitus" in the next chapter, since this has important implications for everyday aesthetic existence—the embodied and affective seemingly "meaningless" and "fun" activities that are in fact deeply formative, implying a necessary relation with discipleship and ethics. But here it is important to note that for Ward it is precisely these "dispositions" and "biases" that constitute belief.[35]

---

29. Ward, *Unbelievable*, 13.

30. Ward, *Unbelievable*, 11.

31. "Kihlstrom recognises . . . three forms of nonconscious activity: automatic responses, where we have learnt something by practice such that it requires little conscious attention . . . subliminal perception, where stimuli too weak to be consciously detected . . . impact on our impressions, judgements and actions . . . and implicit memory, where events that cannot be consciously remembered have a palpable effect upon our experience, thought and action" (Ward, *Unbelievable*, 11).

32. Ward, *Unimaginable*, 93.

33. Ward, *Unbelievable*, 12.

34. Ward, *Unbelievable*, 12.

35. Ward, *Unbelievable*, 12.

Since belief operates on this dispositional level, it follows that "belief is unavoidable."[36] Belief not only undergirds knowing, and the subsequent response, but it is inextricably bound up within the (nonlinear) cognitive, affective, and embodied processes that yield both preconscious and conscious apprehension. Ward maps out this processing through the economy of "anticipation–projection–reception–recognition–response."[37] It is a rather obvious claim that sentient reception plays a role in knowing, but the critical point is that reception is always preceded by intentional anticipation and projection. "Sentience means that the body is continually receiving an input of information, but anticipation is directing and focusing that information in specific ways . . . only a small percentage of what is being received is adequately lit by our consciousness."[38] This is necessary in order to make meaning of the world, amid the mass of stimuli presented through dynamic sensory experience, creating representation (left hemisphere) from fluid presentation (right hemisphere) by "generating associative narratives."[39]

Anticipation then, the ability to "*see as*," offers an imaginative narrative through which stimuli are selectively processed. Based on this narrative, we *project* meaning. This is the intention that drives perception, the "going out of oneself" in order to read meaning into experience.[40] "As phenomenologists from Edmund Husserl onwards have recognised, human beings perceive intentionally. They see meaning."[41] The operation of anticipation and projection, to draw connections between one phenomenon and another (whether an experiential memory, or an abstract rule), requires the creation of an inferential connection, which can be a conscious process but can also be unconscious, thereby forming a disposition. The implication is that we may not be fully aware, or even aware at all, of how we arrived at the disposition.[42] In order for meaning to be shared, these dispositions are then subject to the human trait of *recognition*.[43] This is most obvious in the articulation of belief as common

---

36. Ward, *Unbelievable*, 77.
37. Ward, *Unbelievable*, 47–77.
38. Ward, *Unbelievable*, 46.
39. Ward, *Unbelievable*, 48.
40. Ward, *Unbelievable*, 54.
41. Ward, *Unbelievable*, 51.
42. Ward, *Unbelievable*, 49.
43. Ward uses the term "recognition" as "expounded by the nineteenth-century German philosopher G. W. F. Hegel in his groundbreaking *Phenomenology of Spirit*

AESTHETIC EXISTENCE AS FUNDAMENTAL IN FAITH FORMATION 159

symbolic language, but even recognition cannot be reduced to left-hemisphere abstraction, since it includes emotional and implicit knowledge, essentially being "an understanding of the other, myself, *and* the relation of meaning binding both other and self."[44]

For our purposes, the most significant aspect of Ward's economy of human interaction with the world and formation of meaning (anticipation-projection-reception-recognition-response) is the pervasive, integrated, and fundamental role of both belief and aesthetic engagement. Belief is the lens through which we interact with the world, central to anticipation (*seeing as*) and the subsequent projection of possibilities.

> Belief is evident not only in these projected possibilities—the belief of their possibility based on previous occurrences which are not simply recalled in order to predict. It also determines how what is seen is seen. Furthermore, belief also resides in the abstraction process itself—the construction of how things work in the world. More fundamentally, belief is evident throughout the cognitive processes in ways that inform both the disposition to anticipate and the projection of possibilities.[45]

The influence of belief at this fundamental cognitive level is often preconscious, operating in the aesthetic realm of the embodied and affective. Not only McGilchrist's research but also findings from the field of embodied cognition confirm this, as we have seen.[46] Further, while cognition is embodied, it is also embodied on a social and cultural level, not solely on a personal level. The implications of this are that personal and communal, embodied and affective experiences affect belief, shaping the ways we see, our anticipation, and our projection of possibilities.[47] Everyday aesthetic experiences, as embodied and affective, therefore influence not only our beliefs but consequently our formation as a whole.

(1807). Himself something of an early anthropologist, the word he used was *Anerkennung*. The German word is subtle. *Erkennung* is 'knowledge', but the prefix *an* lends that word an incompleteness. It is 'almost' knowledge or 'on the way to' knowledge, pre-knowing, intuitive, in ways that bear some similarities with what many neuroscientists refer to as 'emotional knowledge'. Nevertheless it announces a cognition regarding what is outside the ego, the one perceiving. It is as if from an external stimulus the self provokes a knowledge that is not quite knowledge within itself: a déjà vu. Hence the translation 'recognition'" (Ward, *Unbelievable*, 53).

44. Ward, *Unbelievable*, 53.
45. Ward, *Unbelievable*, 48.
46. Ward, *How the Light Gets In*, 257.
47. Ward, *How the Light Gets In*, 118.

This does not mean that we should fall into the trap of attempting a neat, propositional equation, quantifying the role that everyday aesthetic experiences play in the formation of belief. The problem here would be that we attempt to use left-hemisphere abstraction to quantify right-hemisphere embodied and affective formation. Precisely because much of this dynamic is preconscious, a comprehensive analysis lies beyond rational, empirical reach, just as our understanding of consciousness itself is limited. While neuroscience, for instance, can offer important clues to our understanding of belief, we should also acknowledge the limitations of this approach. "The irreducibility of belief to the physics and chemistry of the brain draws our attention to a lacuna that cannot be disassociated from the lacuna of consciousness itself. We cannot account fully for belief, and belief cannot fully account for itself. We don't always (possibly most of the time) know believing's secret operations, its secret selections among our memories, emotions and understandings."[48] Any attempt, therefore, to offer a neat formula capturing the exact role aesthetic experience plays in the development of belief will be inevitably reductionist. Admittedly, this may seem to be precisely the task at hand in delineating the aesthetics of discipleship. However, even while we are not able to neatly *quantify* the role of aesthetic existence in the formation of belief, thereby suggesting that the process has been captured in its entirety, with scientific certainty, there remains great value in paying attention to the undeniable evidence for the significant role that everyday aesthetic existence plays in the formation of belief. The important role everyday aesthetic experience plays in belief raises important implications, even while not offering the tidy, illusory certainty that would come with being able to quantify the role of everyday aesthetic experiences in believing.

While we therefore want to avoid the reductionist illusion that it is possible to comprehensively map the causal connections between aesthetic existence and belief: to even attempt such a mechanical account would represent a misunderstanding of the process, and ultimately a misunderstanding of the nature of meaning in relation to being itself. As we have seen, belief (or ethics, for that matter) is not merely to be equated with ratiocination. Belief is indeed a pivotal component in the human creation of meaning, but seeing this demands approaching understanding as relational, not propositional in essence (even though the

---

48. Ward, *Unbelievable*, 112.

propositional plays an important role). Along the lines of "Heidegger's analysis of 'being there', or *Dasein*," understanding is "not simply a cognitive act in our coming to know something, but . . . a mode of being in itself. As a mode of being, understanding enables us to relate to the world, make sense of the world and our exchanges with it, and give shape to that world. It is in this way that understanding is existential."[49] But as Ward notes, Heidegger "did not pay enough attention to the way understanding as a mode of knowing passes into understanding as a mode of being."[50] Belief operates at this nexus of knowing and being; it is lived, the one organically shaping the other in embodied, affective, and sometimes preconscious ways. Consequently, belief, as a living, enacted, relational commitment of trust creates a *seeing as*, not while disconnected from the world in abstract contemplation, but amid existential reality. "For beliefs are (and have) lived conditions for the possibility or impossibility of certain imaginative experiences of the world."[51] These "lived conditions" are embodied, creating a dynamic, symbiotic, and complex relationship between consciousness, aesthetic existence, and belief—one that is not driven only by conscious volition, but by affective desire embedded in embodiment. Belief "motivates and energizes as it issues from the swirl within embodiment itself in relation to and in response to all that is given to it."[52]

The Existential "Seeing As" of Belief

The preceding exploration of Ward's architecture of belief reveals the fundamentally integrated nature of aesthetic existence and belief, thereby highlighting a weakness in McGilchrist's otherwise helpful account. McGilchrist's description of belief, in an effort to be stylistically neat, unintentionally returns belief to the left-hemisphere realm of cognitive choice, thereby eliminating the preconscious aspects of belief. But as we have seen, the dispositional nature of belief means that it does not have a linear relationship with cognition and action, but functions within a "complex set of feedback and feedforward loops."[53] This is not to say

---

49. Ward, *Unbelievable*, 7.
50. Ward, *Unbelievable*, 8.
51. Ward, *How the Light Gets In*, 134.
52. Ward, *How the Light Gets In*, 257.
53. Ward, *Unbelievable*, 13.

that belief is disconnected from conscious volition. It is simply to point out that volition itself is more complicated and multifaceted than the Lockean perspective allows. In this regard, it may be helpful to consider belief through a broader, more inclusive framing, describing it, for instance, as a "mental state (where 'state' can cover 'thought', 'perception' and 'experience', all of which are dynamic, not static conditions)," noting that, first, "not all mental states are brought to consciousness," and second, that mental states are not disassociated from sensory perception (remembering that sensing itself may have "intentional content").[54]

Both Ward and McGilchrist agree that belief is essentially relational, and thus concerns "recognition" (in the sense of Ward's use of the term). Further, that this disposition of "care" necessarily entails response-ability (it comes with ethical implications). They also concur that preconscious, implicit, and embodied experience of the world affects belief and thereby has implications for concrete action. Commenting on McGilchrist's findings, Ward notes that, "working together, the left and right hemispheres of the brain make believing a mode of cognition associated with imagination, motivation, desire, intuition and feeling."[55]

Nevertheless, Ward suggests that McGilchrist's description of belief in terms of "acting as if" situates it firmly within "left-hemisphere ratiocination."[56] It is indeed a curious description that McGilchrist employs, incongruent with his larger project. For example, "Some people *choose* to believe in materialism; they *act 'as if'* such a philosophy were true."[57] Ward's observation that this phrasing provides stylistic neatness may well be McGilchrist's motivation here, for it seems to allow for a clear articulation of the operation of belief.[58] Not only is this description inconsistent with McGIlichrist's own work, but it also fails to do justice to the complex and integrated nature of belief as further articulated by Ward. McGilchrist himself suggests that preconscious "seeing as" fundamentally shapes conscious choice, challenging the fallacy of independent ratiocination in a disembodied vacuum.[59] However, not only can "acting as if" be construed as a somewhat condescending phrase (acting on

---

54. Ward, *Unbelievable*, 91.
55. Ward, *Unbelievable*, 77.
56. Ward, *Unbelievable*, 81.
57. McGilchrist, *The Master and His Emissary*, 170 (italics added).
58. Ward, *Unbelievable*, 78.
59. McGilchrist, *The Master and His Emissary*, 162.

AESTHETIC EXISTENCE AS FUNDAMENTAL IN FAITH FORMATION

fantastical "wishful thinking" and associated with untruth), but the notion of "choice here is far too locked into the assumption of a Cartesian, monadic ego who does the choosing."[60] "I can choose to believe that, rationally calculated, materialism or Marxism best fit the facts as we have them. But this form of believing is much more akin to Locke's account of knowledge . . . it is believing very much in service to the probability calculus of left-hemisphere thinking. It cannot be equated, as McGilchrist does, with faith."[61] We will shortly be turning to the relationship between faith and belief in general, but here we can note the problematic nature of describing religious belief as "acting as if." Christianity bears

> witness to an experience not of choosing God but being chosen by God. Such a re-cognition is based in something familiar, something half-known, known intuitively, known in the very substructures of our being human . . . In seeing *as* there is always a moment of what is given in seeing . . . In McGilchrist's characterisation of believing, choosing and the 'as if', neither does justice to the rich complexity of belief in a creator God nor fully describes the disclosive nature of what comes with such a belief.[62]

What Ward is describing here is the givenness, or even the Otherness, that is always present in a relational understanding of belief. Receptivity to this givenness, or Otherness, is often intuitive and implicit. It is receptivity within the realm of the aesthetic. This is not a two-stage process, wherein we first, intuitively and implicitly *see as*, shaped by embodied and affective, preconscious engagement with the world, but then, second, go on to consciously *act as if*. It is a complex unity of "feedback and feedforward" loops wherein preconscious *seeing as* informs conscious *seeing as*, thereby initiating a relational commitment (belief) and subsequent action on the basis of this (both implicit and explicit) knowledge of reality. The implication is that everyday aesthetic existence is not a separate realm of existence, distinct from ethical or religious existence governed by ratiocination. Aesthetic existence, being in the moment bodily and affectively, generates an *as if* that informs ethical and religious being and doing, believing and acting.

---

60. Ward, *Unbelievable*, 79–80.
61. Ward, *Unbelievable*, 80.
62. Ward, *Unbelievable*, 80–81 (italics original).

To illustrate this we can return to neuroscientific research on mirror neurons. As pointed out in the last chapter, our imitative and empathic ability stem from our brain's capacity to vicariously live out, in our very nervous system, an experience external to our body, merely by perceiving it. Ward suggests that research on mirror neurons has significant implications for understanding the deeply integrated relationship between belief, embodiment, and the imagination. Mirror neurons

> write the "as if" of belief into our physiologies because they evoke the "simulation, in the brain's body maps, of a body state that is not actually taking place in the organism," amplifying the "functional resemblance" (Damasio). In this way, and with the help of what another neuroscientist, Antonio Damasio, terms CDZs (convergence-divergence zones at the microscopic level that assemble neurons within feedforward–feedback loops of information) and CDRs (convergence-divergence regions located at strategic areas in association cortices where major pathways for information come together), *belief is not only embodied but inseparable from the capacity to imagine.*[63]

Further, Ward's exposition of this "biology of belief" that neuroscientific research offers shows that a dispositional understanding of belief is not only a theoretical construct but a neurological reality. Damasio himself describes a "dispositional space" in brain function, the brain encoding previous perceptions and representations as dispositions. These dispositions function at a lower level of consciousness (similar to the body's autonomic system), thereby not requiring conscious memory, and freeing up brain space in a sense.[64]

> While the contents of images can be accessed by consciousness, we can never have direct access to the contents of our dispositions. They are encrypted and dormant. Nevertheless, *this dispositional space is the source of images in the process of imagination and reasoning* and is also used to generate movement. It is located in the cerebral cortices that are not otherwise occupied by the image [mapping] space (the higher-order cortices and parts of the limbic cortices) and in numerous subcortical nuclei. The point of all this for an architecture of belief is that

---

63. Ward, *Unbelievable*, 95 (italics added).
64. Ward, *Unbelievable*, 98.

the foundations for the very edifice of believing itself lie in a knowledge base that is implicit, encrypted and unconscious.[65]

In other words, not only is believing fundamentally and inextricably connected to embodiment, the human faculty of imagination (*seeing as*, which feeds off and into belief) is shaped at a preconscious level. It is therefore unhelpful to talk of two separate processes—*seeing as* and *acting as if*—as McGilchrist does. Clearly, acting is related to *seeing as*, and conscious volition plays an important role both in *seeing as*, as well as acting, but reduction to a two-step process is too simplistic, not accounting for the complex and organic nature of the process. Rather, an intricate web of "imagination, motivation, desire, intuition and feeling" affects belief and its consequent abstract articulation, in a nonlinear and multi-directional manner.[66] The implication here is a fundamental link between everyday aesthetic existence and belief. While a Lockean perspective of belief centers on conscious volition, based on (weak) knowledge, "the aesthetic appreciation of the act of believing introduces aspects of the structure of belief hitherto concealed: most explicitly, the work of the imagination."[67]

Spotlight on Music: Aesthetic Existence as Propulsive, Mythic Sensibility

It is worth pausing at this point to illustrate the power of aesthetic existence in belief formation by looking, once again, at the case of musical sensory immediacy. If belief is not merely a weak form of knowledge but stems from embodied and affective, often preconscious engagement with the world, then sensory immediacy is not merely an obstacle to be overcome in the development of belief, but rather shapes the imagination, thereby playing a role in the very trajectory of belief formation. A brief look with Ward at two musical examples illustrates, first, the visceral, propulsive force of musical sensory immediacy, and. second, the imaginative myth-formation that ensues.

Ward points out that before we can speak of sensing and imaginative "making sense," we need to consider sentience itself, which neuroscientists

---

65. Ward, *Unbelievable*, 98 (italics added).
66. Ward, *Unbelievable*, 77.
67. Ward, *Unbelievable*, 17.

consider to be "'core' or 'primal' consciousness."[68] Discussion of the human faculty of imagination can easily become cerebral, when in fact it is deeply biological, rooted in "the body at the border of the instinctive and the intuitive."[69] Sentience provides "primal awareness" from which consciousness arises.[70] It is the birthplace of "elemental passion." Simply, "Bodies feel, that is their nature, and feeling is 'propulsive.'"[71] Between sentience and conscious articulation there is a "formed response."[72] This formed response is not merely animal reflex but "an intentional propulsion prior to agency, prior to the will of a commanding ego."[73] This is the realm of aesthetic existence, expressed, for example, in the arts such as dance, music and film, or even in everyday play. "These propulsive intentions have no single aim or directedness. As in play, they have no instrumental end other than to display themselves."[74]

To illustrate the propulsive power of musical sensory immediacy, Ward turns to a performance by singer James Arthur in *The X Factor* (2012) and in particular his rendition of Shontelle's "Impossible." The song mourns a broken relationship, and Shontelle's version, while at times "angry, regretful, even hurt," ends neatly in resignation, "the singing . . . beautifully in tune, the words clearly enunciated."[75] By contrast, Arthur brings all of his "complex biography" and existential brokenness to the performance. Beginning with "a series of soft moans," by the second verse his "breathing begins to rasp," then "anger erupts, which is accompanied by him hitting his chest on 'empty promises . . . I know, I know.'"[76] In repetition beyond Shontelle's version, he sings a "reiteration of the opening, his breathing becomes unregulated, the lines of the lyrics break, and their articulation is half-formed . . . [he] then launches into a third iteration of the chorus. The notes, shouted, invoke the disturbing as he carves into himself . . . Arthur just wails and howls that brokenness while a backing chorus repeats 'Impossible. Impossible.' When he picks up their words,

68. Ward, *Unimaginable*, 84.
69. Ward, *Unimaginable*, 29.
70. Ward, *Unimaginable*, 85.
71. Ward, *Unimaginable*, 87.
72. Ward, *Unimaginable*, 87.
73. Ward, *Unimaginable*, 87.
74. Ward, *Unimaginable*, 87.
75. Ward, *Unimaginable*, 88.
76. Ward, *Unimaginable*, 88.

'Impossible' is dark with sunken depths of despair."[77] Ward notes that it is not Arthur's musical performance that is compelling as much as it is his expression of pain, "both visceral and immediate."[78]

It is the sheer affective propulsion of this "formed response" that we need note here, since it cannot simply be discarded as insignificant emotion in the quest for a Lockean development of belief. Arthur has been existentially moved through this aesthetic expression, but significantly, so have the audience. By listening to, or perhaps better, by *partaking in* his performance, "we are forced to hear an elemental passion that is prior to language. It leaves us breathing, but breathless; and not a little frightened for him."[79] In resonance with our conversation on mirror neurons above, not only is imagining "profoundly affective and somatic," but "the imagination, as a dynamic process of affects in the body's immersion in the world, emerges in this coming-to-form that is prior to and beneath all public communication."[80]

Further, this affective propulsion is a potent force in the creation and sustenance of presiding myths, thereby shaping belief.[81] It can provide an attunement of the senses to ultimate reality in what Ward describes as "mythic sensibility."[82] The imagination and mythic sensibility go hand in hand as we "make" sense of sensation.[83] Here, Ward turns to the composer Gerald Finzi's *Dies Natalis* to illustrate the point. *Dies Natalis* is a five-movement cantata featuring settings of Thomas Traherne's poetry. The theological nature of Traherne's writing stems from his own experience of mythic sensibility, of "epiphanic quality."[84] Finzi draws from Traherne in an effort to produce a composition of "emotional force that eschews the darknesses of late Beethoven and Wagner as much as it eschews the sentimentalities and coyness of the Romantic child."[85] It is music that tests the range of any soloist and "demands superhuman breathing discipline."[86]

---

77. Ward, *Unimaginable*, 89.
78. Ward, *Unimaginable*, 89.
79. Ward, *Unimaginable*, 89.
80. Ward, *Unimaginable*, 89–90.
81. Ward, *Unimaginable*, 59.
82. Ward, *Unimaginable*, 156.
83. Ward, *Unimaginable*, 157.
84. Ward, *Unimaginable*, 159.
85. Ward, *Unimaginable*, 160.
86. Ward, *Unimaginable*, 160.

The result defies articulation; it is a "metamorphosis of the everyday."[87] Finzi, drawing from Traherne, and inspired by Botticelli's *Mystic Nativity*, works with everyday sensation, and through "an orchestration of the sensed" evokes an elemental response in the hearer.[88]

> Our response to what is elemental here feebly gropes for names. "Sublime" won't help. It's dogged down now in philosophical niceties. But Traherne's "ravishment" is suggestive—for it has the immediacy of the unimaginable; capturing that moment as it excites the imagination. Sensing (*aesthesis*) opens into aesthetics, and immediately the effect is a transformation not just of perspective but also of the way existence is experienced: gusto, ravishment, wonder, delight are the affective registers of beauty.[89]

Propulsive sensory immediacy in service of mythic awareness here produces a new way of seeing reality, and consequently a change in disposition toward the world. In short, it shifts the imagination, which affects belief. However, we cannot discuss the formative power of the imagination without acknowledging its pathologies. Just as mythic sensibility can lead to wonder and transcendence, it is the selfsame human faculty that produces horror.[90] In other words, such a shift is not, by default, a shift in a positive direction, towards apprehending reality more accurately. As we have noted, the imagination can be harnessed both toward the cultivation of virtuality as well as toward the apprehension of reality. In order to distinguish the difference, we need to turn to the relationship between aesthetic existence and faith formation.

Relating Dispositional Belief to the Formation of Faith

The human ability, then, to *see as*, the faculty of the imagination, lies at the heart of belief. This is a point we need to look at more closely in order to understand the implications for aesthetic existence. But before we do so, we need to clarify the relationship between belief and faith. The aesthetics of discipleship, after all, seeks to probe the question of the interaction between everyday aesthetic existence and faith, but up until this

---

87. Ward, *Unimaginable*, 160.
88. Ward, *Unimaginable*, 160.
89. Ward, *Unimaginable*, 161.
90. Ward, *Unimaginable*, 162–67.

point we have been considering belief in general, as a universal human disposition, not specifically *religious* belief, and the consequent relationship between faith and belief.

Religious belief is an acknowledgement that reality contains hiddenness, that which is obscured from view, beyond the realm of left-hemisphere certainty. However, hiddenness is not only an attribute of divine transcendence, but is equally immanent, this-worldly. We can turn, with Ward, to phenomenology to clarify the point.[91] In his last essay, "The Visible and the Invisible," Maurice Merleau-Ponty argues that he is dealing with the "'invisible of *this* world,' underscoring the immanence of his project."[92] To illustrate this, Merleau-Ponty works with an example stemming from Edmund Husserl's *Logical Investigations*: a cube. When we perceive a cube, we can actually only see two or three sides, and yet we know it to be a cube. We *believe* the other sides to be there. In order to make sense of it, we *project* all six sides of the cube. Along with the visual perception of the object, Merleau-Ponty suggests that this projection is co-present, allowing us to see a cube, and the hiddenness involved, in an act of (this-worldly) intentional transcendence (as opposed to absolute transcendence). We *see as*, seeing the two or three sides present to us as a six-sided cube, in what Husserl describes as "apperceptive transcendentalism."[93] Merleau-Ponty develops this notion as "perceptual faith." Note the "theological or quasi-theological language" used in Merleau-Ponty's work here, which highlights the inconsistency of Merleau-Ponty's insistence that this does not have religious implications, a consequence of the "cultural politics" ("securing phenomenology as a secular philosophical science") from which Merleau-Ponty is speaking.[94] "It is a 'faith' that is co-posited with perception itself."[95] Such "perceptual faith' is the seeing of meaningful form (what has been referred to as Merleau-Ponty's 'gestalt ontology') through intentional expectation and projection."[96]

Using the work of Jean-Louis Chrétien and Dominique Janicaud, Ward questions whether there is indeed grounds for Merleau-Ponty to

---

91. Ward, *How the Light Gets In*, 226–33.
92. Ward, *How the Light Gets In*, 228.
93. Ward, *Unbelievable*, 195.
94. Ward, *How the Light Gets In*, 229–30.
95. Ward, *Unbelievable*, 196.
96. Ward, *How the Light Gets In*, 229.

make a distinction between this-worldly "intentional transcendence" and divine "absolute transcendence."[97] Does the process of "perceptual faith" not apply equally to the operation of religious faith? This is an important question for the aesthetics of discipleship, since it probes the relationship of belief, as a fundamentally embodied and affective disposition, to faith. On the one hand, it would be a theological error to conflate God and this-worldly reality; to do so would simply be pantheism. Yet, as the incarnation makes clear, there is an undeniable connection between divine transcendence and embodied, this-worldly immanence. While projecting the sides of a physical cube (intentional transcendence) and projecting the divine from material reality (absolute transcendence) may not operate on the same continuum, it would be equally erroneous to suggest that there is no relationship between the two. The created world carries a necessary connection to the uncreated Creator, as distinct as these two entities are. Merleau-Ponty's "radical and unbridgeable difference" rests on the irrational assumption of "an hermetically sealed realm named the immanent."[98] While the exercise of "perceptual faith" in relation to a cube offers a neat, immanent conclusion, an attempt to apply the same process to the human body, for example, offers "much more complex and irreducible invisibilities" around the nature of being human.[99] How then do we best understand the relationship between everyday hiddenness and divine hiddenness? If everyday aesthetic existence shapes our beliefs about everyday hiddenness, how does this relate to divine hiddenness?

Connecting Embodiment with Transcendence: The Analogical Worldview

Ward's answer to this question is analogy.[100] As with McGilchrist's use of metaphor that we explored in the previous chapter, by *analogy* Ward means something quite different from the modern, left-hemisphere perception of analogy as a mere figure of speech—a decorative addition solely for the purpose of making a propositional statement more colorful—a helpful addition, at best, but not ultimately necessary. Such

---

97. Ward, *How the Light Gets In*, 231–33.
98. Ward, *How the Light Gets In*, 233.
99. Ward, *How the Light Gets In*, 231.
100. Although it undergirds much of his work, Ward deals with the analogical worldview at length in Ward, *Cities of God*.

an understanding of analogy would be of no help in relating the uncreated divine to this-worldly reality. Analogy, from this left-hemisphere perspective, is in service of, and therefore bound within, a closed system of signs, producing self-referential "certainty." Rather, as with our discussion of living metaphors, for analogy to break out of modern, left-hemisphere virtuality, it needs to be *lived*. It needs an embodied and affective engagement, a *participation* in the created world, which allows for right-hemisphere, implicit, and intuitive openness to the hiddenness that lies beyond. Such a framing of living analogy draws from the theological concept of *analogia entis*—participation in created being offering an analogous participation in divine hiddenness. The concept of *analogia entis* has a long, complex and controversial history (Barth called it an invention of antichrist), but a full articulation of this fractious history need not detain us here.[101] For our purposes, it will be sufficient to outline Ward's perspective before framing the broader principle that undergirds it, which arguably holds traction across the ecumenical spectrum, and contributes to understanding the role of aesthetic existence in faith formation.[102]

The analogical is a bridging worldview. However, it is a bridge that needs to be carefully understood. As with metaphor, this bridging capacity is only functional to the extent that right-hemisphere, meaning-making aesthetic engagement with reality is embraced. The metaphorical, to which McGilchrist refers, and the analogical for Ward are not merely theoretical tools, the product of abstraction. They are formative modes of engaging reality, or perhaps better articulated, *living* reality. As McGilchrist notes, co-opting embodied and affective experience into the hegemonic economy of left-hemisphere abstraction and then, for example, approaching ritual and icon as representations of explicit theory means that they lose their transparency as metaphors. Instead, a right-hemisphere approach demands that they "are always incarnate and therefore must be left to act on us intuitively—neither just material or just immaterial, but bridges between the two realms."[103] Both McGilchrist and Ward point here to the Eucharist as an example—McGilchrist showing that through the Reformation living metaphor, as presence, was substituted with simile, "'this is my body' becomes 'this *signifies* (is like)

---

101. Barth, *Church Dogmatics I*, xiii.
102. Ward, "Radical Orthodoxy."
103. McGilchrist, *The Master and His Emissary*, 444.

my body."[104] Ward, likewise, contrasting Aquinas and Calvin's notions of "presence" in the Eucharist, and the consequent movement from the analogical to the univocal.[105]

The analogical therefore lies at the heart of the sacraments, and further, a sacramental understanding of all of life, including everyday aesthetic existence, to which we will shortly return. But before we can do so, we need to clarify the nature of this analogical relation. Theologically, it is founded in the "analogy that pertains between the uncreated God and creation, Christ and human beings. It is an analogy that can pertain because we are made in the image of God and therefore, as Jean-Louis Chrétien understands, 'it is the transcendence in us that knows the transcendent.'"[106] The analogical worldview thus stems from the foundational theological truth that there is a necessary (and from a Christian perspective, mutually participatory) connection between a creating, active God and his creation—a connection that both is logically necessary and also supersedes logic in its mysterious operation.

> Analogy as *ana*-logical is theologically freighted. It bears the weight of a profound cosmological significance. It is profound because creation is related to an uncreated creator, who not only inaugurates but maintains a world-order within which analogy is an index of participation . . . It is cosmological because analogy traces an order that is dependent upon a creating God, an active God.[107]

It is precisely in the mystery of this participation that the value of the analogical worldview lies. It is therefore hardly surprising that the perspective largely collapsed (at least in Protestant circles) following the rejection of the medieval enchantment of the world, amid subsequent theological abstraction dominated by left-hemisphere attention. In the binary categorization and controversy that followed, the analogical worldview has been at times understood to locate God and creation within the same category of being. But as David Bentley Hart succinctly clarifies,

> The analogy of being does not analogize God and creatures under the more general category of being, but is the analogization of being in the difference between God and creatures; it is as

---

104. McGilchrist, *The Master and His Emissary*, 319.
105. Ward, *Cities of God*, 157–65.
106. Ward, *Christ and Culture*, 17.
107. Ward, *Cities of God*, ix.

> subversive of the notion of a general and univocal category of being as of the equally "totalizing" notion of ontological equivocity, and thus belongs to neither pole of the dialectic intrinsic to metaphysical totality: the savage equivalence of univocity and equivocity, Apollo and Dionysus, pure identity and pure difference (neither of which can open a vantage upon being in its transcendence).[108]

Ward affirms that an analogical understanding needs to be prefaced by emphasizing the dissimilarity of Creator and created being, lest the two become conflated, through a distorted understanding of analogy.[109] Further, that in navigating the relationship between embodied this-wordliness and divine transcendence, it is all too easy to slip into univocity, equivocity, or dualism.[110] But are these pitfalls not the consequence of navigating this-worldliness, God, and the analogical from the perspective of left-hemisphere abstraction rather than right-hemisphere participation?

While the dangers are noted, the point remains that a necessary analogical connection exists between God and creation, which is affirmed by the incarnation. Like Bonhoeffer, Ward concurs that Christology lies at the center of understanding reality, and consequently the relation between aesthetic existence (as a fundamentally embodied mode of existence) and reality.[111] This is because Christ is the essence of all relationality ("in him all things hold together" [Col. 1:17])—or the "betweenness" of the world, as McGilchrist would name it—which is at the core of mature aesthetic existence: the presencing of the Other. "Christ, as second person of the Trinity, is the archetype of all relation. All relations, that is, participate in and aspire to their perfection in the christological relation. Not only in him is all relation perfected, but the work and economy he is implicated in is relation: that is, the reconciliation of the world to God."[112]

Ward writes at length on the "displaced body of Christ," his argument being, not only that the incarnation itself unites divine and embodied reality in the person of Jesus, but that this incarnational relation

---

108. Hart, *The Beauty of the Infinite*, 241.
109. Ward, *Unbelievable*, 191.
110. Ward, *Cities of God*, 254.
111. Ward, *Christ and Culture*, 5.
112. Ward, *Christ and Culture*, 1.

continues following the ascension through the "mapping" or displacement of Christ's own body on to other bodies.[113]

> When I say all bodies are "in some sense" incarnational they are not identical repetitions of Christ's body, but nevertheless participate in that incarnation in their own creaturely way. Embodiment therefore is analogically related to incarnation, and it is, as such, that Paul's *soma* can refer both to (a) the historical and physical body each possesses, even Christ and (b) the transhistorical, spiritual body that is Christ's alone but which is made of several members constituting the Church.[114]

The challenging task of articulating the precise nature of embodied participation in the body of Christ is not necessary here; for our task at hand the important point to note is that such a relation necessarily exists. However, if the argument thus far holds true, then the precise nature of this relation is beyond the realm of abstract, propositional articulation in any case. Something of its living nature will inevitably be lost in such a reduction. This wondrous incarnational relation raises significant implications for the aesthetics of discipleship: First, this relation is bound up within our very bodies (as opposed to our minds, souls, spirits or any other disembodied aspect of being human one could argue for). Second, this embodied relation holds true across all spatial and temporal boundaries since "all places and times are sustained by God's Being," as Anselm affirms.[115] In other words, this embodied relation transgresses any sacred or secular boundaries we may artificially impose on everyday life. Everyday aesthetic experiences are all within the realm of the sacred in this sense. Third, this relation is not something to be grasped as an abstract concept, but one to be lived, to be participated in; this is how it is known.[116]

The intention here is not to ground theological validation of aesthetic existence in Ward's analogical worldview or in any particular

---

113. Ward, "The Displaced Body of Jesus Christ."

114. Ward, *Christ and Culture*, 157.

115. Ward, *How the Light Gets In*, 205.

116. This resonates not only with McGilchrist's neuropsychological explanation of how we know reality, but also the biblical, and particularly ancient Israelite, perspective of knowing. "Knowing God in the Hebrew sense arises from lived experience." Rudolf Bultmann observes that in the Old Testament, "knowledge is not thought of in terms of a possession of information. It is possessed only in its exercise or actualization" (Bultmann, "γινώσκω, κτλ," 698).

stripe of participatory metaphysics for that matter, but merely to harness the paradigm to point toward a foundational theological truth: there is a necessary relation between this-worldly embodied existence and the revelation of God. As James Smith points out, mention of a sacramental ontology and the associations some make with it inevitably provokes a skittish response, but the main point being raised here is simply that of "the psalmist's claim that 'The earth is the Lord's and all that is in it, the world, and those who live in it' (Ps. 24:1), echoed in Paul's claim that in the Creator God 'we live and move and have our being' (Acts 17:28)."[117] Revelation of God cannot be disconnected from this-worldly embodiment; God speaks through created things. Even the reduction of revelation to truncated, left-hemisphere abstraction demands embodiment. The communal reading of Scripture, for instance, requires eyes, ears, and tongues. The sacraments of bread and wine can only have significance if the broader principle applies that God uses these specific channels of grace because the material matters. The intensified sacramentality of the bread and wine is only possible because the entire world is a sacrament. Seeing it thus reconfigures our understanding of materiality, confronting naturalism by illuminating that the world as "a means of worship and means of grace is not accidental, but the revelation of its meaning, the restoration of its essence, the fulfillment of its destiny."[118] But we are getting ahead of ourselves: we will return to the sacramentality of all earthly existence in the next chapter—all of life as worship, and the implications for aesthetic existence. Here, the point is that "God meets us in materiality, and that the natural world is always more than just nature—it is charged with the presence and glory of God."[119] Therefore, the sacramental imagination is not bound within the naturalistic confines of this-worldly transcendence, nor does it serve a gnostic, disembodied belief in the supernatural; rather, "it walks the tightrope of a 'theological materialism' that both affirms the goodness of materiality but also [affirms] that the material *is* only insofar as it participates in more than the material."[120] The skittish reaction to speaking of the world as sacrament stems from a concern for heresy, from nervousness about "blurring the Creator/creature distinction," prompting a retreat to the safe certainty of

---

117. Smith, *Desiring the Kingdom*, 141.
118. Schmemann, *For the Life of the World*, 121.
119. Smith, *Desiring the Kingdom*, 143.
120. Smith, *Desiring the Kingdom*, 143.

propositional abstraction, which can clearly explain the mystery of God's relationship with embodied materiality. However, those that undertake this retreat to ratiocentric certainty "unwittingly evacuate the world of its charge and grandeur. In the name of avoiding the so-called paganism they find here, they end up with a flattened 'nature' that is only a symbol or pointer rather than being creation that is charged with the Spirit's presence which makes it more than material."[121] If our commitment is to house disembodied doctrine, and faith in general, within the safe certainty of rational proposition, "we shouldn't be surprised that it is poets who better intuit and express the elements of a Christian social imaginary and the sacramental imagination."[122]

In summary, this-worldly hiddenness, or everyday invisibilities, are an accepted part of navigating material reality. We continuously project to make meaning of these invisibilities through the operation of our imagination, *seeing as* being a fundamental aspect not only of belief, but also subsequently of all human being and understanding. The way we *see as* is shaped by the embodied, affective, often preconscious attention we offer the world. In other words, everyday aesthetic existence affects belief, playing a significant role in the meaning we project into the invisibilities of this world. However, the impact of aesthetic existence is not limited to this-worldly believing. Even though divine invisibility cannot be conflated with material invisibility, a necessary relation exists between uncreated Creator and creation, a relation underscored by the incarnation. As a consequence of this relation, embodied existence and everyday aesthetic experiences not only shape this-worldly belief but also thereby have the potential to analogically participate in transcendent reality, thus shaping religious belief and ultimately faith formation. In other words, embodied and affective practices as experienced in everyday aesthetic existence are formative not only from a neuropsychological perspective but also from a theological one, as informed by the incarnation—the sacramental imagination being shaped by divine revelation even through navigating the earthly realities of embodied existence. Here it should be noted that just as McGilchrist argues regarding the perception of living metaphor, it is particularly right-hemisphere attention that allows for awareness of and reception to this formative transcendent relation. It is necessarily an embodied and affective mode, an aesthetic mode of

---

121. Smith, *Desiring the Kingdom*, 147–48.
122. Smith, *Desiring the Kingdom*, 147–48.

engaging incarnational reality. Yet, while all belief is inherently connected to aesthetic existence, not all belief culminates in faith formation. To understand why, we need to revisit the two types of attention we offer the world, and the consequences for the relationship between aesthetic existence and faith formation.

Two Expressions of Belief: Faith and Virtuality

Historically and etymologically, the relation of belief to faith is a close one. "*Fides* is both a mode of knowing *and* the content or object of that knowing, but the emergence of two separate terms from the twelfth century introduced new epistemological possibilities."[123] The word *belief* can be traced back to the old Saxon *ga-lauben*, meaning "to greatly desire or esteem," thus not directly related to God or faith.[124] Ultimately, the Lockean secularization of belief uncoupled it from faith, hermeneutically situating it within a "different semantic field."[125] Belief thus, as we have seen, came to be understood as a weak form of knowledge, while faith became largely "associated with religious piety."[126] This fracturing of belief from faith (particularly alongside this same epistemological shift giving rise to the dominance of left-hemisphere, disembodied abstraction in modernity) opened up a new avenue for the function of belief in human existence: the endorsement of a pseudoreality, a virtuality. In the last chapter, we noted that aesthetic existence does not by default aid an accurate understanding of reality. Potentially, it can serve left-hemisphere sensationalism, thereby endorsing and validating a virtual perception of reality. By contrast, mature aesthetic existence, as a manifestation of the right hemisphere → left hemisphere → right hemisphere progression, has the potential to break out of the self-referential system of left-hemisphere abstraction, to transcend this insularity, and thereby cultivate a healthy understanding of Reality. We are now in a position to elaborate on the implications for belief. In the former (left-hemisphere sensationalism), belief simply fuels pervading virtuality. In the latter (*mature* aesthetic existence), we find a form of believing conducive to faith, which we will briefly consider, before returning to virtuality.

---

123. Ward, *How the Light Gets In*, 248.
124. Ward, *How the Light Gets In*, 248.
125. Ward, *How the Light Gets In*, 253.
126. Ward, *How the Light Gets In*, 250.

Faith: A Commitment to Relational Belief

Essentially, this form of belief is an acknowledgement of reality as a mode of belonging, constituting more than the atomized individual. It is embedded in right-hemisphere relationality. It is "a believing *in*—there is an object, a relation, and an active commitment."[127] Three points clarify the distinctiveness of faith and belief, but also how they work together. First, "religious faith is a specific commitment to belief, to the invisible that pertains to and subtends the visible."[128] By acknowledging the fundamental role belief plays in understanding reality (both visible and invisible), faith is simply an acknowledgement of the way things are: we always *see as*, all knowledge being built on the foundation of belief.

Consequently and secondly, faith is not the embrace a specific type of belief—*religious* belief; it is a commitment to the "primordial disposition to believe. It is not a different type of believing. It is the same disposition framed by and exercised within specific religious practices."[129] This means that aesthetic existence and faith formation are inextricably intertwined. Since faith embraces both the relational disposition of belief, and also the commitment to exercise this disposition through practices, faith is a manifestation of the right hemisphere → left hemisphere → right hemisphere progression. Faith relies on the aesthetic as it feeds our dispositional beliefs through embodied, implicit, and preconscious means (right hemisphere); it also requires explicit articulation (left hemisphere) and a return to embodied practice (right hemisphere) in order to be communicated. "Religious faith, Christian or otherwise, is a practice of belief . . . Belief could not be articulated, would have no content, and therefore remain highly amorphous, if it were not communicated through gestures, images, concepts, narratives etc."[130] Our definition of "religious practices" is highly significant for the relationship between everyday aesthetic existence, faith formation, and ethical action. We will return to this in the next chapter as we discuss aesthetic existence in relation to everyday liturgy. Here we simply need note the integral connection between faith and practice. Aesthetic practices provide the primal orientation of faith (through the process of belief formation) as well as expressing the outworking of faith, which again provides faith orientation in a circular

---

127. Ward, *How the Light Gets In*, 264.
128. Ward, *How the Light Gets In*, 264.
129. Ward, *How the Light Gets In*, 265.
130. Ward, *How the Light Gets In*, 124.

AESTHETIC EXISTENCE AS FUNDAMENTAL IN FAITH FORMATION 179

(but not closed, and not necessarily linear) fashion. "Praxis is both the acting that issues from a believing and the acting that issues in coming to believe."[131]

Third, "if believing is constitutive of knowing *as* and seeing *as*, then religious believing is a mode of perception."[132] Faith is the acknowledgement that Reality lies beyond the realm of certainty. This does not mean that faith is an endorsement of a postmodern epistemological vacuum. "Faith is not . . . some intellectual suicide leaping into the void, but an intellectual and affective, somatic engagement with the invisible in the visible."[133] As both a relational commitment to the Other, and the concomitant mystery which this entails, "religious believing is a way of responding to the world that recognizes and valorizes the invisible operative within what is materially visible of that world."[134] But comprehending this invisibility demands interpretation; rightly *seeing as* requires discernment. Religious believing, as a mode of perception, demands a "reading" of the world—a reading of the world that functions on both a conscious and unconscious level. It is a reading that is less about comprehensive and systematic control of abstract epistemology and more about a relational orientation, a commitment to believing *in*, fueled by implicit and intuitive perception of the visible. It is a "reading" that is inextricably bound up within aesthetic experience, an attunement of the senses, to which we will shortly return.

Virtuality: "Belief" Fueled by Aesthetic Sensationalism

We have already discussed the problem of virtuality, through the work of McGilchrist, as left-hemisphere hegemony of aesthetic existence in the form of sensationalism. We have also seen, through Ward's work, how virtuality applies to belief: Ward recovers the visceral and aesthetic nature of belief, but in the contemporary world belief as visceral and aesthetic is disconnected from meaning, devoid of any connection to reality. In contrast to faith, virtuality is the condition of Lockean belief once the illusion of certainty has been destroyed, as is the case in postmodern epistemology. Rather than faith as relational commitment to belief *in*,

---

131. Ward, *How the Light Gets In*, 276.
132. Ward, *How the Light Gets In*, 265.
133. Ward, *How the Light Gets In*, 226.
134. Ward, *How the Light Gets In*, 266.

it is an artifact of Lockean belief *that*, adrift amid simulacra. It "lacks an object, relation, or commitment. It is a passive residual state when the gods have fled and in their place is a profound distrust in what one is told to be certain."[135] The embodied and affective nature of belief is co-opted in service of a visceral commitment to a brand. "Nominalism becomes rampant as signs and logos, image and icon are increasingly detached from material entities and take on an independent life."[136] The loss of a necessary connection to the real creates a pervading confusion about what to believe amid the plethora of sensationalist aesthetic stimuli bombarding our imagination. It is a "mediatization of the real" creating confusion around

> what to believe—in Christ, the saviour of the world, or the anti-ageing properties of a new cosmetic mousse—because although believing is an embodied cognitive process, an anthropological a priori, in cultures that prize high levels of self-consciousness and therefore awareness of embodied cognitive processes, believing can be manufactured, consciously so. Advertising is only one of the blatant forms of making a belief believable. Ours is an age of galloping dematerialization. Virtual realities proliferate. They are not just on our desktops, our TV screens, our movie DVDs, and our theme-parks, demanding our interactive involvement. They populate our high streets where company logos (Starbucks, Nike, Virgin, etc.) float free of the goods they brand.[137]

Belief is hijacked by a commoditized world, subject to the market forces of consumerism. In a powerful distortion of Lockean belief as a weak

---

135. Ward, *How the Light Gets In*, 264.

136. While offering a detailed account of the rise of nominalism, Ward suggests that the main point here is not plotting the rise and history of the concept (as has become popular recently), but the implications it has for our understanding of reality. Ward shows that it has become "intellectually fashionable to examine the genealogy of this nominalism as a causal force in a narrative of the decline in Christian orthodoxy," and that, "Frequently, critics of these narratives of decline, this eclipse of sacramental realism where signs participate in their materialities they signify and God's communicative relations, argue that they are exercises in nostalgia; haunted by a theological desire to return to and re-establish the pre-Ockhamite ontology upon the basis of which theological knowledge and ethics can once more flourish." But through the work of de Certeau, Ward shows that the origin of this decline stems right back to the ascension, to the loss of the "historical body of Jesus," and the subsequent *mediated* "dissemination of the *Logos*" (Ward, *How the Light Gets In*, 267).

137. Ward, *How the Light Gets In*, 281.

form of knowledge, our world is saturated by these "aestheticized knowledges," all working on our imaginations—sensory rhetoric persuading our "belief."[138]

Here, in the context of our discussion of faith formation, and with particular relevance to the aesthetics of discipleship, we can note two particular implications: First, this distinction between faith and virtuality, as two forms of belief, does *not* mirror the practice of belief in sacred-versus-secular environments. In other words, "religious" belief, or at least that which is perceived as religious belief, is not immune to a nominalist worldview and the consequent commodification of belief amid virtuality. In fact, quite the reverse holds true. It is precisely in religious contexts, and distorted manifestations of Christendom, where this virtuality can be most potent, since it operates by subtle, implicit, and preconscious means under the guise of religion, albeit an artificial, self-serving distortion of it. If what is called religious practice becomes less about acknowledging the Other and more about the creation of a left-hemisphere, self-referential system of signs that produces certainty (a virtual reality), then the so-called religious Other, or the god made in one's own image, becomes as much a commodity, a simulacrum floating free from reality as Nike, whether god or brand. The question then follows as to whether aesthetic experience in this religious context (whether manifest, for instance, as rationalized liturgy, the rapture of a Christian worship concert, or ecstatic euphoria serving the prosperity gospel) should be understood as virtual sensationalism rather than an expression of faith. Second, and consequent to this, we need to probe the inverse: if virtuality is not by default excluded from institutional religion, then genuine faith too can and will be both formed and expressed outside the walls of a church and the overt sacred practices embodied therein. In short, everyday aesthetic existence can serve either virtuality or faith formation.

Everyday Aesthetic Existence as Discipleship

"Believing matters; right believing matters even more. And both the access to and the formation of that right believing for Christians is discipleship."[139] It is this "access to" and "formation of" belief that we

---

138. Ward, *How the Light Gets In*, 282.
139. Ward, *How the Light Gets In*, 284.

have been exploring in an effort to clarify the role of everyday aesthetic existence in discipleship. We have found that at the heart of this is the imagination, the human ability to *see as*, which is impacted by embodied and affective experience through implicit and intuitive means.

The world as we make sense of it, the way we *see as*, is imaginatively mediated to us through sensory engagement with reality. Arguably then, the aesthetic is the most potent force in this formation, working on our imaginations consciously and unconsciously, implicitly and explicitly.[140] "We exist . . . individually and collectively within streams of presentations that are somatic as well as psychic and so also inseparable from affects, intentions, drives and desires. Individually and collectively we create and transform our worlds out of the operations of this imaginary."[141] Ward is here following in the wake of Benedict Anderson, Cornelius Castoriades, Paul Ricoeur, and Charles Taylor, among others, showing that the imagination is foundational not only to individual formation but to common societal understanding and practices through a social imaginary.[142]

Not only is the imagination fundamentally connected to the sensory, but it is integral to belief, as we have seen. "Imagination is belief in action, projecting and anticipating, receiving and responding."[143] Faith cultivates the imagination such that a relational commitment to the Other is nurtured through embodied and affective practices. This is at times consciously intentional, but the intentionality carried within embodied and affective experience does not need to be consciously processed to be effective, as we have seen. Herein lies the power of the imagination, since it provides a bridge between affect and cognition, the visible and invisible, performing a crucial role in formation and sanctification, to the extent that it provides a *seeing* and concomitant *participation* in christological reality.[144]

In other words, there is a symbiotic, multidirectional relationship between aesthetic existence, the imagination, and faith formation. We noted earlier that aesthetic practices are both outworkings of faith (or virtuality) as well as orienting influences in the formation of faith (or virtuality). Another way to put this would be to say that the way we *see*

---

140. Ward, *Unimaginable*, 114.

141. Ward, *Cultural Transformation and Religious Practice*, 144.

142. Ward, *Cultural Transformation and Religious Practice*, 119–72; Ward, *Unimaginable*, 153–233.

143. Ward, *Unbelievable*, 150.

144. Ward, *How the Light Gets In*, 141.

as, individually and collectively, both is shaped by our aesthetic experience and shapes our aesthetic engagement with the world. This is what Kierkegaard described as the "poeticizing" nature of mature aesthetic existence.

The paradigmatic power of the imagination points not only to the significance of poetic living in faith formation but also to its manifestation as ethical action. Drawing on the work of Paul Ricoeur, Ward shows the inherent connection between the imagination and poiesis.[145] Since social imaginaries are constructions, having no ontological basis in and of themselves, they "are ways of *making* sense, they are forms of *poiesis.*"[146] The implications of this are profound. Admittedly, aesthetic existence as mere sensationalism is effectively only formative in the generation of virtuality (the work of "fancy," in Samuel Coleridge's taxonomy of the imagination). However, poetic living, as a mature form of aesthetic existence, not only plays a significant role in faith formation, but consequently has an ethical *telos*. This is because Ward is here arguing for a connection between poiesis and praxis, thereby acknowledging the role of the imagination in personal and cultural formation and transformation.[147] Ward returns to

> Aristotle's understanding of *poiesis*, for *poiesis* is the name he gives to "making" as in "creating." The noun relates to the verb *poieo*—to produce, perform, execute, compose or, more generally, be active. *Poiesis* is an historically specific operation concerned with creative action. As such, it would constitute one aspect of a theory of action—cultural and moral action—and in this way it is associated with praxis, from the Greek *prasso*, meaning to act, manage, do or accomplish. For Aristotle there appears to have been a distinction between a specific form of making (*poiesis*) and the more general notion of doing and being involved in an activity (*praxis* or *pragma*). *Praxis* would be associated with ethics, politics, and the formation of character. But the distinction between *poiesis* and *praxis* cannot hold strictly; not if we accept what I have outlined about the psychobiology of believing and desiring. So I wish to take *poiesis* in a

---

145. Admittedly, *poiesis* is a theologically loaded term used in quite diverse ways. Here we employ it as Ward expounds it in what follows.

146. Ward, *Christ and Culture*, 129–30.

147. Ward, *Cultural Transformation and Religious Practice*, 141.

complex sense that would not isolate aesthetic production from political and ethical activity.[148]

It is mature everyday aesthetic existence, as poiesis, which draws one outside of the virtuality of the atomized individual into relationship with the Other, thereby cultivating a participation in reality and consequent ethical action. It is poetic faith, as Coleridge notes, as "transcendence that . . . has both theological and ethical significance; we will be shaken from our 'selfish solitude'. The constitution of this poetic faith is transformative. Belief is not only given expression, it is created."[149]

As we have previously noted, the ability of the arts to draw us outside of ourselves, to transcend our own virtual realities and point toward the divine, are commonly noted contributions to faith formation within the field of theological aesthetics. But our focus here is *everyday* aesthetic existence. Yes, this includes the profound sensory encounters with the Other through awe-inspiring music, dance, or visual art, for example, but a particular focus here is also the aesthetic (as we have broadly defined it) amid ordinary experiences of play, food, friendship, and daily engagement with the popular arts. While the formative nature of everyday aesthetic existence may be less explicit, as we have already seen, the implicit is also operative as poiesis, *making* sense, building belief. An experience of playing with one's children or sharing a walk with a friend, for example, may not be explicitly or consciously an experience of absolute transcendence, but these experiences of everyday transcendence nevertheless have the potential to draw us out of ourselves and into relation with the other, *making* sense of the world implicitly and intuitively, through our embodied participation in this-worldly reality. These everyday moments of aesthetic existence are then both productive in the formation of belief and also themselves the very outworking of that belief.

The organic, nonlinear, "feedback-and-feedforward-looping" nature of this belief formation and expression speaks to a key point in understanding the role of aesthetic existence in discipleship. It is formation through *living*, through everyday aesthetic *existence*. It is precisely in this embodied, analogical *participation* in this-wordly reality that faith formation occurs. It is not primarily the product of an abstract, linear

---

148. Ward, *Unbelievable*, 146 (italics added); see also Ward, *Cultural Transformation and Religious Practice*, 6–8.

149. Ward, *Unbelievable*, 136.

process dominated by ratiocination.¹⁵⁰ If Bonhoeffer helped us to appreciate the christological validity of celebrating aesthetic existence, Ward makes it clear that the *living* of aesthetic existence is not only a right response theologically, but it is also a significant component of the formation of faith. In other words, as we have noted, the embrace of aesthetic existence is not only the consequence *of* faith, it is formative *for* faith. Mature aesthetic existence as poiesis is the creation not only of art, play, friendship, and so forth, but thereby, of a world, an embodied way of being *in* the world, of *seeing* the world—which celebrates and participates in christological reality. Such existence is a mode of discipleship, an incarnational *mimesis*, that sacramentally participates in the divine through embodied reality.

> One can see the form of God not only in the works of human beings—the music of Mozart, the paintings of Christ-clowns by Rouault—but in the style of the lives of those who have given themselves over to imitating him. The life of Elizabeth of Dijon 'became a sacrament' . . . the track of her becoming, her vocation, announces a doctrine, a teaching, carved out in, through and upon her body.¹⁵¹

Ward draws attention to the "complex character of *mimesis*" through the work of Aristotle, for whom art "does not strictly mirror what is but imitates what should be or will be," therefore mediating "between presentation, representation and absence."¹⁵² By extension then, we could say that aesthetic existence has the potential to engage one in a way of being and relating that offers a window onto the way things should be, thereby reframing reality and forming faith.

Discerning Mature Aesthetic Existence: Embodied Attunement

The vital question, which we have been following as a thread throughout, is how we distinguish between mature aesthetic existence (forming faith) and sensationalist aesthetic existence (forming virtuality). Ward

---

150. Again, this is not to deny the crucial role that abstract theorization plays in faith formation, as in systematic theology for example. But as Ward shows, such abstraction needs to always occur within the context of embodied existence, as an "embedded" and "engaged" theology, which is at the heart of Ward, *How the Light Gets In*.

151. Ward, *Christ and Culture*, 203.

152. Ward, *Christ and Culture*, 32–33.

contributes to this through his description of discernment and its connection to an embodied "reading" of the world. The process of coming to believe is itself a process of discernment, as the verb *credo* historically would have been understood (the way in which Anselm used it, for example, as in *credo ut intelligam*).[153] This discernment process of coming to believe takes place amid what Charles Taylor describes as the "immanent frame," which is "the sensed context in which we develop our beliefs."[154] Not only does the discernment process take place within the immanent frame, but beliefs themselves "are (and have) lived conditions for the possibility or impossibility of certain imaginative experiences of the world. 'All beliefs are held within a context or framework of the taken-for-granted.'"[155]

Because this framework operates in the preconscious world of the taken-for-granted, carefully evaluating one's belief solely through logical analysis is not sufficient for discerning right belief. Rather, discernment is a matter of holistic "reading," specifically learning how to "read well."[156] All creatures having consciousness (from plants to human beings) must "read" their environment, reading the "signs, signals and communicative relations" that surround them and respond or adapt appropriately in order to live.[157] This reading is "not simply a matter of consciousness; the reading goes on at emotional and somatic levels not lit by consciousness."[158] Embodied reading as discerning is thus a fundamental aspect of being human, a prerequisite for mental and physical well-being. Discernment "is an aspect of what neuroscientists call the 'cognitive imperative': the demand made by the brain to make order, to search for causes, and to question."[159] It is the "seeking" in Anselm's "faith seeking understanding."[160] In other words, discernment is a process inextricably bound up within embodied living; faith formed, and the truth being "learned as it is lived. That is the beating pulse of Christian discipleship. As it is learned so there must be a deepening of discernment,

---

153. Ward, *How the Light Gets In*, 242.
154. Ward, *How the Light Gets In*, 124.
155. Ward, *How the Light Gets In*, 134.
156. Ward, *How the Light Gets In*, 237.
157. Ward, *How the Light Gets In*, 237.
158. Ward, *How the Light Gets In*, 237.
159. Ward, *How the Light Gets In*, 237.
160. Ward, *How the Light Gets In*, 237.

a continual reading of the world in the light of Christ and by the breath of the Spirit."[161] Such a process of discernment is a form of prayer—the process of bringing Christ to the world and the world to Christ—an act of faith seeking understanding, engaging "all those human facilities which enable any understanding: sensory perception, emotional experience, imagination, intuition, will, memory, reasoning etc."[162]

Ward explores this prayerful form of sensory discernment through comparing radical embodiment in sports and the embrace of "radical incarnation."[163] An athlete's experience of entering "the zone" is a place of deeply attuned embodiment, "pushing beyond left hemisphere knowledge to right hemisphere instinct," the consequence not primarily of determination or willpower but of disciplined practice.[164] "One enters one's body more deeply; eased into it such that there is a new level of relaxation and composure."[165] It is an experience often described as transcendence.[166] This radical embodiment of the sportsperson or dancer is akin to the experience of "radical incarnation—that immersion into the very depths of the material and the particular, in Christ, in order to 'hear', 'recognise' (these are both metaphors, you understand) the groaning of all creation for its creator."[167] Such "radical incarnation" results in a perception of reality that is not merely known; it is lived.

The consequence is that the aesthetic category of "'fittingness' or 'attunement' of the body is a possible entry into a deeper form of the ethical," which Ward names "ethical life."[168] Fundamentally this is so, because, as an incarnational expression of faith, such prayerful "attunement" exposes participation in christological reality for what it is—"the immersion of the world in Christ."[169] "Prayer is not the means of tran-

---

161. Ward, *How the Light Gets In*, 213.
162. Ward, *How the Light Gets In*, 213.
163. Ward, "Sport and Incarnational Theology."
164. Ward, "Sport and Incarnational Theology," 55.
165. Ward, "Sport and Incarnational Theology," 56.
166. Ward, "Sport and Incarnational Theology," 56. For a discussion on how an encounter with beauty can parallel this transcendent entry into "the zone," see Ward, *Unimaginable*, 120.
167. Ward, "Sport and Incarnational Theology," 52.
168. Ward, "Sport and Incarnational Theology," 51.
169. Ward, "Sport and Incarnational Theology," 63.

scending the material but of entering the materiality of our condition more profoundly."[170]

Discerning mature aesthetic existence then, is a matter of embodied attunement to this-worldly, incarnational life in Christ. "Attunement is both the source and goal of discipleship."[171] Reading our environments is not merely a process of ratiocination but includes intuitively discerning aesthetic "fittingness."[172] Discerning mature aesthetic existence from sensationalist aesthetic existence cannot be solely a conscious process. It is a prayerful engagement, which incorporates the whole being, in an intuitive concern for fittingness, a resonance, or in Bonhoeffer's terms, a harmonic polyphony of christological reality.

Attuned aesthetic existence, as a celebration of christological reality, is therefore liturgical, "where liturgy is not just something that goes on in church, but a way of being church beyond buildings, institutions, lectionaries, and orders of service."[173] In this sense, there is no line to be drawn between liturgy and living.[174] However, poetic living, as a form of liturgy for the Christian, is not only an expression of faith. It is also formative *for* faith, as we have seen. In other words, poetic living is a form of poiesis, not only *making* films, music, fine art, play, or communal meals, but thereby *making* sense of the world, forming belief.[175] Further again, this poiesis, as living, cannot but have an ethical *telos*. Believing, as a relational disposition, as participation in reality, is ethically oriented.[176] If in the living, in the making, the personal imagination and the social imaginary are being shaped and formed, it will have cultural and material effects; it will change the way we act. It is this integration of aesthetic, ethical, and religious life that we need to probe further, our understanding of everyday aesthetic existence as liturgy being central to this exploration.

---

170. Ward, "Sport and Incarnational Theology," 61.

171. Ward, "Sport and Incarnational Theology," 63.

172. *Fittingness* is a term with rich Christian heritage, one that Anselm uses, for example, "in his work *Cur Deus Homo* . . . to describe God's suitable accommodation to the human and created order" (Ward, *How the Light Gets In*, 235).

173. Ward, *How the Light Gets In*, 120.

174. Ward, *How the Light Gets In*, 122.

175. Ward, *How the Light Gets In*, 193.

176. Ward, *Unbelievable*, 148.

6

The Liturgical Orientation of Mature Aesthetic Existence

MATURE AESTHETIC EXISTENCE PLAYS a significant role in a life of discipleship because *all* of such a life is oriented towards worship. *Being* Christian means that aesthetic experience, commitments of faith, and action in the world are interwoven, reciprocally feeding off and into one another, in what we can describe as everyday liturgical life. Just as right belief is not solely intellectual, ethical action is not merely the consequence of measured ratiocination, the imposition of "moral codes, implicit or explicit," but the embrace of "ethical life," a "radical incarnation," an attunement of the body embedded in living.[1] In other words, mature aesthetic existence coheres with ethics and faith in a holistic understanding of being Christian, an embodied life oriented by love and worship of God.

Understanding mature aesthetic existence as liturgical clarifies the connections between aesthetics, faith, and ethics. The lens of liturgy offers two important contributions to the aesthetics of discipleship. First, it elucidates the nature of mature aesthetic existence as a *fitting* expression of Christian living, distinguishing it from potentially deforming modes of aesthetic existence. If there is no line to be drawn between liturgy and Christian living (liturgy thus not limited to activity within the walls of a church), then a liturgical understanding of daily aesthetic engagement becomes a means of ethical discernment, akin to Bonhoeffer's

---

1. Ward, "Sport and Incarnational Theology," 51.

polyphonic living. The litmus question for right Christian living, whether understood religiously, ethically, or aesthetically, is thus fundamentally relational. Mature aesthetic existence has a liturgical orientation, with holistic implications for the direction of desire, service, and worship.

Second, understanding mature aesthetic existence as everyday liturgy underscores the observation that aesthetic engagement is inextricably bound up with both faith formation and ethical action. The aesthetic category of poiesis is not separate and distinct from the ethical category of praxis. On the one hand, "praxis is both the acting that issues from a believing and the acting that issues in coming to believe."[2] On the other, poiesis, as aesthetic engagement in the world (*making* music, dance, a meal, play), also, at the same time, plays a role in *making* sense of the world, forming belief. Aesthetic engagement in the world is best understood then as both praxis and poiesis. Aesthetic practices contribute not only to faith formation but also to the formation of ethical categories and ultimate action. In short, aesthetic practices have ethical consequences. Here, a liturgical understanding of aesthetic existence clarifies this relationship, particularly when framing it within the relational and ethical context of social practices.[3]

In this chapter then, drawing on the work of Nicholas Wolterstorff, the argument is that, on the one hand, liturgy is embedded in a socially constructed "script," while on the other, aesthetics, too, is best understood in the context of social practice (rejecting the modern narrative of aesthetics as disinterested contemplation). By bringing both of these paradigms together, a liturgical approach to aesthetic existence foregrounds not only its formative contribution but also the inseparable relationship between aesthetic experience, faith formation, and ethical action, which collectively function as a *fitting* expression of shalom.

---

2. Ward, *How the Light Gets In*, 276.

3. As mentioned in the introductory chapter, three interrelated theoretical models inform our discussion as whole, but undergird this chapter in particular, and our understanding of "practice" and "social practice." Firstly, *practice theory*, as delineated by the likes of Pierre Bourdieu, which highlights the formative role of practice, accentuated through *habitus* and the shaping of culture by practice. Second, the related theory of *social practice*, as developed by Alasdair MacIntyre, which highlights the normative nature of "socially established cooperative human activity" toward a specific *telos*. And finally, the interrelated conceptualization of a *social imaginary*, as expressed by Charles Taylor and others. While this chapter will at times stretch the strict boundaries of these models, they offer the foundation for the trajectory of the argument. Bourdieu, *The Logic of Practice*; MacIntyre, *After Virtue*, 187; Taylor, *Modern Social Imaginaries*.

Christian Action as Liturgy

The concept of liturgy with which we are working is not limited to that which takes place within ecclesial "buildings, institutions, lectionaries, and orders of service."[4] Rather, we are considering liturgy as a way of being; marking the entire gamut of Christian living. Simply, Christian action is liturgical.[5] We will delineate a definition of *liturgy* shortly, but before we do so, it will be helpful to outline the essence of Ward's argument for understanding Christian action as liturgy.

Ward turns to Aristotle's use of *leitourgia* (from which we derive "liturgy") as a helpful starting point. Aristotle engages the term in his *Nicomachean Ethics,* wherein he considers the ethics of an action (*praxis*). Significantly, here ethics is not divorced from aesthetics, the Greek "*to kalon*" being equally "the Good" and "the Beautiful."[6] In this context, and in keeping with the etymology of the term (*litos ergos* literally being the "work of the people" or "public service"), Aristotle's use of *leitourgia* is employed in both a narrow sense as "a technical political term for a service rendered to the city or state," but also more broadly and "nontechnically to refer to any act of service."[7] Aristotle's use of *leitourgia* thus points to two significant observations regarding this early use of the term. First, a close relationship exists between action and liturgical practice. Second, and consequently, describing *leitourgia* as *to kalon* brings together both ethics and aesthetics in the liturgical act.

Understood through this lens, Christian liturgy, as an act of service, *relationally* orients action, since it is a proclamation of that to which one is committed. Liturgy so construed is the embodied and active extension of belief, as a relational disposition, the expression of a commitment of trust. The Catholic catechism describes liturgy as God's people participating in the *work* of God.[8] It is therefore fundamentally active. If, "to swim is a verb [and] swimmer is the noun [then] liturgy is a verb, Church (plural) or Christian (singular) is the noun."[9] Liturgy is thus simply the active life of the Christian, Aidan Kavanagh describing liturgy as "doing

---

4. Ward, *How the Light Gets In*, 120.
5. Ward, *The Politics of Discipleship*, 181–220.
6. Ward, *The Politics of Discipleship*, 182.
7. Ward, *The Politics of Discipleship*, 183.
8. Fagerberg, "Liturgical Theology," 10.
9. Fagerberg, "Liturgical Theology," 9.

the world as the world was meant to be done."[10] In this sense, as the active extension of the relational disposition of belief, liturgy as a Christian act of service cannot be confined within the walls of a church but needs to be understood within the relational context of being Christian, *being in Christ*. The Christian act can thus only be understood in light of the church being the body of Christ. So construed, worship is the "life of the church, the public act which eternally actualizes the nature of the Church as the Body of Christ."[11] Action here is bound up within a relational ontology, which

> is summed up in Christ's words to his disciples: "he dwells in me, and I in him" (John 6:56 KJV). This statement can be taken as axiomatic for an account of a Christian act. In this act, therefore, we are not dealing with an autonomous subject who, in full knowledge of the facts of a situation, acts consciously in and for himself or herself. In the conception of a Christian praxis, there is no room for such a modern notion of self-sufficiency... In fact, what characterizes this Christian agent is a surrender, a sacrifice, in which he or she is bound by what Augustine calls a "*vinculum caritatis*" [bond of love].[12]

Christian action, then, is not merely the *consequence* of this relational orientation, discipleship is "not simply following the example of Christ; it is formation *within* Christ, so that we become Christlike. And the context of this formation is the church in all its concrete locatedness and eschatological significance."[13] This formation takes place in the concrete everyday, all action, including aesthetic engagement, indicative of a relational commitment. "Interrelationality," therefore, is fundamental to the becoming of the Christian self, actions an expression of this. "The Christian embodied agent always lives beyond himself or herself in and toward other bodies (the eucharistic body, the ecclesial body, social bodies of various kinds, the civic body, and the body of Christ)."[14] In this sense, action should not be seen, first and foremost, through the lens of utility, but through the relational lens of participation. Rather than the I-It modern transaction of the self with material existence (leading to

---

10. As quoted in Fagerberg, "Liturgical Theology," 15.
11. Schmemann, *Introduction to Liturgical Theology*, 12.
12. Ward, *The Politics of Discipleship*, 184.
13. Ward, *The Politics of Discipleship*, 184 (italics added).
14. Ward, *The Politics of Discipleship*, 190.

aestheticism), an I-Thou orientation to embodied existence celebrates mature aesthetic existence as integral to discipleship. Here, we can recall Augustine's distinction between "use" and "enjoyment," and his argument that enjoyment has "a higher theological purpose: to enjoy a thing is to participate in the worship of God. God must be enjoyed; he cannot be used."[15] A liturgical understanding of Christian action is thus not oriented by utility but by enjoyment of "the goodness, beauty, justice and truth of God," thereby uniting faith, ethics, and aesthetics.[16]

In other words, rather than create categories of action such as "teaching, commanding, obeying, entertaining," or aesthetic enjoyment for that matter, "because all Christian action participates in the economy of love, all action becomes liturgical."[17] All Christian action, oriented by love of God is doxological; it is a proclamation of worship and ultimate allegiance.[18] Doxology thus understood is "much more than a moment in a service of worship; it is, or should be, the Christian's everyday mode of being-in-time."[19] Resonating with Alexander Schmemann's liturgical approach to a sacramental understanding of all of life, Graham Ward suggests that the aesthetic and ethical natures of the Christian act cohere, and are inseparable when located in the common *telos* of life in Christ.[20] All believers are priests, all Christian actions sacraments, the objective of which "is to articulate what is just, good, beautiful, and true," thus incarnationally participating "in the unfolding of God's grace."[21]

For the aesthetics of discipleship, this means that first, mature aesthetic existence is a right response, a doxological response to being in Christ. To use an aesthetic category, there is a fittingness to such a response. However, as is illustrated through the Greek term *to kalon*, such fittingness is as much ethical as it is aesthetic. Ethical action is equally a fitting response, and the modern notion of severing the two categories points to a failure to understand the relational and participatory nature of discipleship, the liturgical nature of *all* Christian living.

15. Ward, *The Politics of Discipleship*, 195.
16. Ward, *The Politics of Discipleship*, 195.
17. Ward, *The Politics of Discipleship*, 190.
18. Ward, *The Politics of Discipleship*, 190.
19. Vanhoozer, "Praising in Song," 118.
20. Schmemann, *For the Life of the World*. This liturgical approach to all of life has a rich history in the tradition, going right back to the church fathers, as shown by von Balthasar's treatment of Maximus the Confessor in *Cosmic Liturgy*.
21. Ward, *The Politics of Discipleship*, 195.

Second, a liturgical understanding clarifies that in their mutual coherence, aesthetic existence and ethical action are not only right responses to faith, but they are also formative for faith. It is in the midst of Christian action, as liturgy, that faith is formed. The implication here is that the liturgical nature of Christian actions should be understood as practices (in the sense of contributing to a *habitus*), along with the social, historical, and cultural contexts that inform them. In sum, Christian action as liturgy is not only a fitting doxological expression of discipleship, but operates as formative practice, thereby itself playing a role in becoming Christian. In order to elaborate on this claim, it is helpful to turn to the work of Nicholas Wolterstorff.

Liturgical Existence as Practice

Wolterstorff may seem worlds away from Ward, since they are operating from distinctly different theological traditions, but this is precisely the richness of bringing their perspectives of liturgy and aesthetics into dialogue with one another.[22] Wolterstorff himself models the value of engaging diverse interlocutors, acknowledging that one of the primary influences on his own work regarding liturgy is the Orthodox theologian Alexander Schmemann.[23]

Before turning to Wolterstorff's philosophical analysis of both liturgy and aesthetics, we need to briefly acknowledge the foundation from which Wolterstorff is working—his epistemological grounding of belief in "entitlement" (as opposed to rationality) fundamentally connecting faith with responsible action.[24] Wolterstorff argues for the pretheoretical

---

22. There is commonality too. Epistemologically, for instance, both are responding to the vacuum left by the demise of modern logical positivism, seeking a recovery of the metaphysical. Both acknowledge the limits of Enlightenment rationality in this enterprise, "belief" for neither limited to the realm of objective certainty characteristic of "classical foundationalism" (to use Wolterstorff's phrase). The paths that they have taken in response are clearly different, Wolterstorff and Plantinga's articulation of Reformed epistemology certainly distinct from Ward and Radical Orthodoxy's postmodern Augustinian epistemology. Yet, as Smith notes, while "these different schools of thought are not often associated . . . these tensions represent a kind of sibling rivalry," Smith's work itself functioning as something of a bridge between the two worlds. Smith, *Thinking in Tongues*, 109.

23. Wolterstorff, *Acting Liturgically*, 6n12.

24. While Wolterstorff concedes that there is merit in approaching belief from the perspective of both rationality and "warrant" (Alvin Plantinga's project), he argues

nature of founding "control beliefs," which are not consciously and rationally reflected upon.[25] Belief is intimately tied to practice. Specifically, Wolterstorff highlights the significance of "practices of inquiry," the formation of belief embedded in social practice.[26] Since beliefs are not simply the consequence of ratiocination, Wolterstorff acknowledges the existence of "immediate beliefs" (or "basic beliefs," as Plantinga names the concept), those beliefs that are held "immediately," not on the propositional basis of "reasons for."[27] There is a clear parallel here between Wolterstorff's description of "immediate beliefs" and Ward's articulation of belief as a partly preconscious disposition, even if they resolve the observation in different ways. For our purposes, the important point to note is the mutual grounding of belief in practice. While we will be limiting our engagement with Wolterstorff to his articulation of liturgy and aesthetics, as mutually framed by social practice, it is worth noting the epistemological weight of practice that underlies Wolterstorff's larger project.

Wolterstorff will help us to test the argument that mature aesthetic existence is best understood as liturgical, thereby integrating faith with aesthetics and ethics, through a doxological orientation of embodied action. If such a claim is valid, then the implications are that mature aesthetic existence has a circular relationship with faith formation and ethical action. Mature aesthetic existence is both an *expression* of worship (it is a fitting celebration of being Christian, a polyphonic embrace of this-worldly, christological reality) and also *formative* for becoming Christian. Approaching aesthetic existence through the lens of this liturgical cycle (expression-formation-expression-formation and so forth) highlights not only the formative and celebratory aspects of mature aesthetic existence but consequently that faithful aesthetic practices have ethical consequences.

---

that human beings largely do not subscribe to a belief on the basis of a rational decision, and yet we hold people responsible for what they believe. The reason people are held responsible for their beliefs is founded not in the rational, volitional basis of the particular belief (as one might expect), but rather in the belief's genesis being located in social practice. Wolterstorff, *Practices of Belief*, 6–7, 62–117.

25. Wolterstorff, *Reason within the Bounds of Religion*.

26. Wolterstorff, *Practices of Belief*, 7.

27. Importantly, even though "immediate beliefs" are not held on the basis of ratiocination, this does not make such belief irrational. In fact, the possibility exists that immediate beliefs, including religious belief, can be explored rationally and be shown to be cogent. Wolterstorff, *Practices of Belief*, 338–41.

Wolterstorff's Model: Liturgy as Performative

We need to note at the outset that Wolterstorff understands *liturgy* in the strict sense, as the doxological actions performed by a community of Christians gathered to worship on a Sunday. While he is not closed to extending the term "analogically" to actions in the broader life of the world, his treatment is in the context of this narrow sense.[28] By contrast, for our purposes, we are approaching liturgy in the extended sense, understanding mature everyday aesthetic existence as liturgical. However, despite these differing parameters, the argument here is that the principles of Wolterstorff's analysis remain valid for an extended understanding of liturgy, a point that will be clarified as the argument unfolds.

Wolterstorff's unique analysis of liturgy stems from his pioneering philosophical dissection of the performative nature of liturgy. While much theological work has been done over the centuries regarding both the expressive and formative aspects of liturgy, liturgy has not been explored through the lens of analytic philosophy, particularly as a performative act.[29] Wolterstorff's focus is on the enactment itself, on "what is done," his argument being that by looking closely at this performative dimension, light will be shed on both the expressive and formative aspects of liturgy.[30] His approach is thus particularly relevant to understanding the connections between liturgy and the aesthetics of discipleship because it is not ratiocentric; he is exploring what is going on in the liturgical action itself rather than that which can be distilled from it to rational proposition. It is for this reason that Wolterstorff specifically chooses to focus on Orthodox liturgy for his analysis, since "unlike the liturgies of the West, the Orthodox liturgy has never been subjected to what one might call 'rationalization.' In Western liturgies the thought has been simplified, the language clarified, complexity reduced, hyperbole diminished, metaphors eliminated. The Orthodox liturgy is prolix, poetic, excessive, wild, hyperbolic, highly metaphorical, complex, often obscure, much of it clearly the production of poets rather than theologians."[31]

---

28. Wolterstorff, *Acting Liturgically*, 11.
29. Wolterstorff, *Acting Liturgically*, 5.
30. Wolterstorff, *Acting Liturgically*, 5.
31. Wolterstorff, *Acting Liturgically*, 9.

Liturgy Is "Scripted" Activity

At the heart of Wolterstorff's dissection of liturgical enactment is his observation that liturgy is a form of "scripted" activity. He argues this by first noting that there is a distinction between types of acts and instances of acts. Or, in philosophical terminology, there are act-types and act-tokens.[32] Act-types can recur; they are universals.[33] Wolterstorff suggests that liturgy is best understood as a sequence of act-types. In other words, liturgy is not the random expression of worship. Rather, an instance of worship is liturgical when it conforms to the sequence of act-types prescribed as universal. Wolterstorff names this the "script"; scripted activity being a type "of activity for which there are prescriptions in force."[34]

To clarify what this means, it is helpful to consider other types of scripted activity. Liturgy is only one "species" within the "genus" of scripted activity.[35] Wolterstorff considers two examples: American football and music.[36] In American football, plays are conducted according to a playbook. If a quarterback calls play number 9, there is a script prescribed for the sequence of actions to be accordingly followed. Play number 9 can be executed correctly or incorrectly. However, this does not mean that every instance of play number 9 is identical. There are instances of play number 9 that are better and worse, but that are not necessarily correct or incorrect. Likewise, a musical performance follows a script. The most obvious manifestation of the script is the score.

However, the key point of relevance for us is that the script is not *merely* the score or the playbook. Wolterstorff is stretching the term "script" beyond "instructions written down in words" or diagrams or musical notations for that matter.[37] In fact, as we will see, the most determinative aspects of the script are exactly those that cannot be so articulated. The playbook cannot possibly articulate every aspect of every action that is to be performed in the play within the diagrams or words that constitute it. In addition to the rational articulation of the

---

32. Wolterstorff, *Acting Liturgically*, 13.

33. Strictly, it is not accurate to say that *all* act-types are universals, as Wolterstorff explains, but for our purposes, as the concept applies to liturgy, it is sufficient to treat them as such. Wolterstorff, *Acting Liturgically*, 13.

34. Wolterstorff, *Acting Liturgically*, 14.

35. Wolterstorff, *Acting Liturgically*, 18.

36. Wolterstorff, *Acting Liturgically*, 14–18.

37. Wolterstorff, *Acting Liturgically*, 17.

playbook, *a history of practice* contributes to the script. All of the athletic components—running, catching, tackling, throwing, and so forth—have a history of embodied practice through which appropriate action is prescribed. Partly this can be (and is) articulated through technique (hence, coaching), but partly this transcends cognitive expression and is learned via embodied practice, immediate sensory fittingness, attunement, or experiences of "being in the zone," manifest in terms such as "muscle memory," entrenching what has been named "automaticities."[38] We could say then, that apart from the prescriptions specified in the playbook, the script for the particular play also draws upon prescriptions specified through embodied practice, and further, as Wolterstorff highlights, the meaning communally attributed through social practice. In music, for instance, "The script for a musical performance is the total set of prescriptions holding for that performance, both those specified in the score and those embedded within the relevant social practice."[39] Beyond the score, the social practice of violin playing, or conducting, for example, emerge from the social practice of the particular society. This holds true also for organically composed music such as jazz, which may not be operating from a score but nevertheless submits to the script of what constitutes a jazz performance.

Since social practices contribute to the scripting, the script that informs liturgical action is not shaped simply by explicit and direct means but also through the implicit and indirect. Evidence of this lies in the reality that no liturgy is explicitly composed from scratch. Rather, since the birth of the early church, liturgy has emerged from, and contains, implicit belief.[40] Liturgy, even understood in the narrow sense of congregational enactment in a worship service, is formed not only by the dynamics of the specific congregation and its religious tradition but also by society more generally.[41] Here we should recall that it is in *living*, through embodied, aesthetic, relational interaction with the world, that imaginative paradigms are formed through which we see the world. Again, we should recall that these imaginative paradigms do not operate solely or even primarily on an individual level, but they are communal: they are social imaginaries. These social imaginaries inform the nature of social

---

38. Smith, *Desiring the Kingdom*, 80–82.
39. Wolterstorff, *Acting Liturgically*, 17.
40. Wolterstorff, *The God We Worship*, 12–13.
41. Wolterstorff, *Acting Liturgically*, 20.

practices that become normative for scripted action. The implication of this progression is that aesthetic engagement not only is an aspect of liturgical enactment itself but also contributes to the script that determines liturgical action.

Liturgical Activity Has "Count as Significance"

If liturgical enactment belongs to the genus of scripted activity (along with many other scripted activities), it is specifically to be identified within this genus with those activities that have *count as* significance.[42] In other words, it is an activity performed not for the sake of itself, like an American football game, but for the significance it holds beyond the act itself. Speech-act theory has illuminated the reality that in human life one act can *count as* another. For instance, raising one's hand at an auction *counts as* making a bid. Within the liturgical script of a worship service, being sprinkled with water, or immersed in water, or raising one's hands, or eating bread and wine, are not merely acts in themselves, they have *count as* significance. The critical question for us is whether it is possible for this *count as* significance to extend to actions beyond the context of a worship service, into the actions of everyday life. This depends on the script that informs those actions (assuming a script does inform those actions; not all action, of course, is scripted). We will return to this momentarily, but before we can do so, we need to note a second specific attribute of liturgical enactment.

Liturgical Activity Is for Direct Engagement with God

If liturgical enactment falls within the genus of scripted activity, and is further, specifically categorized by actions of *count as* significance, then the particular species of liturgy is uniquely marked by being *for* direct engagement with God.[43] "When we orient ourselves toward God by enacting a liturgy we engage God directly and explicitly. When we kneel, there is no creature before whom we are kneeling; we are kneeling before God. When we stand with hands upraised, there is no creature before

---

42. Wolterstorff, *Acting Liturgically*, 24.
43. Wolterstorff, *Acting Liturgically*, 26.

whom we are standing with hands upraised; we are standing with hands upraised before God."⁴⁴

Wolterstorff suggests that by understanding liturgy according to these criteria, staring in awe at the "starry heavens" is not a liturgical act, since it is mediated. The object of attention here is the stars, not God—the potential worship of God being indirect and implicit in this act. Similarly, in relating to fellow human beings as bearers of God's image, while these interactions may point toward the wonder of God, the engagement here, again, is indirect and implicit; directly and explicitly, the object of action is one's fellow human being.⁴⁵

In sum, Wolterstorff identifies liturgy as a sequence of act-types that conforms to a script, but specifically scripted activity that has *count as* significance, and which is for direct engagement with God.

Applying the Model: Liturgy as Lived in the Everyday

Wolterstorff's articulation of liturgical action not only is helpful for understanding the fundamentally embodied nature of a strict sense of liturgy but also is insightful for understanding mature, everyday aesthetic existence as liturgical. However, the applicability of extending Wolterstorff's model to action in all of life rests on two criteria: first, whether such action can carry *count as* significance, and second, whether such action can be construed as direct engagement with God. On both counts, particularly the second, Wolterstorff suggests that extending a liturgical understanding to action in all of life is untenable. Nevertheless, by taking a closer look at these criteria it is evident that excluding everyday aesthetic existence from liturgical enactment is not only an unnecessary move, but to the contrary, these qualifications are useful for defining the boundaries within which *mature* aesthetic existence *can* be understood as liturgical.

Aesthetic Existence as Direct Engagement with God

While delineating liturgy as being *for* direct engagement with God is a helpful contribution to our quest, Wolterstorff's application of the notion is reductionist, thereby unnecessarily eliminating everyday

44. Wolterstorff, *Acting Liturgically*, 27.
45. Wolterstorff, *Acting Liturgically*, 27.

aesthetic enactment from the realm of the liturgical. We need to qualify Wolterstorff's criteria here by noting that "direct" engagement with God is: first, always mediated; second, never purely direct and explicit; and consequently, third, best understood not as a binary, but on a continuum. Simply, in an effort to articulate an argument that is analytically neat, care needs to be taken to allow for the complex and organic nature of human existence, lest artificial dichotomies are created that do not accurately reflect an embodied life of faith.

In fairness, by "direct" engagement with God, Wolterstorff is not suggesting that liturgical engagement with God is *not* mediated through our sensory engagement with material reality, only that God is here the primary object of our attention. Nevertheless, it is important to note that since all engagement with God is mediated due to our finite nature, in a strict sense, engagement with God cannot be purely "direct." As we noted earlier, "the mystery of the ultimate is glimpsed not grasped, for it is always mediated in the penultimate polyphony of life."[46] Hence, we need note the fundamentally sensory nature of even a strict sense of liturgy, mediated through material engagement with the bread and wine, vocal cords and sound waves, water and oil. Wolterstorff's point is that the object of attention here is not the oil or the water or the wine, but God. Or, to put it differently, this is not a mode of immature aesthetic existence, or sensory immediacy, being lost in the moment of aesthetic experience, purely for the moment, but *for* direct engagement with God. But framing it in this way is reductionist. It is precisely the embodied nature of this engagement that makes it meaningful, being present in the moment of *tasting* the wine, *feeling* the water, *smelling* the oil. As we have seen, Kierkegaard describes this as immediacy that is characteristic of faith, a second immediacy, or an immediacy after reflection; being present in the moment, but the sensory moment carrying significance beyond itself. The implication here is that in speaking of "direct" engagement with God, we need to acknowledge not only the necessarily mediated nature of that process (since we are embodied, finite beings) but also the *gift* that this is, the sensory goodness of an encounter with God through the sacraments.

Acknowledging the fundamentally embodied, and thus mediated, nature of all "direct" engagement with God points to a second clarification we need to make: all such liturgical enactment will always be a complex, symbiotic combination of being direct and explicit while also

---

46. De Gruchy, "The Search for Transcendence," 10.

being indirect and implicit. Engagement with God can only be direct and explicit to the extent that it is a conscious process, as a function of left-hemisphere attention. However, as we have learned, the implicit and indirect embodied cognition of right-hemisphere attention is not comprehensively articulated in consciousness. Aspects of paradigmatic formation remain largely unconscious. In other words, by engaging the whole being in liturgy, the significance and meaning of a particular act is only partially accessible through the abstraction of direct and explicit propositional thought and language. The power of liturgy lies precisely in unifying the cognitive, affective, and embodied aspects of being human, thereby engaging both the explicit and implicit, the right and left hemisphere in worship of God. While this accounts for the richness of liturgy in Christian living, it makes left-hemisphere analysis of what is going on here challenging.[47] For our purposes, the key point to elucidate is that in speaking of liturgical enactment as *for* "direct" engagement with God, it is helpful to clarify that Wolterstorff is essentially describing a focus of attention or orientation.[48] Rather than speak of "direct engagement with God," we could therefore say that liturgical enactment *orients one's whole being in focus on God*.

By affirming that "direct" engagement with God is actually mediated, and that what we are essentially describing here is a holistic *orientation*, we have clarified that this delineation of liturgy is best understood not as a binary distinction but on a continuum. Not all action is equally liturgical; taking Holy Communion is not liturgical in the same sense as gazing at the stars, to use Wolterstorff's example. However, this is not to say that enjoying the stars is *not* liturgy, as a binary application of Wolterstorff's model would assert. Rather, some liturgical enactments orient one's whole being more completely and comprehensively in worship of God than others. Or, to return to a recurrent Bonhoefferian theme, if liturgy in the strict sense (such as celebrating the Eucharist or baptism) is the fundamental and required liturgical cantus firmus affirming the ultimate, then gazing at the stars or enjoying the sunset are the penultimate liturgical counterpoints, offering all of human existence as polyphonic

---

47. In concluding his analysis of a performative understanding of liturgy, Wolterstorff notes that work needs to be done on better understanding the relationship between liturgy and life-meaning. This is true precisely because in the complex relation between liturgy and existence, analysis can only partially explain the total and holistic "life-meaning" of what is going on here. Wolterstorff, *Acting Liturgically*, 293–94.

48. Wolterstorff, *Acting Liturgically*, 26.

worship. At the heart of such a stance is a christological understanding of all of reality, as we have seen. "The liturgy, which is celebrated at certain moments but lived at every moment, is the one mystery of the Christ who gives life to human beings."[49] Schmemann is helpful in further articulating this point.[50] Liturgical enactments strictly understood, or the "instituted acts called 'sacraments,'" are not magical in and of themselves, but pivotal for allowing one "to see" the world and "to 'live' it *in Christ*."[51] Is this not Wolterstorff's point, that liturgical enactment is orientation of one's whole being in Christ? But Schmemann further clarifies that the implication of this orientation in Christ affects *all* perception and engagement in the life of the world.

> A Christian is the one who, wherever he looks, finds Christ and rejoices in Him. And his joy *transforms* all his human plans and programs, decisions and actions, making all his mission the sacrament of the world's return to Him who is the life of the world.[52]

The institutional sacraments are the pinnacle of liturgy, representing the one end of the continuum, embodied participation in the Eucharist, for example, a manifestation of life in Christ. However, rather than a binary perspective that locates secular aesthetic experience outside of this liturgical enactment, the Eucharist is an "entrance into a fourth dimension which allows us to see the ultimate reality of life. It is not an escape from the world, rather it is the arrival at a vantage point from which we can see more deeply into the reality of the world."[53] The Eucharist, along with other liturgical practices of the institutional church, are not *the* expressions of liturgy as distinct from secular life in the world. This is not what makes them pivotal. Rather they are crucial because they are the entryway, the "vantage point," the paradigm from which *all* Christian action in the world can be understood as liturgical.

While we then need to necessarily expand Wolterstorff's strict delineation of liturgy, we can affirm that not all liturgical enactments are "*for* direct engagement with God" in the same way. Or, to reformulate it as discussed above, not all liturgical enactments orient one's whole

---

49. Corbon, *The Wellspring of Worship*, 141.
50. Schmemann, *For the Life of the World*, 76.
51. Schmemann, *For the Life of the World*, 113.
52. Schmemann, *For the Life of the World*, 113.
53. Schmemann, *For the Life of the World*, 27.

being in focus on God to the same degree. Wolterstorff himself points out that some liturgical enactments (even in his strict delineation of liturgy—passing the peace, for example) are "ancillary and subordinate" to being "directly" engaged with God.[54] By his own admission, their ancillary and subordinate status does not eliminate these actions from being considered liturgical. In the same way, mature aesthetic existence in the everyday, in the life of the world, is indeed "ancillary and subordinate." It is not the cantus firmus, but this does not exclude it from being considered liturgical. However, it is critical that we not confuse this "ancillary and subordinate" status for peripheral and insignificant. Such a misunderstanding stems from underestimating the impact of the indirect and implicit in human existence. As we have seen, everyday aesthetic existence is formative in ways that are most often precisely indirect and implicit. In other words, ancillary and subordinate liturgical enactments in everyday life can not only impact faith formation but also further action in the world. To expand on this, we need to turn to Wolterstorff's second criterion for understanding scripted action as liturgical, its *count as* significance.

Aesthetic Existence Can Count as Worship

In Wolterstorff's model, while liturgical enactment orients one's whole being in focus on God, it also has *count as* significance, as informed by a script. It would seem, then, that everyday aesthetic existence (strictly understood as sensory immediacy, or being in the moment) cannot be considered liturgical, since it is engaged for itself, not for significance beyond itself. However, a closer look at both what qualifies as *count as* significance as well as the nature and role of the script shows that by rejecting a reductionist view of this dynamic, everyday aesthetic engagement can indeed carry an element of *count as* significance, as informed by (and in turn contributing to) a socially constructed script.

While certain actions, such as raising one's hand at an auction, are enacted solely for their *count as* significance, it does not follow that actions outside of this set do *not* carry any *count as* significance. In other words, in the context of our discussion of liturgy here, it is possible for an action to be enacted for its own sake *and* to also carry *count as*

---

54. Wolterstorff, *Acting Liturgically*, 27.

significance.[55] To use Wolterstorff's example, playing in the football game may well be solely for the pleasure of the game itself (aesthetic existence), in accordance with the script as operative for the game itself. However, it is too simplistic not to acknowledge that there may well be multiple scripts in operation here. A father may join his son in playing the game specifically because he desires to build a relationship with his son. The father may enjoy the game, he may at times be entirely in the moment, but this does not mean that the game has no significance beyond itself. In fact, the father's primary motivation for playing the game is the *count as* significance: the message of love thereby communicated.

Gazing at the stars in wonder may not orient one's whole being in focus on God to the same degree as explicit liturgy enacted in a church on Sunday morning. It may not carry the same intensity of *count as* significance, but to say that it neither orients one toward God nor *counts as* a worshipful act (a fitting response to the shared beauty of incarnational reality) would be reductionist and inaccurate. Granted, the nature of the *count as* significance may be more implicit than explicit (although more than likely both), but as we have seen, this implicitness does not indicate irrelevance. The pivotal question is what determines *count as* significance. Intention clearly plays a role, but as Wolterstorff shows, even intention is not a prerequisite for a particular liturgical act to be meaningful.[56] Rather, it is the relation between intention and adherence to the broader script that proves insightful.

The Implicit "Scripting" of Liturgical Aesthetic Existence

The presiding script is the key element in determining the *count as* significance of liturgical enactments. As we have seen, the script carries both explicit instruction (in the form of words or diagrams, such as lectionaries or orders of service) and implicit prescription (in the form of ecclesial

55. In parallel to this question of whether an act can both carry *count as* significance and at the same time be engaged for itself, one can consider whether, according to Alasdair MacIntyre's model, it is possible for practices to produce both internal *and* external goods. Wolterstorff's argument is that the goods gained by a practice can at times be *both* internal and external, or even defy such categorization. Wolterstorff, *Art Rethought*, 92–96.

56. Wolterstorff deals extensively with the question of what is going on, first, when a person does not understand the particular liturgical enactment they participate in, and, second, when a person without faith participates in liturgy; on both counts he does not find the liturgy invalid. Wolterstorff, *Acting Liturgically*, 42, 97.

and broader cultural social practices). In a strict understanding of liturgy, a congregation collectively submits to such a script when they gather on a Sunday morning to worship. However, a broader understanding of liturgy acknowledges that humans, as essentially beings-in-relation, are necessarily always participating in one or other form of communally "scripted" activity in everyday life.

This claim draws on the work of narrative theory in cognitive science (referred to as "cognitive narratology," by Smith, for example) and narrative theology, in conjunction with the notions of social imaginaries and social practices that undergird this chapter and inform our understanding of the aesthetics of discipleship as a whole.[57] Therefore, if Wolterstorff has already stretched the meaning of the term "script," we are here stretching it even further by equating it with a presiding cultural narrative or social imaginary. However, for the purposes of articulating the formative and expressive nature of a liturgical understanding of aesthetic existence, we will continue to use the term "script" since it highlights the communally (*ekklesia* in the fullest sense of the term) prescribed nature and significance of mature aesthetic existence.

Such broader scripts, as presiding narratives or social imaginaries, always carry implicit elements, although at times they also contain explicit prescription, such as in an auction, football game, musical performance, or court of law. Scripts define whether prescribed actions carry *count as* significance or not, and what such an action *counts as*, when raising one's hand in an auction, a classroom, or a church, for example. For our purposes, the main point here is that the church's liturgical script (and consequent enactment that has *count as* significance) does not only operate in the more "direct" and explicit setting of a Sunday morning, as Christians physically gather in community, but the "script" continues to operate in every time and place, as prescribed to the body of Christ in the everyday. Individual enactment is thus embedded in the communal enactment of liturgy, just as it would be on a Sunday morning. When the church gathers on Sunday, every individual does not uniformly enact communal enactments of liturgy; there is space for individual roles in communal enactment. Liturgy encapsulates the interplay between individual and communal identity, Wolterstorff describing this as "joint action."[58] As the church disperses into the life of the world, we can extend

---

57. Smith, *Imagining the Kingdom*, 130–33.
58. Wolterstorff, *Acting Liturgically*, 63.

this notion of joint action more broadly, to individual Christians in the everyday, acting "jointly" in the world as the collective body of Christ.

Therefore, gazing at the stars *does* have *count as* significance in accordance with a broader liturgical script. This broader script is informed both by explicit and implicit elements. Explicitly, for example, there is a biblical injunction connecting engagement with the beauty of creation and worship of the Creator (Pss 8:3–5; 19:1, in relation to the stars, are obvious instances, among many others). Further, a theological tradition may make an explicit doctrinal prescription (as in the Catholic Catechesis on Creation). Implicitly, through the social practices of a particular theological tradition, local church community, or family, the importance of worshiping God through celebrating the beauty of creation may be affirmed. In such a case, the Christian person living within this script cannot help but worship God when encountering the starry sky. It is a moment of sensory immediacy, a moment of aesthetic existence, informed by a larger liturgical script, offering *count as* significance to the moment.

However, as we have noted, this broader Christian liturgical script is not the only script at play in the everyday. In fact, we could say that it is not even the only broader liturgical script at play. Multiple liturgical scripts are operative in everyday life as informed by the largely implicit prescriptions of social practice. In this sense we can talk, as Smith does, of "cultural liturgies"; not all holistic orientation, or worship is directed at Christ, or even at a religious deity.[59] As Smith notes, there are rival kingdoms vying for our desire and enacted worship. Each of these kingdoms is driven by a set of social practices that prescribe their respective operative liturgy. By way of example, Smith offers a vivid description of the temple of the contemporary shopping mall, along with the worship of iconography (brands), and communal enactments that a pilgrimage to the mall entails.[60] The same liturgical mode is operative in the modern sports stadium. The script here, while it can be explicitly deduced, is largely operative on the level of implicit social practices.

Bonhoeffer's call for a recovery of aesthetic existence in the life of the church amid the horrors and atrocities of Nazi Germany, is a countercultural, explicit naming of a liturgical script he had implicitly embraced up until that point. He is not here suggesting an aesthetic escapism from

---

59. See Smith's Cultural Liturgies project: Smith, *Desiring the Kingdom*; Smith, *Imagining the Kingdom*; Smith, *Awaiting the King*.

60. Smith, *Desiring the Kingdom*, 17–27.

reality into a moment of sensory immediacy *for* itself. Rather, as informed by a broader christological script, he suggests it is fitting to celebrate aesthetic existence as a manifestation of faithful Christian living. While having music constantly playing at Bonhoeffer's Finkenwalde seminary may not be liturgical in Wolterstorff's strict sense (it is not explicitly *for* direct engagement with God, and does not obviously have *count as* significance, as operative within an overt and explicit liturgical script, such as an order of service), in the broader sense it is indeed a liturgical enactment. To use the broadened criteria we have drawn from Wolterstorff, there is no doubt that the Finkenwalde seminarians

1. oriented their lives holistically in focus on God (as grounded in the practice of institutional sacraments; belief manifest here as a life disposition, not a weak form of knowledge);

2. subscribed to a liturgical script, which proclaimed all of their "life together" as worship to God.

Consequently, the enjoyment of music not only functioned as a *moment* of rich aesthetic existence, but also *counted as* a worshipful celebration of incarnational living, in polyphonic harmony with their explicit affirmation of this truth. An important point in this example is that the seminarians may not themselves have explicitly named their playing of music as worship. In Wolterstorff's strict understanding of liturgy, this disqualifies the act from being categorized as liturgical enactment. However, at the heart of this chapter (and the broader argument for a robust understanding of the aesthetics of discipleship) is the suggestion that the implicit and indirect are not dissociated from the explicit and direct. Implicitly, Bonhoeffer and the seminarians embraced the playing of music as congruent with their holistic liturgical project of "life together," thereby affirming a sense of polyphonic resonance.

Further, by considering this *performative* manifestation of mature aesthetic existence as a liturgical enactment (to continue the example of the Finkenwalde seminarians playing music), it points not only to the *expressive* nature of their everyday liturgy (a polyphonic celebration of christological this-worldliness) but to the *formative* nature of such everyday liturgy. This formative nature is easily underestimated due to its indirect and implicit operation. It does not lend itself to being measurable by means of rational abstraction, as it is nonlinear, organic, and complex. However, as we have seen through the example of Bonhoeffer's musical metaphors, the formation of his theological categories through his musical experience is an insightful example of the formative impact of aesthetic existence as everyday liturgy.

Throughout our discussion thus far, we have noted that in order to understand why everyday aesthetic enactments such as these are formative, we need to reject the modern epistemological narrative, as expressed through the likes of Locke in favor of models that acknowledge the impact of embodied and affective interaction with the world on human understanding. There is another modern narrative—the aesthetic narrative—that we now need to confront, through the work of Wolterstorff, in order to appreciate that aesthetic existence, as everyday liturgy, is fundamentally connected to action in the world.

Aesthetic Engagement as Practice

We have distinguished *mature* aesthetic existence as liturgical: as anchored in life oriented by focus on God, thereby conforming to a broad liturgical script wherein aesthetic existence is not for its own sake, but for the significance it carries beyond the aesthetic act itself as polyphonic worship of the Creator. But according to the modern narrative of aesthetics this is a contradiction in terms. The aesthetic has no obligations beyond itself. Art exists for its own sake, not for significance and responsibility outside of its realm.

Severing Aesthetics from Action: Modern Disinterested Contemplation

Wolterstorff names this the "grand narrative of art"—the pinnacle of the aesthetic in modern life being disinterested contemplation, as manifest in the rise of art institutions, such as museums and galleries.[61] On the same continuum, modern everyday aesthetic enjoyment is for itself. As Kierkegaard's pseudonym Climacus observed regarding an outing to Deer Park, according to this narrative, aesthetic frivolity is distinct from ethical life. Such aesthetic experience is peripheral to the serious business of life. The narrative separates aesthetics from action, poiesis from praxis. Consequently, aesthetic engagement is distinct from ethics. Wolterstorff challenges this narrative by suggesting that aesthetic engagement is best

---

61. Wolterstorff, *Art Rethought*, 5–82.

understood as action.[62] Artistic creation and presentation are best seen as social practice. While Wolterstorff's focus is on art rather than aesthetics more broadly, the principles from his focus on the subset of art apply to the broader category of aesthetics as we are discussing it.

Wolterstorff suggests that while aestheticians and philosophers no longer support the veracity of this modern, grand narrative on art, it continues to influence our thinking in contemporary life, as is evident in our everyday engagement with aesthetics and the privileged place of high art.[63] The narrative emerged due to the rise of "a middle class with considerable leisure time . . . [alongside] a secular civil society" and rests on two theses.[64] The first is the progressivist idea that in this modern conception of disinterested contemplation, as the pinnacle of aesthetic engagement, art had finally come into its own; it had reached its ultimate *telos*.[65] The second is that the arts offered an escape from the "causal instrumental rationality" that dominated modern life, "The arts are liberated from service to extraneous values and freed to come into their own"; as such they are "socially other and transcendent."[66] Hence, as we have seen with Kierkegaard's interaction with Romanticism and Bonhoeffer's response to Nietzsche, the aesthetic was seen as a means to escape the fragmentary everyday and recover the ideal whole. Consequently, the highest form of the aesthetic, as socially other and transcendent, is venerated, seen as distinct from the finitude and utility of everyday action, cementing a distinction between true art and that which is merely craft.[67] This salvific approach to the aesthetic causes friction between faith and modern aesthetics (impelling Kierkegaard's critique of immature aesthetic existence), as Max Weber pointed out, for in this modern narrative

> art becomes a cosmos of more and more consciously grasped independent values which exist in their own right. Art takes over the function of a this-worldly salvation, no matter how this may be interpreted. It provides a salvation from the routines of everyday life, and especially from the increasing pressures

---

62. This is comprehensively argued in Wolterstorff, *Art in Action*.

63. Wolterstorff, *Art Rethought*, ix–x, 1–16.

64. Wolterstorff, *Art Rethought*, 7.

65. Strictly, Wolterstorff identifies three theses, not two, underlying this narrative, but for our purposes it is sufficient to conflate his first two theses into one. Wolterstorff, *Art Rethought*, 27.

66. Wolterstorff, *Art Rethought*, 32.

67. Wolterstorff, *Art Rethought*, 17.

of theoretical and practical rationalism. With this claim to a redemptory function, art begins to compete directly with salvation religion.[68]

Wolterstorff rejects both theses as untenable. On the former—that the aesthetic has reached its *telos* in disinterested contemplation—he argues that this is not only impossible to prove, but it is highly dubious when one considers the state of modern art. Fundamentally, too, it is fallacious on the basis that reaching a *telos* requires *stasis*, which is clearly not the case as seen over the last three hundred years, where notions and expressions of "art" continue to evolve.[69] But it is specifically Wolterstorff's response to the second thesis—that at its pinnacle, the aesthetic is socially other and transcendent—which is of interest to us, since he suggests that rather than "socially other and transcendent," art (and by implication, the aesthetic more broadly) is always socially embedded in practices.

Wolterstorff shows that the argument for the socially other and transcendent nature of art rests on the fallacy that art is clearly and distinctly concerned with "internal finality in place of external causal finality; unity in place of fragmentation."[70] Internal finality is here understood as the sole internal concern for "unity of the parts with parts and parts with the whole" rather than concern for any external causation.[71] The binary basis of this thesis needs to be rejected based on three counts: First, even works of fine art are created for both disinterested attention *and* causal effect (remuneration, appreciation, and so forth). While such causal effects may in some cases not be immediately apparent, they inevitably exist on closer inspection. Second, a work can be socially other and transcendent even though it is not made for disinterested contemplation (Orthodox icons, for example). Third, the distinction between external and internal finality is blurred even in the process of artistic creation. Every artistic action, every compositional technique contains an element of means-end rationality. Applying paint *so that* it is seen to be a tree, for instance, is a process necessarily driven by external causation.[72] "To eliminate all

---

68. Weber, *From Max Weber*, 342.
69. Wolterstorff, *Art Rethought*, 70–73.
70. Wolterstorff, *Art Rethought*, 76.
71. Wolterstorff, *Art Rethought*, 80.
72. Wolterstorff, *Art Rethought*, 73–82.

'servitude' from the artist's compositional choices, all means-end rationality, one's work has to be purely abstract."[73]

Uniting Aesthetics and Action as Social Practice

The grand narrative of art, therefore, needs to be rejected, along with understanding the aesthetic as socially other, and the concomitant severance from action. By contrast, it is more accurate to acknowledge that the aesthetic is fundamentally grounded in social practice. Wolterstorff is not alone in this assessment. Informed by a broader, contemporary philosophical and sociological understanding of the nature of being human, in recent years a number of writers about aesthetics and the arts "have brought to light the many ways in which art is enmeshed in the social dynamics of our societies rather than transcending those dynamics."[74] The field of theological aesthetics, however, is still very much influenced by the legacy of modern "transcendent and socially other" perceptions of the aesthetic in faith life. While these insights remain valuable, it is important to acknowledge that over the last century, classical thinkers in the field of theological aesthetics have been influenced by this modern narrative. As Wolterstorff points out, "it's because they accept the narrative without question that [Clive] Bell, [Gerardus] Vander Leeuw, [Paul] Tillich, and their cohorts focus exclusively on the contemplative mode of engagement with art in their discussion of art and religion."[75] Again, without dismissing the immense contribution of this cohort, and the value of the aesthetic for engaging the transcendent (which is indeed extremely important, as we have seen, for encountering the Other), it is vital to counterbalance this perspective with an accurate account of the this-worldly implications of aesthetic existence. In other words, while not dismissing the value of the aesthetic as a gateway to the transcendent, we need to reject the notion that this is a function of the "socially other" nature of the aesthetic itself. On the contrary, the power of the aesthetic lies in its ability to bridge worlds, precisely because it is fundamentally connected to embodiment and this-worldly social relatedness.

---

73. Wolterstorff, *Art Rethought*, 79.
74. Wolterstorff, *Art Rethought*, 84.
75. Wolterstorff, "The Religious Dimension," 334.

Wolterstorff articulates this social embeddedness through the lens of social practices.[76] He suggests that if we pay close attention to the inherent connection between aesthetics and human action, we will see that we engage the aesthetic in different *ways*. By "ways" he means act-types or sequences of act-types (just as with liturgy above).[77] There are "ways" of violin playing, to use the same example again. As we have seen, these "ways" are informed by shared societal practices. Violin playing is both the product of, and *for* that particular social practice. Because of this shared practice, violin playing has social-practice meaning.[78] If one were to play the violin in a way discordant with its social practice, it would be meaningless, if not cacophonous, to the hearers.[79] Social practices inform not only the making and presenting or performing of art but also engagement with such works.[80] For instance, composing, performing, and appreciating classical music as presented in an opera house requires familiarity with the respective social practices involved.

However, this does not mean that the social practices of art as disinterested contemplation (or absorbed attention, in Wolterstorff's phrasing) have a monopoly on "ways" of engaging the aesthetic more broadly, or even the arts more narrowly. Wolterstorff highlights a few of the many other social practices that inform aesthetic making, presenting, and engaging, such as memorial art (a manifestation being the mural art of Belfast), art for veneration (Orthodox icons), protest art (*Uncle Tom's Cabin*), and so forth.[81] We will take a closer look at one of these examples—work songs—shortly. The point here is that the vast majority of our everyday aesthetic engagement in the world is governed by a constellation of social practices and the social-practice meanings that accompany them. Further, while such aesthetic engagements may well (and indeed do) offer experiences of transcendence at times, this is not the function of their being socially other, disconnected from action in the world, or even being disconnected from means-end rationality for that matter. In resonance with the incarnational understanding of being Christian, we

---

76. Wolterstorff is not the first to acknowledge this link. Both Julius Moravcsik and Noël Carroll have written about approaching the arts as social practices. Wolterstorff, *Art Rethought*, 85.

77. Wolterstorff, *Art Rethought*, 86.

78. Wolterstorff, *Art Rethought*, 112–13.

79. Wolterstorff, *Art Rethought*, 87.

80. Wolterstorff, *Art Rethought*, 96–97.

81. Wolterstorff, *Art Rethought*, 123–303.

have outlined thus far, transcendence and action in the world are not mutually exclusive. To the contrary, the formative potency of aesthetic practice is underscored by ackowelding that aesthetic engagement as everyday action has the ability to offer experiences of transcendence.

Aesthetic Practices Sustain a Vision of the Good Life

Understanding aesthetic engagement through the lens of social practice highlights that all aesthetic engagement contains means-end rationality. This statement is only problematic if we equate means-end rationality with "causal instrumental rationality." However, while many aesthetic practices are not engaged in this latter sense—"to *cause* some event"—they have a more implicit sense of means-end rationality in the form of *counting as*.[82] Thus, on the one hand, there are clearly certain actions that carry more explicit means-end rationality, enacted *for* causal instrumental rationality. We describe such actions as utilitarian. However, on the other hand, rather than locating the aesthetic in a separate and distinct set (that of "transcendent and socially other") entirely disconnected from utility, approaching aesthetic enactment through the lens of social practice highlights the pervasive implicit sense of means-end rationality. Social practices have a *telos* and the *count as* significance implicit in aesthetic action is ordered by the presiding *telos*. Even though much aesthetic enactment is not considered overtly *for* utility—it is considered *for* itself—on closer inspection it becomes apparent that such enactment nevertheless plays a role in affirming an orientation to a certain *telos*. Acts of aesthetic existence, such as walking on the beach, playing football, or listening to music, may explicitly be labeled by the participant as being *for* the moment; expressions of pure nonutilitarian sensory immediacy. However, such actions perform a role in a larger life-narrative. Walking on the beach may be predominantly simply *for* itself, for the pure pleasure of it, but even here it can also *count as* a liturgical celebration of incarnational existence. There may be other narratives at play too. It may *count as* exercise, even if not performed *for* exercise. Listening to music may be simply seen as an experience of sensory immediacy, but even as such, it can potentially *count as* a polyphonic embrace of created goodness. Or in relation to other ordering life-narratives at play, it may also *count as* rest, for example.

82. Wolterstorff, *Art Rethought*, 78.

To put it differently and return to our earlier discussion on scripts, multiple life-narratives, or scripts, are operative, whether implicit or explicit, with multiple *teloi*, including the ultimate *telos* of the good life (however construed), which order the *count as* significance of aesthetic practices therein. Or, as Smith describes it in Augustinian terms, what one worships is betrayed by the "liturgies" of one's everyday practices, disclosing how one's desires are ordered in orientation toward respective "kingdoms."[83] Just as liturgical enactment on a Sunday, strictly understood, orients one toward the kingdom of God, so cultural liturgies, such as the deeply aesthetic practice of a consumer's outing to the mall, may orient one toward a different "kingdom." The key point to note here is that since the *count as* significance of aesthetic practices is often implicit, it is possible to participate in and thereby subscribe to a particular "liturgical" script and its accompanying social-practice meaning without being fully cognizant of this subscription.

Mature Aesthetic Existence as Fitting Shalom

Mature aesthetic existence requires an embrace of a broad liturgical script that guides all of life's actions as aesthetic-ethical-religious practices. This is not to say that such action is always permeated with conscious and explicit liturgical intention. Inevitably, by definition, this cannot be the case if we understand aesthetic enactment as being marked by sensory immediacy.[84] Rather, aesthetic-ethical-religious practices are recognized as liturgically oriented by their *fittingness* to the *telos* of shalom. Fittingness is usually understood to be an aesthetic category, but as we briefly explored earlier, if we are to take the relationship of embodiment to meaning seriously, then fittingness has not only aesthetic but ethical and religious implications too. At the end of the last chapter, we noted through Ward's work that embodied attunement, or fittingness, is an entryway into a deeper actualization of ethical life. This is so because it offers holistic sensitivity to and participation in christological reality—thus Ward's assertion that "attunement is both the source and goal of discipleship."[85]

83. Smith, *Desiring the Kingdom*.

84. However, as should be apparent by now, a neat distinction between immediacy and reflective intentionality exists only in theoretical abstraction. Immediacy and explicit intentionality have a complex, multidirectional relationship, thus challenging a rigid binary between a Kierkegaardian first and second immediacy.

85. Ward, "Sport and Incarnational Theology," 63.

If mature aesthetic existence is liturgically oriented, so discerned by the fittingness of aesthetic-ethical-religious practices to the *telos* of shalom, then it is important to clarify our definition of *shalom*, and consequently the significance of fittingness for not only aesthetics but ethics. Wolterstorff's articulation of shalom is holistically relational:

> Shalom is flourishing in all one's relationships: to God, one's fellow [human beings], to oneself, to the natural world, to society and culture. It has both a normative component, being *rightly* related, and an affective component, finding *joy* in being so related.[86]

Wolterstorff emphasizes the validity of this affective component, in resonance with an Augustinian "enjoyment" of God: "Shalom at its highest is *enjoyment* in one's relationships . . . To dwell in shalom is to *enjoy* living before God, to *enjoy* living in one's physical surroundings, to *enjoy* living with one's fellows, to *enjoy* life with oneself."[87] It is clear that orienting one's life by such a relational and affective understanding of shalom demands not only abstract left-hemisphere attention but the embodied and affective "betweenness" contributed by right-hemisphere attention. Note that there are not two types of shalom: normative or ethical shalom and affective or aesthetic shalom. Rather these two components, this dual understanding of the good life, of the *kalos* life, cohere in this aesthetic-ethical-religious understanding of shalom. The embodied and affective nature of shalom demands a measure such as fittingness to adequately discern appropriate action.

The strength of fittingness as a means of discernment is the integration of embodiment, affect, and reason in everyday evaluation.[88] Significantly, it is a mode of discernment that does not discount ratiocination but also goes beyond it, harnessing aesthetic sensitivity to an environment. For instance, a jagged line simply *fits* better with restlessness, and a smooth line *fits* better with tranquility.[89] Light *fits* better with "ping," and heavy *fits* better with "pong."[90] In a sense, we could describe fittingness as "expanded synesthesia" which is common to all.[91]

---

86. Wolterstorff, "Human Flourishing and Art," 164.
87. Wolterstorff, *Hearing the Call*, 110.
88. For a detailed theory of fittingness, see Wolterstorff, *Art in Action*, 96–121.
89. Wolterstorff, *Art in Action*, 97.
90. Wolterstorff, *Art in Action*, 97.
91. Wolterstorff, *Art in Action*, 101.

Technically, we can define it as "cross-modal similarity."[92] It is the human ability to intuitively associate one modality with another, drawing from the fullness of the right → left → right-hemisphere-attention progression. It is the same faculty that allows us to understand metaphor, the association of one modality with another.[93] "Metaphors are often (if not always) renditions of perceived fittingness."[94] Here we should recall our discussion on the analogical participation of everyday action in christological reality. Hence, the human ability to discern fittingness is the same faculty that allows one to perceive an embodied action as having liturgical *count as* significance. There is a fittingness to such action.

This is so due to the appropriateness or fittingness of particular actions to a presiding script or narrative. For instance, planting a tree serves as a fitting memorial to a student who has passed away, while vandalizing the classroom wherein he learned is not a fitting memorial.[95] In liturgically orienting one's life toward shalom certain actions may instrumentally further shalom while others may *count as* affirming shalom—both will *fit* the script. Here, fittingness should be understood not only in an aesthetic sense but as a measure of appropriate aesthetic-ethical-religious action. For instance, fittingness-to-shalom can serve as a lens for evaluating justice, where "an unjust act is an unfitting act; it is an act which fails to accord with the status of the person treated."[96] In other words, fittingness is also a means of ethical discernment. An ethic informed by fittingness brings to the fore the strengths of right-hemisphere relational attention to the world.[97] The implication is an enhancement of Wolterstorff's ethic of care, including creation care, founded in love.[98]

92. Wolterstorff, *Art in Action*, 99.
93. Wolterstorff, *Art in Action*, 102.
94. Wolterstorff, *Art in Action*, 116.
95. Wolterstorff, *Art Rethought*, 139.
96. Cupit, *Justice as Fittingness*, 2.

97. Fittingness is fundamentally about relational sensitivity, with ethical implications on multiple fronts. In the words of the Niebuhr scholar Charles McCoy, "In one sense fittingness underscores the importance of particularity—responding to particular persons, situations and issues. In a larger sense, fittingness requires taking account of the encompassing context of the social and natural environment, so that what is done fits with everything else that is happening and avoids causing more problems than it solves." As quoted in Hessel, "Now That Animals Can Be Genetically Engineered" 288.

98. Which Wolterstorff articulates as "care-agapism," see Wolterstorff, *Justice in Love*.

However, to consider fittingness as an ethical versus aesthetic qualifier is to miss the point, for the value of fittingness is precisely in pointing to the integration of mature aesthetic existence and ethical action in a life oriented toward shalom. Kevin Vanhoozer rightly argues for the integrative nature of fittingness as discernment by associating it with wisdom.

> Wisdom—the virtue that orders all other virtues—is intrinsically linked to the imagination, and to beauty, via the theme of fittingness. The wise person perceives and participates fittingly in the ordered beauty of creation. Wisdom thus integrates the true, the good, and the beautiful... Right perception, the capacity to discern, is therefore the connecting link between aesthetics and ethics.[99]

In other words, "the wise person perceives and participates fittingly" in shalom. Such participation, such action, cannot be merely described as "ethical." While it is "right" action, and there is a normativity to such action, it is also affective, as Wolterstorff pointed out in his definition of *shalom*. Vanhoozer affirms here that the affective sense of shalom as the good life is not the giddy heights and agonizing lows of Romantic or Nietzschean aestheticizing self-creation, but the joy of co-poeticizing with Christ in the Kierkegaardian sense of poetic living.[100] "Joy is the perception of, and the participation in, a larger 'fittingness' that satisfies our longing for ultimate meaning. Joy is not a passing feeling so much as a perduring mood or orientation to the whole of life. Christian joy is *being-toward-resurrection*."[101]

To recap, *fitting* aesthetic engagement and action participates in the liturgical script of shalom. It is a performative act that is both formative and expressive. On the one hand, it is expressive of shalom as a function of right-relationship, of being-in-Christ, of being-for-others. Such an incarnational understanding of being human orients play, friendship, art, and all manner of everyday aesthetic existence as liturgical celebration. At the same time, and on the other hand, it is formative *for* shalom. Participation in such practice shapes not only the individual imagination but if enacted collectively the social imaginary. The *count as* significance of such action consciously and unconsciously underscores the script and its *telos*. In other words, if one were to ask, with Wolterstorff, from a

---

99. Vanhoozer, "Praising in Song," 115.
100. Vanhoozer, "Praising in Song," 121–22.
101. Vanhoozer, "Praising in Song," 118.

performative perspective, what is happening in everyday aesthetic action as liturgy, what does it *do*? We could answer with him, simply, it enhances. Liturgy "serves our life in the world" by directing and nourishing it.[102] Mature aesthetic existence, manifest as liturgical action, polyphonically *enhances* everyday experience of shalom. To elucidate this summation, and by way of conclusion, we can turn once again to the example of music as aesthetic existence.

Spotlight on Music: Sung Work as Enhancement toward Shalom

Wolterstorff's analysis of the social practice of work songs not only provides a case study of aesthetic engagement understood as action but clarifies how everyday aesthetic action enhances, through a liturgical orientation toward shalom. Work songs are typically understood to be songs that are sung to accompany work. However, such a fragmented perspective stems from a separation of aesthetics from action, poiesis from praxis. Wolterstorff argues that rather than two distinct entities—songs and work—it is more accurate to speak of the single entity of sung work, "the singing and the working 'coinhere'—to borrow a term from theology of the trinity."[103] The singing is not merely an insignificant accompaniment to the work, but it modifies the work; it changes its nature.[104] Drawing from an interview with a prisoner engaging in sung work, Wolterstorff highlights the sentiment that "singing makes the work 'go so better.'"[105] In other words, work songs *enhance* one's experience of work. The question is why; why does sung work "go so better"?

It is fundamentally because manifestations of sung work can function as "signs" of shalom, "samples of shalom that [point] to a shalom beyond" the humanizing experience of sung work itself.[106] Prisoners attest to singing while working to "uplift themselves . . . as a manifestation of the 'will of the human spirit.'"[107] Conversely, prison overseers may disallow singing in order to crush workers' spirit.[108] Even in the face of denigrating

---

102. Wolterstorff, *Hearing the Call*, 23.
103. Wolterstorff, *Art Rethought*, 259.
104. Wolterstorff, *Art Rethought*, 270.
105. Wolterstorff, *Art Rethought*, 262.
106. Wolterstorff, "Human Flourishing and Art," 169.
107. Wolterstorff, *Art Rethought*, 259.
108. Wolterstorff, *Art Rethought*, 259.

labor, "by singing, the worker manifests an indomitable sense of his or her ineradicable dignity."[109] Pragmatically, sung work may "go so better" because it sustains working rhythm or energizes or cultivates solidarity.[110] However, these utilities only partially explain how singing enhances work. "Singing enhances not only the work itself but the workers' experience of the work. The creative excess of the singing blurs the distinction between work and play by introducing a dimension of play into the work; this enhances their experience of the work."[111] In other words, the introduction of play, an expression of aesthetic existence, modifies the work, allowing it to *count as* an expression of human flourishing.

Drawing from music historian Ted Gioia and his research on work songs, Wolterstorff suggests that workers experience the creativity of singing while working as an intrinsic good. The workers sing "for the joy of creating sung work."[112] Sung work then, as the fusion of poiesis and praxis, functions as a sign of shalom. Or, to put it in the language we have used thus far, sung work may implicitly *count as* an affirmation of shalom, flourishing in the joy of being human.[113]

However, it does not follow that singing while working automatically validates *any* labor as harmonious with human flourishing. Here we need to return to fittingness as a means of holistic discernment. Certain songs fit certain work due to rhythm, tempo, and "expressive character."[114] To use the wrong song would not enhance the work but make it more challenging. To use a musical metaphor, there needs to be harmony between the work and the song. It needs to fit. We can take this further; for sung work to be fully expressive of flourishing, it needs to fit a liturgical life-script of shalom (thus foregrounding the dissonance of inhumane

---

109. Wolterstorff, *Art Rethought*, 259.
110. Wolterstorff, "Human Flourishing and Art," 169.
111. Wolterstorff, "Human Flourishing and Art," 169.
112. Wolterstorff, *Art Rethought*, 265.
113. The objection may be raised that action is here obviously connected to aesthetics simply due to the example chosen, work (action) + songs (aesthetics) = sung work. However, the example merely serves to neatly portray Wolterstorff's point that *all* aesthetic engagement is action. We could also consider Wolterstorff's articulation of hymns as sung work, or "sung praise," the singing of the action of praise making it "go so better." Or even the exercise of absorbed attention *for* listening to classical music will "go so better" when *fitting* shalom, the relational flourishing of *kalos* in its fullest sense, incorporating faith, aesthetics, and ethics. Wolterstorff, "Human Flourishing and Art," 174–79.
114. Wolterstorff, *Art Rethought*, 261.

work). Such fittingness is therefore neither merely aesthetic nor ethical, but a measure of goodness in which the aesthetic and the ethical cohere.

Mature aesthetic existence, as liturgically integrated with both ethical and religious life, thus "contributes to flourishing by enhancing our ordinary activities."[115] With Wolterstorff, we can therefore conclude by asking, "Might it be that, in general, human flourishing is best advanced by enhancing the ordinary rather than by trying to deny it or in some way to transcend it?"[116] Mature aesthetic existence as discipleship embraces the immediacy of the ordinary, orienting such action toward God in a liturgical disposition, thereby *counting as* worship, which not only celebrates being Christian but formatively orients it.

---

115. Wolterstorff, "Human Flourishing and Art," 179.
116. Wolterstorff, "Human Flourishing and Art," 179.

7

Conclusion

Toward Aesthetic Stewardship as a Spiritual Practice

THE CENTRAL CLAIM OF this book is that aesthetic existence is fundamental to being human and becoming Christian. We ignore aesthetic existence at our peril, since it shapes our lives, whether we acknowledge it or not. Yet, in many ways, this book only scratches the surface of the aesthetics of discipleship, or perhaps, more accurately, it offers limited glimpses of what lies below the surface in the hope of highlighting that the stakes are high. There is much more work to be done, particularly from the perspectives of biblical studies and practical theology, toward developing a robust call to aesthetic stewardship as a spiritual practice in contemporary Christian life. Before sketching some of these trajectories that need to be further explored, and their implications for a life of discipleship, it will be helpful to offer a summary of the argument presented here, both for the purposes of clarifying foundational principles of an aesthetics of discipleship, and also, importantly, for emphasizing what is *not* being suggested. It should go without saying that understanding the (penultimate) role of aesthetic existence in discipleship must always be framed in the context of and in dialogue with the core tenets of the faith—notably divine agency manifest in the ultimate joy of God's redeeming grace. Any attempt at recovering everyday aesthetic existence in the Christian life without this grounding is merely a vacuous "Christianized" invention of existential Neo-Romanticism.

CONCLUSION   223

We began our inquiry with Kierkegaard, who helped us to articulate the nature of aesthetic existence as sensory immediacy. A core observation immediately emerged that we have been following as a thread throughout: There are two modes of aesthetic existence in relation to discipleship—one leading to Christian formation, the other to self-created "formation," or the creation of virtuality. Kierkegaard described the former through the concept of "poetic living" and the latter as the *life stage* of aesthetic existence. The life stage, or sphere, of aesthetic existence is a mode wherein the aesthetic becomes absolute. In other words, it is an expression of everyday aestheticism. By contrast, the Christian attitude toward aesthetic existence rejects sensory immediacy as absolute and the Romantic self-creation associated with it. Rather than poeticizing one's own life, one co-poeticizes with Christ in a mode of poetic living as discipleship. It is this mode that we have termed *mature* aesthetic existence, stemming from Bonhoeffer's "mature worldliness," as "a way of being *Christian* in the world that is *fully human, truly of the earth*; one that involves not only living responsibly in the world but also living . . . a genuinely 'aesthetic existence' of creativity, playfulness, freedom and friendship."[1]

Kierkegaard's rhetorical focus is on the immature mode of aesthetic existence, highlighting the deformative danger of such existence, particularly when coupled with Christendom. This dangerous alliance creates a comfortable and apathetic virtuality, disconnected from being a witness to the reality of Christ. Kierkegaard's prophetic critique is arguably more relevant than ever. Not only do we face manifestations of Christendom today in dissonance with costly discipled living, but the postmodern tendency toward self-creation, further enabled by the aestheticization of everyday life and ubiquitous sensory technology supporting such self-creation, provides fertile ground for the proliferation of virtual realities both individual and collective. In resonance with Kierkegaard's aesthetes, for some (as with the "action alone" of Don Juan), such self-creation is a somewhat accidental consequence of absolutizing the aesthetic; here, identities are created via largely unreflective saturation in the sensory delights of social and entertainment media, for example. For others (as with the thoughtful approach of Kierkegaard's Seducer), the process is more intentional: an exploration of identity (notably through gender and sexuality) toward the goal of maximal personal and aesthetic fulfillment.

1. De Gruchy, *A Theological Odyssey*, 60.

What undergirds both these postmodern creations of self is what underlay Romanticism, according to Kierkegaard's critique: the "endless process of experimentation and play with a multiplicity of interpretations"—whether linguistic or existential—fueled by sensory immediacy.[2]

How do we then distinguish *mature* aesthetic existence from such everyday aestheticism? Kierkegaard gives comparatively little attention to the mature mode of engaging the aesthetic, since the rhetorical urgency of his "attack on Christendom" (along with the concomitant immature modes of engaging the aesthetic) dominates his work. However, he does point to the centrality of the imagination in discipleship, and the notion that a "second immediacy" or "immediacy after reflection" may be vital to the Christian life. For Kierkegaard, it appears that reflection and consequent intention are the necessary precursors to mature aesthetic existence as an aspect of discipleship. We will return to this point shortly.

Kierkegaard's limited and qualified endorsement of aesthetic existence stands in vivid contrast to Bonhoeffer's enthusiastic call for a recovery of aesthetic existence in the life of the church. His affirmation of this-worldly immediacy, as manifest in the freedom of art, play, friendship, and *Bildung*, stems from his Christology and the importance of an incarnational approach to imitating Christ. Christological reality is not merely otherworldly. The penultimate celebration of aesthetic existence has value precisely due to the worldliness of Christian reality. In other words, while Kierkegaard's focus is on exposing the Romantic illusion of poeticizing a life that unites the finite and infinite, Bonhoeffer shows that participation in finite reality, even in its fragmentary state, has meaning as it is unified *in Christ*. It is the cantus firmus of Christ, as one is anchored in love for God, that makes the fragments, the moments of aesthetic existence, cohere in polyphonic counterpoint.

An accurate understanding of the aesthetics of discipleship hinges on this point, which cannot be emphasized strongly enough: rightly ordered aesthetic existence cannot be contrived solely by human agency. To the contrary, the starting point for the aesthetics of discipleship is God's love for humankind, manifest in new life being offered through the incarnation, death, and resurrection of Christ. In other words, discipleship is always impelled by divine agency and God's ultimate act of saving grace. Love for God is a fitting response to this life-giving mercy; it is the cantus firmus that orders mature aesthetic existence. While such

---

2. Walsh, *Living Poetically*, 245.

mature aesthetic existence creates "conditions of the heart" and imaginatively nurtures paradigms conducive to receiving God's grace, to making dispositional commitments to believe and trust in God's redemptive work, it is not where discipleship begins.[3] Mature aesthetic existence is a faithful response to God's initiative. It is not ultimate but penultimate. As with all spiritual practices, it is always contingent. It is not the genesis or initiation of discipleship through cultivating habits of the senses, but polyphonic attunement to the ultimate work of the Spirit in one's life. Mature aesthetic existence requires discernment of and participation in christological reality.

Moments of aesthetic existence are always embedded in a particular way of seeing reality (the orientation of desire to a particular vision of the good life), and discipleship is precisely the ability to *see* reality in light of Christ. Bonhoeffer was all too aware of the consequences of the aesthetic gone awry, severed from ethics, amid the rise of Nazi Germany and complicit Christendom. Mature aesthetic existence is neither the untethered free play of the imagination nor something distinct from costly discipleship. Rather, mature aesthetic existence is a polyphonic counterpoint to the committed sacrifices of a discipled life. Herein lies the key to discerning mature aesthetic existence: "Where the *cantus firmus* is clear and distinct, a counterpoint can develop as mightily as it wants."[4]

If one concluding principle to note is that there are two modes of aesthetic existence in relation to discipleship—formative and deformative—then another is that mature aesthetic existence plays a dual role in the Christian life. Just as Kierkegaard introduced us to the *formative* nature of mature aesthetic existence as co-poeticizing with Christ, Bonhoeffer highlights its *expressive* nature, as a celebration of this-worldly, christological reality in the penultimate. Yet, as Bonhoeffer's own life shows, these two roles are not separate and distinct. The formative is always at work, even while one embraces the expressive, as seen through the role Bonhoeffer's own experience of music played in his theological development. The contribution of musical metaphors to Bonhoeffer's late theology points toward the role sensory immediacy can play, collaborating with the imagination in the formation of paradigms, ways of seeing.

Aesthetic existence will necessarily always play such a role because it is fundamental to being human, as an embodied, affective, often

---

3. Bonhoeffer, *Ethics*, 162.
4. Bonhoeffer, *Letters and Papers from Prison*, 394.

preconscious mode of attention that humans universally employ in relating to the world and in making meaning. The classic notion that there are two ways of engaging the world—the Dionysian and Apollonian—is grounded in our very physiologies, having resonance with McGilchrist's argument for two types of attention dominant in the lateralization of brain function. However, and this is another important concluding point, it is not an either/or; *both* are vital. McGilchrist is not suggesting that we do not need the left hemisphere of our brains; simply that right-hemisphere attention has a vital contribution to make. His rhetorical focus is on correcting our misunderstanding and neglect of such right-hemisphere attention. So too, this book is not an argument for aesthetic existence in opposition to rationality. Clearly, both are vital to being human, explicit rational processing playing an indispensable role in apprehension and communication. While it is paramount that we acknowledge the significant role of aesthetic existence in human consciousness, this does not in any way deny the indispensable role of abstract rationality and critical thinking in being human and becoming Christian. One does not come at the expense of the other, but ideally both work together in a symbiotic relationship, feeding off, challenging, and directing each other. The concern is simply that the tendency of modernity has been to prioritize rationality at the expense of the aesthetic, which not only is an error, but leads to an illusory perception of reality.

The perception is illusory since it is precisely embodied and affective attention that offers breadth and relational context, along with an implicit and intuitive sense of how the specifics of detailed abstraction fit into the whole. As we have seen, emerging fields such as embodied cognition, affective neuropsychology, and everyday aesthetics testify to this necessary relationship. While it is obviously impossible for human beings *not* to exist aesthetically—sensory immediacy is the necessary consequence of embodiment, a fundamental aspect of daily human life—illusory notions of reality are created when the primal role of such sensory immediacy is denied. This is exactly why the advertising industry's ideal subjects are those who claim that advertising has no effect on them, since they make choices solely on a rational basis. The aesthetic works largely on our formation through preconscious and implicit means, shaping our paradigmatic imagination, with the consequence that the significance of this influence can be disregarded if subject to ratiocentric hegemony. Immature aesthetic existence, even while indulging the senses, is dominated by this hegemony—the hyper-self-consciousness of left-hemisphere attention—thereby simply offering pseudovital experiences of sensationalism, which serve simulacra rather than breaking out of the self-contained hall of mirrors to encounter the Other. This is most apparent in the rise of sensory technologies to support such sensationalism, situating the subject at the center of so-called reality (as manifest in personal devices, digital gaming, virtual reality, aspects of social media, and even our relationship to fast food).[5] But it is also present in the less obvious social constructions of the prosperity gospel, or in distorted Christendom intoxicated by money and power, for instance. This is immature aesthetic existence in service to a self-seeking, transactional, I-It approach to the world, rather than mature aesthetic existence embracing the possibility and power of everyday transcendence and serving an I-Thou interaction with relational reality. Harnessing mature aesthetic existence is fundamental to understanding the essentially metaphorical nature of all abstraction and language, as it functions analogically, pointing toward ultimate Reality.

The ability of aesthetic existence to open oneself up to the other, to function as a gateway to both this-worldly and otherworldly transcendence, inextricably ties it both to the formation of belief and to action in the world. Belief is not simply a religious category, but plays a role in everyday life. Modern epistemology ranks belief below rational certainty, as a weak form of knowledge, but belief is more holistically and accurately understood as a disposition, as a relational commitment of trust. Such an articulation of belief integrates it with action, "acting as if," in response to the way reality is imagined (seen as). But the interaction between sensation, action, and belief is even more integrated, primal, and preconscious than this neat formula. It is impossible to separate these spheres of being human from one another. Rather, the propulsive nature of aesthetic existence, as it shapes the imagination, plays a significant role in seeing, acting, and believing. Instead of a neat, linear progression (sensory experience → ratiocination → belief → action), anticipation and projection precede conscious ratiocination, affecting one's disposition toward the world at a preconscious level in a complex, multidirectional interaction between action, belief, rational processing, and sensory experience. Not only does aesthetic existence shape the imagination, but

---

5. Smith describes this as the "iPhone-ization of our world." "The world as 'available' to me and at my disposal—to constitute the world as 'at-hand' for me, to be selected, scaled, scanned, tapped, and enjoyed" (Smith, *Imagining the Kingdom*, 143).

we *live into* these paradigms as embodied beings, our desires molded by these "mythic sensibilities."[6]

Aesthetic existence is indeed then a form of poiesis, as Kierkegaard introduced it to us, but the way it is involved in *"making* sense" is not distinct from action in the world, or praxis. On the one hand, the end result of immature aesthetic existence is the *making* of simulacra and the celebration of self-referential sensationalism. On the other hand, by contrast, the poiesis of mature aesthetic existence is the creation not only of art, play, friendship, and so forth, but, thereby, of a way of seeing the world, an embodied way of being in the world, which celebrates and analogically participates in christological reality. Such existence is a relational commitment, a mode of discipleship, a christological mimesis, the incarnate body of Christ in embodied reality, integrating aesthetics, ethics, and faith.

The way of discerning such mature aesthetic existence is through the measure of *fittingness* to the liturgical script of shalom-making. Aesthetic engagement is itself a form of action, refuting the modern grand narrative of art, which seeks to locate art itself within a separate sphere of disinterested contemplation, as having no utilitarian purpose, as being only for itself and thereby being socially other, the pathway to transcendence. Rather, aesthetic engagement is embedded in social practices, carrying normative value toward a specific *telos*; practices are oriented toward a particular vision of the good life. While aesthetic engagement may not be explicitly utilitarian, it can be steered by means-end rationality in a number of ways, notably by carrying *count as* significance. Even sensory immediacy, being in the moment, can carry *count as* significance through embodied and imaginative participation in a larger narrative toward a specific *telos*. These larger life-narratives, informed by a social imaginary and embodied as social practices, function as scripts, lending meaning to action. But drawing on all we have discovered regarding the preconscious and implicit significance of aesthetic existence, the key point here is that such sensory participation is not only *expressive* of a particular script but also *formative* for that script. To identify aesthetic existence as harmless fun is thus illusory. There is a reinforcing circularity about such participation, or a discipleship (whether religious or otherwise) oriented by the relevant *telos*. The question is then not *whether* one worships, but *whom* or *what* one worships. While acknowledging that all liturgy is not focused

---

6 Ward, *Unimaginable*, 157.

on God with the same intensity (and therefore carries different weight), in an understanding of *all* Christian action as liturgy, and consequently a holistic orientation—a liturgical script—for all of life, *mature* aesthetic existence functions as both expressive of being Christian in the world, and formative for a life of discipleship, anchored in a full-orbed approach to following Christ. Within this life script distinctions between sacred and secular are nonexistent: the everyday and the ordinary are significant and *enhanced* through mature aesthetic existence as signs of shalom.

This leads us back to the question of agency. By participating in shalom-making, mature aesthetic existence rejects the self-creation of immature aesthetic existence (and the concomitant "kingdoms" thus generated) and embraces an affective and embodied attunement of human agency to divine agency. In other words, it is a fitting response, an attunement to, and participation in God's work in the world. As all true worship does, a liturgical understanding of all of life situates the self as neither the object of attention nor the source of action. Liturgy is "God's action and our faithful reception of that action."[7] This alignment of the self to the agency of God lies at the heart of discipleship and the spiritual practices that serve it. In this sense understanding the aesthetics of discipleship reveals a call for everyday aesthetic stewardship as a faithful liturgical response, a spiritual practice in the Christian life.

Theoretical and Practical Trajectories toward Aesthetic Stewardship

Moving toward the embrace of aesthetic stewardship as a spiritual practice will require wisdom (both a commitment to developing greater understanding of the aesthetics of discipleship, and the practical application of that understanding in the church). Aesthetic existence has a feral nature; it is not easily domesticated. This is because sensory immediacy "lies beneath" rational processing, engaging the imagination as "mythic sensibility."[8] We have explored at length the dynamic, propulsive nature of aesthetic existence, but again, it needs to be clear that the "mythic sensibility" it cultivates can lead to either wonder or horror.[9] There are indeed "hidden pathologies" of the imagination, and the expression of

---

7. Wolterstorff, "The Reformed Liturgy," 290.
8. Ward, *Unimaginable*, 115.
9. Ward, *Unimaginable*, 157–67.

these can be horrific, as evidenced by Nazism.[10] This is why a recovery of aesthetic existence cannot be a Nietzschean abandonment to the Dionysian, beyond good and evil, but rather needs to be the cultivation of *mature* aesthetic existence, anchored in a full-orbed approach to following Christ. However, herein lies the challenge, precisely because aesthetic existence "lies beneath." This is why any discernment of mature aesthetic existence needs to be holistic, going beyond conscious ratiocination to the attunement, or fittingness, discerned by one's whole being, in polyphonic resonance to a broader life-narrative of discipleship.

This raises the need for more work to be done on the aesthetics of discipleship from the perspective of biblical studies. Not only will this necessarily ground a recovery of aesthetic existence within the broader explicit script of being Christian, but it will reveal the unbalanced extent to which contemporary understandings of discipleship prioritize rational processing. An example of this can be seen in our English translations of Heb 5:14. In speaking of spiritual maturity, the writer uses a description consistent with what we have been discussing: a holistic attunement of one's whole being, an embodied sensitivity to Reality as infused by Christ, "But solid food is for the mature, for those whose faculties have been trained by practice to distinguish good from evil." That the whole meaning of this sentence is saturated with understanding discipleship as embodied existence is almost entirely lost in translation, apart from the obvious metaphor of food. The translation of *aistheterion* (note the obvious etymological relation to the English *aesthetic*) as "faculties" rather than "senses" dilutes this embodied thrust. Some translations omit the sensory element entirely, the NIV simply suggesting the mature "have trained themselves." (Arguably, "themselves" is not a poor translation, since it accurately points to the holistic nature of aesthetic perception in the development of the self implied here, but it fails to convey the embodied and sensory weight carried in the original, particularly when we read it through the modern lens of the ratiocentric "self"). Likewise, our reading of the KJV and NKJV will inevitably be just as ratiocentric, as they use the term "senses" but qualify it with "reason": the mature "by *reason* of use have their senses exercised to discern both good and evil." "Reason" is nowhere to be found in the Greek. In fact, as the NKJV footnotes, the word is better translated "practice." It is a practice that is "trained" (*gymnazo*)—a term used for the training in a palaestra,

---

10. Ward, *Unimaginable*, 119.

where the naked exercise of wrestlers, boxers, and other athletes would take place. In other words, the verse is essentially saying that the spiritually mature have attuned their senses, through embodied practice, to discern the distinction between good and evil. But neither is it translated that way, nor do we interpret the more vague translations to have this weight of sensory discernment. This is but one example of how the holistic understanding of discipleship presented in the Bible, incorporating embodiment and affect, is lost through the hermeneutical hegemony of left-hemisphere abstraction. The aesthetic (particularly in the classic sense, as sensory perceptibility) plays an integral role in a biblical account of human apprehension and consequently carries epistemological weight. (For example, consider *aisthanomai* as perception in Luke 9:45, and *aisthesis* as discernment in Phil 1:9.)

Once again, the point here is not to drive a wedge between the aesthetic and the rational, but simply to point to our modern ratiocentrism. For the biblical writers the two were holistically connected, just as ethical and aesthetic goodness are connected in the term *to kalon*. Jesus himself modeled this holistic embrace of the Christian life. Again, to avoid any misunderstanding, the cost of discipleship is indeed a fundamental aspect of the gospel. However, a life of material sacrifice does not necessitate repudiating the material world or the senses. Luke's Gospel in particular highlights how much of Jesus's own connection with others happened in the context of meals together (recall the this-worldly relational transcendence that aesthetic existence fosters), to the extent that his communal enjoyment of food and wine brought accusations of being a glutton and drunkard (Luke 7:34). The point here is simply that a robust account of the aesthetics of discipleship needs further exploration from the perspective of biblical studies, not only to acknowledge that the Bible takes embodiment and the senses seriously (as many studies have shown), but further, to show that such sensory engagement with the world is central to apprehension and formation, and thus is inseparable from being human and the process of discipleship.

Again, however, even in undertaking such a biblical study, we need to resist the temptation to believe that we can comprehensively get a handle on aesthetic existence solely via ratiocination. This is precisely why a book such as this is limited to offering only glimpses of the internal workings of aesthetic existence. Relying solely on tools of rational analysis, one can only intimate at abstract approximations as to its nature, always losing something of the essence of this aspect of being human by such reduction to propositional language. As a result, this mode of inquiry cannot comprehensively articulate the nature and function of aesthetic existence in being human, even while it aims to offer a greater degree of understanding in this regard. Neat encapsulations of aesthetic existence will always elude our grasp, for precisely the same reason that aesthetic existence remains valuable as a gateway to transcendence, wonder, and mystery. Nevertheless, as we have noted, while it is impossible to quantify the role of aesthetic existence in human formation with scientific certainty, this does not mean we cannot point to its fundamental significance; indeed such endeavors are an important step toward its recovery.

Embracing aesthetic stewardship in the life of the church will, therefore, demand more than measured theoretical ratiocination due to the preconscious, embodied, and affective realms within which aesthetic existence operates. It will require *living* aesthetic stewardship—not merely discussing it or speaking about it, but embracing it as an aspect of Christ-centered life, allowing it full voice amid the polyphony of Christian existence. And yet, the slippery nature of aesthetic existence is precisely why the church has often been reluctant to embrace it. If it cannot be controlled, who knows where it will lead? A mature aesthetic existence cannot be programmatized, ordered, or dictated solely by explicit means. In many senses it is easier then to simply reject it. But such a rejection comes at a high price, as we have seen; this formative aspect of being human continues to operate, either for good or ill, even if not explicitly embraced. What might the solutions be?

A helpful starting point would be to revisit Kierkegaard's "second immediacy." On the one hand, we need to reject a linear account of Kierkegaard's notion of a second immediacy, or immediacy after reflection. The relationship between immediacy and explicit reflection is simply more complex than the sequential progression implied here. On the other hand, we should acknowledge the important role of reflection and intention in mature aesthetic existence. Sensory immediacy plays a role in discipleship precisely when it is integrated with reflection, intention, and self-control, just as *playing* a musical instrument cannot be separated from disciplined practice. The crucial point here is the complex, multidirectional, symbiotic relationship between these aspects of human existence. In this sense, we could say that *all* immediacy is (in Kierkegaard's language) a second immediacy. Being in the moment is always informed by paradigms already formed through amalgamation of previous sensory experience, reflection, intention, action, and so forth. In another sense, we could suggest that all immediacy is (to borrow Kierkegaard's term again) a first immediacy; being viscerally in the moment will always, as Ward says, "lie beneath" conscious intention and reflection to some degree at least. Reflection, intention, and volitional action therefore *do* have important roles to play, but due to the complexity of this relationship, the question is how to best engage these aspects of being human in order to cultivate mature aesthetic existence in the everyday.

As noted at the beginning of Chapter 4, its feral nature, the "uncontrollable, even demonic, energies" associated with aesthetic existence, has led to a suspicious response from the church.[11] The irony is that church traditions most careful to avoid aesthetic existence are often precisely those exposed to its deformative nature. By excluding aesthetic existence from their portrayal of the Christian life, they simply abdicate any responsibility to this formative aspect of human existence, handing it over to the cultural liturgies of everyday life for a secular discipleship. But in many ways, this suspicious response is valid. As we have noted, there is indeed a deformative component to aesthetic existence.

However, the church also cannot afford to ignore the formative power of aesthetic existence. In other words, banishing it from the Christian life is not the solution, particularly amid an aestheticized, technologically saturated society with a plethora of consumerist and political agendas calling for "worship." Rather the church needs to cultivate ways of being attuned to a liturgical life toward shalom in the everyday. What does this look like?

A starting point is to acknowledge the power of aesthetic practice, intentionally nurturing and cultivating spaces for individual and communal everyday liturgical practices for the twenty-first century. In a postmodern society rediscovering the spiritual power of aesthetic engagement and embodiment, the church can offer both explicit and implicit affirmation of a script that embraces everyday aesthetic existence. The christological nature of this-worldly reality and consequently the liturgical significance of the everyday should be didactically affirmed. In addition to this explicit affirmation, the church (as Christians in the life of the world) should endorse this by creating spaces that celebrate such practices as communal play, music-making, dancing, hiking, and feasting. At the same time the church must practice costly discipleship. Again, these two realms—explicit and implicit scripting—are ideally not

---

11. De Gruchy, *Christianity, Art and Transformation*, 16.

separate and distinct. Explicit and intentional reflection should be both feeding into and gleaning from the embodiment of liturgical, everyday aesthetic existence.[12]

Nevertheless, again, the nature of aesthetic existence means that such intentional affirmation will form only part of a Christian embrace. Moments present themselves unexpectedly in the everyday, amid the apparently disjointed fragments of life. As Bonhoeffer pointed out, discipleship is the ability to *see*, to be attuned to these moments as the formative experiences that they are. The fragments can here function as lenses through which to perceive the polyphony in greater mysterious fullness. In this sense, there is resonance between Kierkegaard's second immediacy and Paul Ricoeur's second naïveté.[13] Mature aesthetic existence requires firsthand experience of costly discipleship. It requires confrontation with the jarring fragmentation of a fallen world, not theoretically but existentially, to move beyond the critical to a second naïveté, or a second immediacy.[14] Such an embrace of mature aesthetic existence can never be programmatized. However, an attunement is required, a sensitivity, both personally and pastorally (for others), to identify the fragments, the moments, leaning into them as polyphonic living in counterpoint to the cantus firmus of love for Christ. A mature aesthetic existence is therefore integrated with an understanding and mindful practice of spiritual formation.

Finally, any practical articulation of mature aesthetic existence will need to have love at its core (a theme that has been subtly present throughout our study). To orient this project, we turned to Kierkegaard, who noted that aesthetic existence is not an ethical category, in the sense that it is not to be thought of as either permissible or impermissible. Next we saw that Bonhoeffer situated aesthetic existence in the sphere (*Spielraum*) of freedom, in light of God's faithfulness in the incarnation. Further, we could conclude by saying that it is a *relational* question of formation (*Bildung*); a process of becoming, defined *in relation to* the Other. This is why it is core to discipleship; it orients, and manifests an

---

12. For an excellent example of this, see Warren, *Liturgy of the Ordinary*.

13. Ricoeur, *The Symbolism of Evil*, 349.

14. Bonhoeffer, Kierkegaard, de Gruchy, and Wolterstorff's lives all attest to the fundamental, existential shift that intimate pain and death brings—both Wolterstorff and de Gruchy losing sons, and Wolterstorff describing his life as forever being "divided into before and after." Wolterstorff, *Lament for a Son*, 46. See also de Gruchy, *Led into Mystery*.

orientation of one's love. Here we can recall Kierkegaard's description of a first immediacy as sensory-erotic immediacy to be taken up within marriage, alongside Bonhoeffer's suggestion that the passion of Song of Solomon can "develop as mightily as it wants" in counterpoint to the cantus firmus.[15] Mature aesthetic existence therefore reflects the paradox of the gospel; it is kenotic in the denial of self, while being pleromatic in the restoration of full humanity and identity. It is being-for-others even through existential immersion in the sensory moment. It is not the rejection of earthly love, but an orientation of passion, desire, and immediacy as liturgical service of the other in polyphonic resonance with God's love for us.

---

15. Bonhoeffer, *Letters and Papers from Prison*, 394.

Bibliography

Avis, Paul. *God and the Creative Imagination: Metaphor, Symbol, and Myth in Religion and Theology*. London: Routledge, 1999.

Balthasar, Hans Urs von. *Cosmic Liturgy: The Universe according to Maximus the Confessor*. Translated by Brian E. Daley. A Communio Book. San Francisco: Ignatius, 2003.

———. "Revelation and the Beautiful." In *Explorations in Theology*. Vol. 1, *The Word Made Flesh*, 95–126. 4 vols. Translated by A. V. Littledale with Alexander Dru. San Francisco: Ignatius, 1989.

Barsalou, Lawrence, et al. "Embodiment in Religious Knowledge." *Journal of Cognition and Culture* 5/1 (2005) 14–57.

Barth, Karl. *Church Dogmatics I, The Doctrine of the Word of God, Part 1*. Edited by T. F. Torrance. Translated by G. W. Bromiley. Edinburgh: T. & T. Clark, 1975.

———. *How I Changed My Mind*. Edinburgh: St. Andrew Press, 1969.

———. *Wolfgang Amadeus Mozart*. Translated by Clarence K. Pott. 1986. Reprint, Eugene, OR: Wipf & Stock, 2003.

Begbie, Jeremy. *Music, Modernity, and God: Essays in Listening*. Oxford: Oxford University Press, 2013.

———. *Redeeming Transcendence in the Arts: Bearing Witness to the Triune God*. London: SCM, 2018.

———. *Voicing Creation's Praise: Towards a Theology of the Arts*. Edinburgh: T. & T. Clark, 1991.

Benson, Bruce Ellis. *Graven Ideologies: Nietzsche, Derrida & Marion on Modern Idolatry*. Downers Grove, IL: IVP Academic, 2002.

Bethge, Eberhard. "The Challenge of Dietrich Bonhoeffer's Life and Theology." *The Alden-Tuthill Lectures, The Chicago Theological Seminary Register* 51/2 (1961) 1–38.

———. *Dietrich Bonhoeffer: A Biography*. Rev. ed. Translated by Victoria J. Barnett. Minneapolis: Fortress, 2000.

Bonhoeffer, Dietrich. *Creation and Fall*. Edited by John de Gruchy. Translated by Douglas Stephen Bax. Dietrich Bonhoeffer Works 3. Minneapolis: Fortress, 1997.

———. *Discipleship*. Edited by Geoffrey B. Kelly and John D. Godsey. Translated by Barbara Green and Reinhard Krauss. Dietrich Bonhoeffer Works 4. Minneapolis: Fortress, 2003.

———. *Ethics*. Edited by Clifford J. Green. Translated by Reinhard Krauss et al. Dietrich Bonhoeffer Works 6. Minneapolis: Fortress, 2005.

———. *Letters and Papers from Prison*. Edited by John de Gruchy. Translated by Isabel Best et al. Dietrich Bonhoeffer Works 8. Minneapolis: Fortress, 2010.

———. *London, 1933–1935*. Edited by Keith Clements. Translated by Isabel Best. Supplementary material translated by Douglas W. Stott. Dietrich Bonhoeffer Works 13. Minneapolis: Fortress, 2007.

———. *Theological Education at Finkenwalde, 1935–1937*. Edited by H. Gaylon Barker and Mark S. Brocker. Translated by Douglas W. Stott. Dietrich Bonhoeffer Works 14. Minneapolis: Fortress, 2013.

Bourdieu, Pierre. *The Logic of Practice*. Translated by Richard Nice. Stanford: Stanford University Press, 1990.

———. *Outline of a Theory of Practice*. Translated by Richard Nice. Cambridge Studies in Social Anthropology 16. Cambridge: Cambridge University Press, 1977.

Brown, Frank Burch. *Religious Aesthetics: A Theological Study of Making and Meaning*. Princeton: Princeton University Press, 1989.

Brueggemann, Walter. *The Prophetic Imagination*. Philadelphia: Fortress, 1978.

Bryant, David J. *Faith and the Play of Imagination: On the Role of Imagination in Religion*. Studies in American Biblical Hermeneutics 5. Macon, GA: Mercer University Press, 1989.

Bultmann, Rudolf. "γινώσκω, κτλ." In *Theological Dictionary of the New Testament*, by Gerhard Kittel, 1:689–719. Translated by G. W. Bromiley. 10 vols. Grand Rapids: Eerdmans, 1964.

Cavanaugh, William T. *Being Consumed: Economics and Christian Desire*. Grand Rapids: Eerdmans, 2008.

Coakley, Sarah. "Concluding Eirenic (and Mostly "Unscientific") Postscript." In "Engaging Iain McGilchrist: Ascetical Practice, Brain Lateralization, and Philosophy of Mind." Edited by Wesley J. Wildman and Sarah Coakley. Special issue, *Religion, Brain & Behavior* 9/4 (2019) 423–34.

Colapinto, John. "The Interpreter." A Reporter at Large. *The New Yorker*, April 16, 2007, 120–37. https://www.newyorker.com/magazine/2007/04/16/the-interpreter-2.

Connell, George. *To Be One Thing: Personal Unity in Kierkegaard's Thought*. Macon, GA: Mercer University Press, 1985.

Corballis, Michael C. "The Evolution of Lateralized Brain Circuits." *Frontiers in Psychology* 8 (2017). https://doi.org/10.3389/fpsyg.2017.01021/.

Corbon, Jean. *The Wellspring of Worship*. Translated by Matthew J. O'Connell. New York: Paulist, 1988.

Cottingham, John. "Brain Laterality and Religious Awareness." In "Engaging Iain McGilchrist: Ascetical Practice, Brain Lateralization, and Philosophy of Mind." Edited by Wesley J. Wildman and Sarah Coakley. Special issue, *Religion, Brain & Behavior* 9/4 (2019) 362–68.

———. *Philosophy and the Good Life: Reason and the Passions in Greek, Cartesian and Psychoanalytic Ethics*. Cambridge: Cambridge University Press, 1998.

———. "What Is Humane Philosophy and Why Is It at Risk?" *Royal Institute of Philosophy Supplement* 83/65 (2009) 233–55.

Cupit, Geoffrey. *Justice as Fittingness*. Oxford: Clarendon, 1999.

Damasio, Antonio. *Descartes' Error: Emotion, Reason, and the Human Brain*. London: Vintage, 2006.

———. *The Feeling of What Happens: Body, Emotion and the Making of Consciousness*. London: Vintage, 2000.

De Gruchy, John W., ed. *The Cambridge Companion to Dietrich Bonhoeffer*. Cambridge Companions to Religion. Cambridge: Cambridge University Press, 1999.

———. *Christianity, Art and Transformation: Theological Aesthetics in the Struggle for Justice*. Cambridge: Cambridge University Press, 2001.

———. *Led into Mystery: Faith Seeking Answers in Life and Death*. London: SCM, 2013.

———. "The Search for Transcendence in an Age of Barbarism: Bonhoeffer, Beethoven, Mann's 'Dr Faustus' and the Spiritual Crisis of the Present Time." In *Polyphonie Der Theologie: Verantwortung Und Widerstand in Kirche Und Politik*, edited by Matthias Grebe, 195–208. Stuttgart: Kohlhammer, 2019.

———. *A Theological Odyssey: My Life in Writing*. Beyers Naudé Centre Series on Public Theology 7. Stellenbosch, South Africa: Sun Media, 2014.

Dewey, John. *Art as Experience*. 1934. Reprint, New York: Perigee, 2005.

Dreyfus, Hubert, and Charles Taylor. *Retrieving Realism*. Cambridge: Harvard University Press, 2015.

Dunning, Stephen N. *Kierkegaard's Dialectic of Inwardness: A Structural Analysis of the Theory of Stages*. Princeton Legacy Library. Princeton: Princeton University Press, 2014.

Dykstra, Craig R. *Growing in the Life of Faith: Education and Christian Practices*. 2nd ed. Louisville: Westminster John Knox, 2005.

Eagleton, Terry. *The Ideology of the Aesthetic*. Oxford: Blackwell, 1991.

Ellis, George, and Mark Solms. *Beyond Evolutionary Psychology: How and Why Neuropsychological Modules Arise*. Culture and Psychology. Cambridge: Cambridge University Press, 2018.

Evans, Anna. "Gestalt: A Tale of Two Hemispheres." *Gestalt Journal of Australia and New Zealand* 16/1 (2019) 4–18.

Everett, Daniel L. *Don't Sleep, There Are Snakes: Life and Language in the Amazonian Jungle*. New York: Vintage Departures, 2009.

———. "What Does Pirahã Grammar Have to Teach Us about Human Language and the Mind?" *Wiley Interdisciplinary Reviews: Cognitive Science* 3/6 (2012) 555–63.

Fagerberg, David W. "Liturgical Theology." In *T. & T. Clark Companion to Liturgy*, edited by Alcuin Reid, 3–22. London: Bloomsbury T. & T. Clark, 2015.

Ferreira, M. Jamie. *Transforming Vision: Imagination and Will in Kierkegaardian Faith*. Oxford: Clarendon, 1991.

Fesmire, Steven. *John Dewey and Moral Imagination: Pragmatism in Ethics*. Bloomington: Indiana University Press, 2005.

Forrester, Duncan B. *Truthful Action: Explorations in Practical Theology*. Edinburgh: T. & T. Clark, 2000.

Gallagher, Shaun. *How the Body Shapes the Mind*. Oxford: Clarendon, 2005.

Goldie, John. "The Implications of Brain Lateralisation for Modern General Practice." *British Journal of General Practice* 66/642 (2016) 44–45.

Gouwens, David J. *Kierkegaard's Dialectic of the Imagination*. American University Studies. Series 5, Philosophy. New York: Lang, 1989.

Green, Garrett. *Imagining God: Theology and the Religious Imagination*. Grand Rapids: Eerdmans, 1998.

Güntürkün, Onur et al. "Brain Lateralization: A Comparative Perspective." *Physiological Reviews* 100/3 (2020) 1019–63.

Harrison Warren, Tish. *Liturgy of the Ordinary: Sacred Practices in Everyday Life*. Downers Grove, IL: InterVarsity, 2016.

Hart, David Bentley. *The Beauty of the Infinite: The Aesthetics of Christian Truth*. Grand Rapids: Eerdmans, 2003.
Hessel, Dieter T. "'Now That Animals Can Be Genetically Engineered: Biotechnology in Theological-Ethical Perspective.'" In *Ecotheology: Voices from South and North*, edited by David G. Hallman. 1994. Reprint, Eugene, OR: Wipf & Stock, 2009.
Holland, Scott. "First We Take Manhattan, Then We Take Berlin: Bonhoeffer's New York." *CrossCurrents* 50/3 (2000) 369–82.
Horn, Stacy. *Imperfect Harmony: Finding Happiness Singing with Others*. Chapel Hill, NC: Algonquin, 2013.
Johnson, Howard A. "Kierkegaard and the Church: A Supplement to the Translator's Introduction." In *Kierkegaard's Attack upon "Christendom," 1854–1855*, edited by Walter Lowrie, xix–xxxiii. Princeton: Princeton University Press, 1968.
Johnson, Mark. *The Body in the Mind: The Bodily Basis of Meaning, Imagination, and Reason*. Chicago: University of Chicago Press, 1987.
———. *The Meaning of the Body: Aesthetics of Human Understanding*. Chicago: University of Chicago Press, 2012.
Jones, Carolyn M. "Dietrich Bonhoeffer's *Letters and Papers from Prison*: Rethinking the Relationship of Theology and Arts, Literature and Religion." *Literature and Theology* 9/3 (1995) 243–59.
Jothen, Peder. *Kierkegaard, Aesthetics, and Selfhood: The Art of Subjectivity*. Ashgate Studies in Theology, Imagination, and the Arts. Burlington, VT: Ashgate, 2014.
Kelly, Geoffrey B. "Kierkegaard as 'Antidote' and as Impact on Dietrich Bonhoeffer's Concept of Christian Discipleship." In *Bonhoeffer's Intellectual Formation: Theology and Philosophy in His Thought*, edited by Peter Frick, 145–66. Tübingen: Mohr/Siebeck, 2008.
Kelly, Geoffrey B., and John D. Godsey. "Editor's Introduction to the English Edition." In *Discipleship*, by Dietrich Bonhoeffer, 1–33. Edited by Geoffrey B. Kelly and John D. Godsey. Translated by Barbara Green and Reinhard Krauss. Dietrich Bonhoeffer Works 4. Minneapolis: Fortress, 2003.
Kierkegaard, Søren. *The Concept of Anxiety: A Simple Psychologically Orienting Deliberation on the Dogmatic Issue of Hereditary Sin*. Translated with introduction and notes by Reidar Thomte, in collaboration with Albert B. Anderson. Kierkegaard's Writings 8. Princeton: Princeton University Press, 1981.
———. *The Concept of Irony*. Edited and translated with introduction and notes by Howard V. Hong and Edna H. Hong. Kierkegaard's Writings 2. Princeton: Princeton University Press, 1992.
———. *Concluding Unscientific Postscript*. Translated by David F. Swenson and completed after his death and provided with an introduction and notes by Walter Lowrie. Princeton: Princeton University Press, 1941.
———. *Concluding Unscientific Postscript to Philosophical Fragments*. 2 vols. Edited and translated with introduction and notes by Howard V. Hong and Edna H. Hong. Kierkegaard's Writings 12. Princeton: Princeton University Press, 1992.
———. *Either/Or: A Fragment of Life*. 2 vols. Edited by Walter Lowrie. Translated by David F. Swenson and Lillian M. Swenson. Princeton: Princeton University Press, 1944.
———. *Either/Or*. 2 vols. Edited and translated with introduction and notes by Howard V. Hong and Edna H. Hong. Kierkegaard's Writings 3–4. Princeton: Princeton University Press, 1987.

———. *For Self-Examination and Judge for Yourselves! And Three Discourses, 1851*. Translated by Walter Lowrie. Princeton: Princeton University Press, 1944.

———. *For Self-Examination/Judge for Yourself!* Edited and translated with introduction and notes by Howard V. Hong and Edna H. Hong. Kierkegaard's Writings 21. Princeton: Princeton University Press, 2015.

———. *Kierkegaard's Attack upon "Christendom," 1854–1855*. Edited with an introduction by Walter Lowrie. Princeton: Princeton University Press, 1968.

———. *"The Moment" and Late Writings*. Edited and translated with introduction and notes by Howard V. Hong and Edna H. Hong. Kierkegaard's Writings 23. Princeton: Princeton University Press, 2009.

———. *Practice in Christianity*. Edited and translated with introduction and notes by Howard V. Hong and Edna H. Hong. Kierkegaard's Writings 20. Princeton: Princeton University Press, 1991.

———. *Sickness unto Death: A Christian Psychological Exposition for Upbuilding and Awakening*. Edited and translated with introduction and notes by Howard V. Hong and Edna H. Hong. Kierkegaard's Writings 19. Princeton: Princeton University Press, 2013.

———. *Søren Kierkegaard's Journals and Papers*. Vol. 2. 7 vols. Edited and translated by Howard V. Hong and Edna H. Hong. Assisted by Gregor Malantschuk. Bloomington: Indiana University Press, 1970.

———. *Søren Kierkegaard's Journals and Papers*. Vol. 3. 7 vols. Edited and translated by Howard V. Hong and Edna H. Hong. Assisted by Gregor Malantschuk. Bloomington: Indiana University Press, 1975.

———. *Søren Kierkegaard's Journals and Papers*, Vol. 5. 7 vols. Edited and translated by Howard V. Hong and Edna H. Hong. Assisted by Gregor Malantschuk. Bloomington: Indiana University Press, 1978.

———. *Søren Kierkegaard's Journals and Papers*. Vol. 6. 7 vols. Edited by Howard V. Hong and Edna H. Hong. Bloomington: Indiana University Press, 1978.

———. *Stages on Life's Way: Studies by Various Persons*. Edited and translated with introduction and notes by Howard V. Hong and Edna H. Hong. Kierkegaard's Writings 11. Princeton: Princeton University Press, 1988.

———. *Training in Christianity*. Translated by Walter Lowrie. Princeton Legacy Series. Princeton University Press, 2015.

———. *Works of Love*. Edited by Howard V. Hong and Edna H. Hong. Kierkegaard's Writings 16. Princeton: Princeton University Press, 1998.

Kirkpatrick, Matthew D. *Attacks on Christendom in a World Come of Age: Kierkegaard, Bonhoeffer, and the Question of "Religionless Christianity."* Princeton Theological Monograph Series 166. Eugene, OR: Pickwick Publications, 2011.

Kirmmse, Bruce H. "'Out with It!': The Modern Breakthrough, Kierkegaard and Denmark." In *The Cambridge Companion to Kierkegaard*, edited by Alastair Hannay and Gordon D. Marino, 15–47. Cambridge Companions to Philosophy. Cambridge: Cambridge University Press, 1998.

Kivy, Peter, ed. *The Blackwell Guide to Aesthetics*. Blackwell Philosophy Guides. Malden, MA: Blackwell, 2004.

Koerner, Joseph Leo. *The Reformation of the Image*. Chicago: University of Chicago Press, 2004.

Kosslyn, Stephen, and G. Wayne Miller. *Top Brain, Bottom Brain: Harnessing the Power of the Four Cognitive Modes*. 2nd ed. New York: Simon & Schuster, 2015.

Kundu, Prantik, and Derek Alexander Smith. "The Relationship of Lateralization and Phenomenology to Neural Circuits." In "Engaging Iain McGilchrist: Ascetical Practice, Brain Lateralization, and Philosophy of Mind." Edited by Wesley J. Wildman and Sarah Coakley. Special issue, *Religion, Brain & Behavior* 9/4 (2019) 380–86.

Lacewing, Michael. "What Reason Can't Do." In *The Moral Life: Essays in Honour of John Cottingham*, edited by Nafsika Athanassoulis and Samantha Vice, 139–63. Basingstoke, UK: Palgrave Macmillan, 2008.

Lakoff, George, and Mark Johnson. *Metaphors We Live By*. Chicago: University of Chicago Press, 2003.

———. *Philosophy in the Flesh: The Embodied Mind and Its Challenge to Western Thought*. New York: Basic Books, 1999.

Lewis, C. S. "Bluspels and Flalansferes: A Semantic Nightmare." In *Selected Literary Essays*, edited by Walter Hooper, 251–65. London: Cambridge University Press, 1969.

Lovin, Robin W. *Christian Realism and the New Realities*. New York: Cambridge University Press, 2008.

Lyon, David. *Jesus in Disneyland: Religion in Postmodern Times*. Cambridge: Polity, 2000.

MacIntyre, Alasdair. *After Virtue: A Study in Moral Theory*. Notre Dame, IN: University of Notre Dame Press, 1984.

McGilchrist, Iain. "Author Response to Trimble Book Review." *Cognitive Neuropsychiatry* 16/3 (2011) 284–88.

———. "Cerebral Lateralization and Religion: A Phenomenological Approach." In "Engaging Iain McGilchrist: Ascetical Practice, Brain Lateralization, and Philosophy of Mind." Edited by Wesley J. Wildman and Sarah Coakley. Special issue, *Religion, Brain & Behavior* 9/4 (2019) 319–39.

———. "Exchange of Views: Top Brain, Bottom Brain; A Reply to Stephen Kosslyn & Wayne Miller." https://channelmcgilchrist.com/exchange-of-views/.

———. "A Response to Commentators." In "Engaging Iain McGilchrist: Ascetical Practice, Brain Lateralization, and Philosophy of Mind." Edited by Wesley J. Wildman and Sarah Coakley. Special issue, *Religion, Brain & Behavior* 9/4 (2019) 399–422.

———. "Split Brain, Split Views—Debating Iain Mcgilchrist." *Pandaemonium* (blog), 2013. https://kenanmalik.com/2013/02/24/split-brain-split-views-debating-iain-mcgilchrist/.

———. *The Master and His Emissary: The Divided Brain and the Making of the Western World*. New Haven: Yale University Press, 2009.

———. *The Master and His Emissary: The Divided Brain and the Making of the Western World*. New expanded ed. New Haven: Yale University Press, 2019.

Mithen, Steven. *The Singing Neanderthals: The Origins of Music, Language, Mind, and Body*. Cambridge: Harvard University Press, 2007.

Moseley, David J. R. S. "'Parables' and 'Polyphony.'" In *Resonant Witness: Conversations between Music and Theology*, edited by Jeremy S. Begbie and Steven R. Guthrie, 240–70. The Calvin Institute of Christian Worship Liturgical Studies. Grand Rapids: Eerdmans, 2011.

Niebuhr, Reinhold. *Christianity and Power Politics*. New York: Scribner, 1940.

Nietzsche, Friedrich. "The Anti-Christ." In *The Anti-Christ, Ecce Homo, Twilight of the Idols, and Other Writings*, edited by Aaron Ridley, 1–68. Translated by Judith Norman. Cambridge Texts in the History of Philosophy. Cambridge: Cambridge University Press, 2005.
———. *Beyond Good and Evil: Prelude to a Philosophy of the Future*. Edited by Rolf-Peter Horstmann and Judith Norman. Translated by Judith Norman. Cambridge Texts in the History of Philosophy. Cambridge: Cambridge University Press, 2002.
———. *The Birth of Tragedy, and The Case of Wagner*. Translated, with commentary, by Walter Kaufmann. New York: Vintage, 1967.
———. *The Birth of Tragedy*. In *The Birth of Tragedy and Other Writings*, edited by Raymond Geuss and Ronald Speirs, 1–116. Translated by Ronald Speirs. Cambridge: Cambridge University Press, 1999.
———. *Ecce Homo*. In *The Anti-Christ, Ecce Homo, Twilight of the Idols, and Other Writings*, edited by Aaron Ridley, 69–152. Translated by Judith Norman. Cambridge Texts in the History of Philosophy. Cambridge: Cambridge University Press, 2005.
———. *The Gay Science*. Edited by Bernard Williams. Translated by Josefine Nauckhoff and Adrian Del Caro. Cambridge Texts in the History of Philosophy. Cambridge: Cambridge University Press, 2001.
———. *On the Genealogy of Morality*. In *"On the Genealogy of Morality" and Other Writings*, edited by Keith Ansell-Pearson, 1–120. Translated by Carol Diethe. Cambridge Texts in the History of Political Thought. Cambridge: Cambridge University Press, 2006.
O'Connell, Maureen H. *If These Walls Could Talk: Community Muralism and the Beauty of Justice*. Collegeville, MN: Liturgical, 2012.
O'Connor, Flannery. "The Church and the Fiction Writer." In *Mystery and Manners: Occasional Prose*, selected and edited by Sally and Robert Fitzgerald, 143–53. New York: Farrar, Straus & Giroux, 1969.
Osolsobe, Petr. "Kierkegaard's Aesthetics of Music: A Concept of the Musical Erotic." *Sbornik Praci Filozoficke Fakulty Brnenske Univerzity*, no. 27–28 (1993) 97–106.
Pangritz, Andreas. "Point and Counterpoint—Resistance and Submission: Dietrich Bonhoeffer on Theology and Music in Times of War and Social Crisis." In *Theology in Dialogue: The Impact of the Arts, Humanities, and Science on Contemporary Religious Thought: Essays in Honor of John W. de Gruchy*, edited by Lyn Holness and Ralf K. Wüstenberg, 28–42. Grand Rapids: Eerdmans, 2002.
———. *The Polyphony of Life: Bonhoeffer's Theology of Music*. Edited by John W. de Gruchy and John Morris. Translated by Robert Steiner. Eugene, OR: Cascade Books, 2019.
Panksepp, Jaak. *Affective Neuroscience: The Foundations of Human and Animal Emotions*. Series in Affective Science. Oxford: Oxford University Press, 2004.
Panksepp, Jaak, and Günther Bernatsky. "Emotional Sounds and the Brain: The Neuro-affective Foundations of Musical Appreciation." *Behavioural Processes* 60/2 (2002) 133–55.
Pattison, George. *Kierkegaard: The Aesthetic and the Religious*. London: SCM, 1999.
———. *Kierkegaard and the Quest for Unambiguous Life: Between Romanticism and Modernism; Selected Essays*. Oxford: Oxford University Press, 2013.
———. *Kierkegaard and the Theology of the Nineteenth Century: The Paradox and the "Point of Contact."* Cambridge: Cambridge University Press, 2015.

———. *Poor Paris! Kierkegaard's Critique of the Spectacular City*. Kierkegaard Studies Monograph Series 2. Berlin: de Gruyter, 1999.
Pickstock, Catherine. *Repetition and Identity*. The Literary Agenda. Oxford: Oxford University Press, 2013.
Pinker, Steven. *How the Mind Works*. A Norton Paperback. New York: Norton, 2009.
Price, George H. *The Narrow Pass: A Study of Kierkegaard's Concept of Man*. New York: McGraw-Hill, 1963.
Ramachandran, V. S. et al. "Comments: Some Responses to *The Master and His Emissary*." https://channelmcgilchrist.com/about/#comments/.
Rasmussen, Joel D. S. *Between Irony and Witness: Kierkegaard's Poetics of Faith, Hope, and Love*. New York: T. & T. Clark, 2005.
Ricoeur, Paul. *The Symbolism of Evil*. Translated by Emerson Buchanan. Boston: Beacon, 1986.
Rowson, Jonathan, and Iain McGilchrist. *Divided Brain, Divided World*. London: RSA Action and Research Centre, February 2013. https://www.thersa.org/reports/divided-brain-divided-world/.
Saito, Yuriko. "Aesthetics of the Everyday." In *The Stanford Encyclopedia of Philosophy*, edited by Edward N. Zalta. Metaphysics Research Lab, Stanford University, 2019. https://plato.stanford.edu/archives/win2019/entries/aesthetics-of-everyday/.
———. *Everyday Aesthetics*. Oxford: Oxford University Press, 2010.
Schleiermacher, Friedrich. *On Religion: Speeches to Its Cultured Despisers*. Translated by John Oman. Louisville: Westminster John Knox, 1994.
Schmemann, Alexander. *For the Life of the World: Sacraments and Orthodoxy*. 2nd rev. and exp. ed. Crestwood, NY: St. Vladimir's Seminary Press, 1982.
———. *Introduction to Liturgical Theology*. Translated by Asheleigh E. Moorhouse. Crestwood, NY: St. Vladimir's Seminary Press, 1966.
Seerveld, Calvin. *Rainbows for the Fallen World: Aesthetic Life and Artistic Task*. Toronto: Tuppence, 1980.
Shapiro, Lawrence. *Embodied Cognition*. New Problems in Philosophy. New York: Routledge, 2011.
———, ed. *The Routledge Handbook of Embodied Cognition*. Routledge Handbooks in Philosophy. New York: Routledge, Taylor & Francis, 2014.
Smith, James K. A. *Awaiting the King: Reforming Public Theology*. Cultural Liturgies 3. Grand Rapids: Baker Academic, 2017.
———. *Desiring the Kingdom: Worship, Worldview, and Cultural Formation*. Cultural Liturgies 1. Grand Rapids: Baker Academic, 2009.
———. *Imagining the Kingdom: How Worship Works*. Cultural Liturgies 2. Grand Rapids: Baker Academic, 2013.
———. *Thinking in Tongues: Pentecostal Contributions to Christian Philosophy*. Pentecostal Manifestos. Grand Rapids: Eerdmans, 2010.
Smith, Robert O. "Bonhoeffer and Musical Metaphor." *Word & World* 26/2 (2006) 195–206.
Smyth, John Vignaux. *A Question of Eros: Irony in Sterne, Kierkegaard and Barthes*. Kierkegaard and Postmodernism. Tallahassee: University Presses of Florida, 1986.
Spezio, Michael. "McGilchrist and Hemisphere Lateralization: A Neuroscientific and Metaanalytic Assessment." In "Engaging Iain McGilchrist: Ascetical Practice, Brain Lateralization, and Philosophy of Mind." Edited by Wesley J. Wildman and Sarah Coakley. Special issue, *Religion, Brain & Behavior* 9/4 (2019) 387–99.

Tallis, Raymond. *Michelangelo's Finger: An Exploration of Everyday Transcendence*. New Haven: Yale University Press, 2012.

Taylor, Charles. *Modern Social Imaginaries*. Public Planet Books. Durham, NC: Duke University Press, 2004.

Thiessen, Gesa Elsbeth, ed. *Theological Aesthetics: A Reader*. Grand Rapids: Eerdmans, 2004.

Trimble, Michael. "Book Review: *The Master and His Emissary: The Divided Brain and the Making of the Western World*, by Iain McGilchrist." *Cognitive Neuropsychiatry* 16/3 (2011) 284–88.

Tseng, Shao Kai. "Kierkegaard and Music in Paradox? Bringing Mozart's *Don Giovanni* to Terms with Kierkegaard's Religious Life-View." *Literature and Theology* 28/4 (2014) 411–24.

Tweedy, Rod, ed. *The Divided Therapist: Hemispheric Difference and Contemporary Psychotherapy*. London: Routledge, 2020.

Vanhoozer, Kevin J. "Praising in Song: Beauty and the Arts." In *The Blackwell Companion to Christian Ethics*, edited by Stanley Hauerwas and Samuel Wells, 110–22. Blackwell Companions to Religion. Malden, MA: Blackwell, 2006.

Walsh, Sylvia. *Living Poetically: Kierkegaard's Existential Aesthetics*. Literature & Philosophy. University Park: Pennsylvania State University Press, 1994.

Ward, Graham. *Christ and Culture*. Challenges in Contemporary Theology. Malden, MA: Blackwell, 2005.

———. *Cities of God*. Radical Orthodoxy Series. London: Routledge, 2001.

———. *Cultural Transformation and Religious Practice*. Cambridge: Cambridge University Press, 2005.

———. "The Displaced Body of Jesus Christ." In *Cities of God*, 97–116. Radical Orthodoxy Series. London: Routledge, 2001.

———. *How the Light Gets In:* Ethical Life 1. Oxford: Oxford University Press, 2016.

———. *The Politics of Discipleship: Becoming Postmaterial Citizens*. Grand Rapids: Baker Academic, 2009.

———. "A Question of Sport and Incarnational Theology." *Studies in Christian Ethics* 25/1 (2012) 49–64.

———. "Radical Orthodoxy: Its Ecumenical Vision." *Acta Theologica* 37/S1 (2017) 29–42.

———. *Unbelievable: Why We Believe and Why We Don't*. London: Tauris, 2014.

———. *Unimaginable: What We Imagine and What We Can't*. London: Tauris, 2018.

Weber, Max. *From Max Weber: Essays in Sociology*. Translated, edited, and with an introduction by H. H. Gerth and C. Wright Mills. New York: Oxford University Press, 1946.

Wildman, Wesley J., and Sarah Coakley, eds. "Engaging Iain McGilchrist: Ascetical Practice, Brain Lateralization, and Philosophy of Mind." Special issue, *Religion, Brain & Behavior* 9/4 (2019).

Williams, Stephen N. *The Shadow of the Antichrist: Nietzsche's Critique of Christianity*. Grand Rapids: Baker Academic, 2006.

Wolterstorff, Nicholas. *Acting Liturgically: Philosophical Reflections on Religious Practice*. Oxford: Oxford University Press, 2018.

———. *Art in Action: Toward a Christian Aesthetic*. Grand Rapids: Eerdmans, 1980.

———. *Art Rethought: The Social Practices of Art*. Oxford: Oxford University Press, 2015.

———. *The God We Worship: An Exploration of Liturgical Theology*. Grand Rapids: Eerdmans, 2015.

———. *Hearing the Call: Liturgy, Justice, Church, and World; Essays*. Edited by Mark R. Gornik and Gregory Thompson. Grand Rapids: Eerdmans, 2011.

———. "Human Flourishing and Art That Enhances the Ordinary." In *Envisioning the Good Life: Essays on God, Christ, and Human Flourishing in Honor of Miroslav Volf*, edited by Matthew Croasmun et al., 163–80. Eugene, OR: Cascade Books, 2017.

———. *Justice in Love*. Emory University Studies in Law and Religion Grand Rapids: Eerdmans, 2015.

———. *Lament for a Son*. Grand Rapids: Eerdmans, 1987.

———. *Practices of Belief*. Edited by Terence Cuneo. Selected Essays 2. Cambridge: Cambridge University Press, 2010.

———. *Reason within the Bounds of Religion*. 2nd ed. Grand Rapids: Eerdmans, 1984.

———. "The Reformed Liturgy." In *Major Themes in the Reformed Tradition*, edited by Donald K. McKim, 273–304. Grand Rapids: Eerdmans, 1992.

———. "The Religious Dimension." In *The Blackwell Guide to Aesthetics*, edited by Peter Kivy, 325–39. Blackwell Philosophy Guides. Malden, MA: Blackwell, 2004.

Zelechow, Bernard. "Kierkegaard, the Aesthetic and Mozart's *Don Giovanni*." In *Kierkegaard on Art and Communication*, edited by George Pattison 64–77. London: Macmillan, 1992.

www.ingramcontent.com/pod-product-compliance
Lightning Source LLC
Chambersburg PA
CBHW050850230426
43667CB00012B/2225